THE F.A. CUP

The publishers regret
that the dates and venues
given for the FA Cup
finals are incorrect on
the following pages.

The correct dates and
venues are as follows:

p. 392
12 May 2001 Cardiff

p. 398
4 May 2002 Cardiff

p. 402
17 May 2003 Cardiff

p. 406
22 May 2004 Cardiff

p. 412
21 May 2005 Cardiff.

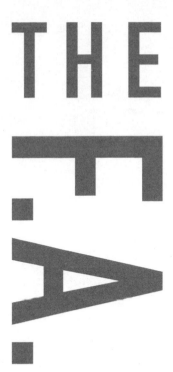

THE F.A. CUP

THE COMPLETE HISTORY

GUY LLOYD
and
NICK HOLT

First published in Great Britain
2005 by Aurum Press Ltd
25 Bedford Avenue, London WC1B 3AT

A catalogue record for this book is available from the British Library.

ISBN 1 84513 054 5

1 3 5 7 9 10 8 6 4 2
 2005 2007 2009 2008 2006

Designed by Ashley Western
Typeset in Joanna and Din by M Rules
Printed by MPG Books, Bodmin, Cornwall

Introduction

Popular opinion relegates the FA Cup to the past tense, in the way that one patronises a faded film star or a prime minister now grazing quietly in the House of Lords. It is tolerated as a once-great performer now reduced to an occasional walk-on part. The glamour, prestige and the ability to hold court are all diminished.

The 2005 final should have been a perfect case in point. Arsenal and Manchester United were two clubs whose *raison d'etre* had been the pursuit of Premiership and European glory. The earlier rounds had seemed no greater an exercise than to blood exotically-named youngsters from the supporting cast. To judge from the reactions of players, supporters and managers, as Patrick Vieira's victorious penalty sparked a joyous scrum, and the Mancunian half of the stadium melted away, it appeared that reports of the tournament's demise had been exaggerated.

The truth is, of course, that the lifeblood of the FA Cup has never been about its biggest participants. A strange premise, when the multiple wins of Manchester United *et al* are taken into consideration. The essence of this most democratic of competitions is its inclusiveness. There is no league and no seeding committee; only its sheer size means that not all teams are thrown together at the same stage. There is but one rule. If you're in the draw, you can meet anyone. Imagine the G14 and Champions League sponsors agreeing to that.

In August, when the extra preliminary round takes place, the likes of Norton & Stockton Ancients and Ford Sports Daventry compete in a tournament that pre-dates the European Cup by eighty-three years. Consult the records and honours' boards of any non-league club, and pride of place will be the season when they battled against the odds to reach the first or third round proper. The lucky few will boast snapshots and programmes telling of visits to Old Trafford, Highbury or Anfield, or photographs of a home draw that saw their own tiny grounds filled to bursting. Ramshackle stadia not worthy of the name are transformed into hothouses of football and media attention. Grounds where the crowd scarcely outnumber the players for a league game acquire a human density where every tree and pylon is crammed with craning spectators.

This appetite for the FA Cup extends not just to fans of clubs at the grass roots. Sunderland boast one of the country's largest grounds, huge support, a history that has seen them dubbed the 'Bank of England club' and a trophy cabinet containing six league titles. Ask any of their fans between nine and ninety to describe the club's crowning achievement, however, and tales of the 1973 final will abound, with its abiding memories of Porterfield, Montgomery, Stokoe and co. True, fans of Liverpool or Manchester United, when asked the same question, will tell tales of Rome, Istanbul and the Nou Camp. But these memories are the preserve of the privileged few, not the majority. Every fan has their own FA Cup moment.

This book can not hope to capture them all. But it will explain why a tournament conceived by a public schoolboy and ratified in a London pub more than 130 years ago became the largest and most glamorous of any in British sport. It will shine the spotlight on Manchester United and Ryhope Colliery Welfare, and explain why the Cup made a hero of Roger Osborne and a villain of Paul Gascoigne, and how it remains forever in the record books of Preston, Hyde and Portsmouth. If this can't convince you of the importance of the FA Cup, consider the words of the late Billy Bremner before Leeds victorious appearance at Wembley in 1972: 'I've got a League Championship medal, a Fairs Cup medal, a League Cup medal and dozens of caps, but sometimes I think I'd swap the lot for a place in a Cup winning side.'

Guy Lloyd and Nick Holt, June 2005.

In The Beginning

V ersions of the beautiful game have existed for thousands of years. Japan, China, Greece and Mexico can all lay claim to the invention of football. It took public school organisation in the Victorian age to transform the spectacle in Britain from inter-village roughhouse to a discipline played by twenty-two players on a marked pitch.

By the early 1860s football's heartlands were in the public schools, South Yorkshire and pockets of Scotland, especially Glasgow. A first attempt had been made by the public schools to formalize playing procedures in 1848. But the 'Cambridge Rules' were never universally adopted.

Local rules were finally unified courtesy of J.C. Thring's blueprint, *The Simplest Game*, published in 1862. A year later, twelve clubs from the London area met at the Freemason's Tavern in Lincoln's Inn Fields, a meeting which culminated in the formation of the Football Association.

What the fledgling game still lacked was competition. No leagues existed; teams competed for local bragging rights only. The solution arrived courtesy of FA secretary, Charles Alcock.

The FA's first secretary, Ebeneezer Cobb Morley, attended its first Wembley Cup final in 1923 at the grand age of 92.

Sheffield FC, formed in 1857, holds the distinction of being the world's oldest football club still in existence.

In 1871 Alcock suggested a knock-out competition based on the inter-house cup at his alma mater, Harrow. His formal proposal contained the historic phrase 'It is desirable that a Challenge Cup should be established'. Fifteen clubs answered the call, a disappointing response from a membership approaching fifty in number, and the world's first football competition was born.

Two of the original entrants, Great Marlow and Maidenhead, have entered every subsequent FA Cup competition.

Charles Alcock made a remarkable contribution to football and to sport in general. In his twenty-five year reign as FA Secretary, he oversaw many of the innovations which shaped the game as we know it. Not only was the FA Challenge Cup the template for all football's major competitions, its concept of the knockout trophy became the blueprint for competition in most modern team sports. Alcock would later nurse through the introduction of professionalism into football. He also refereed a Cup final.

Not content with inventing the thing, Alcock captained the winning side in the first FA Cup, and would have captained England in their first international against

Scotland but was thwarted by injury. He did finally captain his country in a match against Scotland in 1875.

This is impressive enough but he was still not satisfied. In 1880 in his capacity as Secretary of Surrey County Cricket Club, Alcock organised cricket's first Test match at his home ground of Kennington Oval. When Australia beat England two years later and the Ashes were conceived, Alcock was in attendance. Surrey were also at the forefront of the development of the County Championship.

Alcock was an assiduous marketer. The Oval, under his auspices, was home to hockey and baseball matches, and provided the neutral ground for rugby's Varsity match. Alcock also organised and staged the first rugby union international.

Charles Alcock's achievements are down-played by most latter-day writers. He was truly the father of modern competitive sport.

WANDERING STARS

WANDERERS:
Bowen, Alcock, Bonsor, Welch, **Betts (1)**, Crake, Hooman, Lubbock, Thompson, Vidal, Wollaston

RE:
Merriman, Marindin, Addison, Cresswell, Mitchell, Renny-Tailyour, Rich, Goodwyn, Muirhead, Cotter, Bogle

Silliest player's name: Henry Waugh Renny-Tailyour (Royal Engineers)

1871-1872

Although later versions of the FA Cup involved hundreds of clubs and were often a triumph of organisation, the first competition was a shambles. The first round comprised only four games, with two teams progressing via walkovers and a further three courtesy of byes.

Similar chaos in the following rounds saw the Glaswegian side Queen's Park progress to the semi-final without setting foot on a pitch. The farce was compounded when they failed to scrape together the expenses for a replay and withdrew, thus managing to preserve a five-year unbeaten record.

The final, in the absence of any formal football stadium, was played at Kennington Oval. The Royal Engineers started favourites following the elimination of Queen's Park but in a scenario that was to become familiar in pre-substitution Cup finals, they lost a player to injury after ten minutes and never recovered. Five minutes later, Morton Peto Betts became the scorer of the first FA Cup final goal. It proved to be the game's only score. Betts played under the alias A. H. Chequer. He had been registered for Harrow Chequers when the competition began but jumped clubs after they scratched without kicking a ball. Presumably being a member of the organising committee made it easier for him to get away with it.

Best team name: Hampstead Heathens. After a first-round bye, they saw off Barnes 2-0 before succumbing to the Royal Engineers by the same score.

1871-1872

1871-1872

Some of the bizarre features of that first final:
Players were distinguished by caps or garters, and all wore knickerbockers. Let's hope David Beckham doesn't read this!
Throw-ins were taken one-handed. The pitch had no markings apart from the touchlines. Teams changed ends each time a goal was scored.

WANDERING FARCE

Wanderers **2** Oxford University **0**

WANDERERS:
Bowen, Thompson, Welch, **Kinnaird © (1)**,
Howell, **Wollaston (1)**, Sturgis, Stewart,
Kenyon-Slaney, Kingsford, Bonsor

OU:
Kirke-Smith, Leach, Mackarness, Birley,
Longman, Chappell-Maddison, Dixon, Paton,
Vidal, Sumner, Ottaway

1872–1873

Silliest Name:
Cuthbert J. Ottaway
(Oxford University).
The only other
famous sportsman
who was christened
Cuthbert had the
sense to use his
middle name. He
was known by the
more familiar
Gordon Greenidge
when he played Test
cricket for the West
Indies.

1872–1873

Military teams were
common in those
early Cups. In this
season khaki
representatives
included the 1st
Surrey Rifles as well
as the Royal
Engineers.

I f the inaugural competition was beset by teething problems, the second season descended into out-right pantomime. Byes and scratched teams created a permanently lop-sided tournament. Queen's Park were a guilty party again, failing to raise the fare to play their semi-final having generously been given a bye until that stage of the tournament.

The FA hardly helped matters by allowing Wanderers a bye to the final, thus making the rest of the competition a knockout for the right to play the holders. They had realised the error of their ways by the following season.

As holders the Wanderers were allowed choice of venue. Hence the final was staged at Lillie Bridge, then one of London's premier sports complexes. Their opponents would be Oxford University, who had pulled off a minor shock by eliminating the Royal Engineers 1-0 in the third round. Interest in the game was dwarfed by the Boat Race on the nearby Thames later in the day, which nudged forward kick-off time to 11.30am. Much of the 3,000 crowd were Boat-Race enthusiasts killing time before the main event. The Cambridge followers naturally gave their support to Wanderers!

The scorers in the easy victory for Wanderers in the final were Charles Wollaston and Arthur, later Lord, Kinnaird. These two were amongst the few significant footballers of their generation; they would prove to be giants of the FA Cup's early years.

1873

ENGINEERS GET THE BLUES

1874

FINAL, 14 MARCH 1874, KENNINGTON OVAL

Oxford University **2** Royal Engineers **0**

OU:
Neapean, **Mackarness (1)**, Birley, Green, Vidal, Ottaway ©, Benson, **Paton (1)**, Rawson, Chappell-Maddison, Johnson

RE:
Merriman, Marindin © , Addison, Onslow, Oliver, Digby, Renny-Tailyour, Rawson, Blackman, Wood, Von Donop

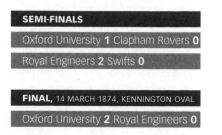

Robert Vidal (Oxford University) became the only man to play in the first three finals, having previously won with Wanderers in 1872. He scored the semi-final winner against Clapham Rovers.

1873-1874

Sheffield's first-round tie against Shropshire Wanderers produced two goalless draws. For the only time in the competition's history, a coin was tossed to decide the winner. Sheffield went through; they were the first Northern team to make an impression on the competition – how that would change in the following decade.

1873-1874

The he organisational chaos receded in 1874, with a much smoother progression for the competition. One notable exception – the perennially disorganised Harrow Chequers. They entered their third FA Cup, only to withdraw for the third time without playing a game.

By now the Royal Engineers must have felt jinxed. The strongest team in England lost their second final in three years having started as favourites in both. They had cruised through to the final, thrashing Brondesbury and Maidenhead 4-0 and 7-0 respectively.

At least the finalists won through on merit, having played in all four of the earlier rounds. By contrast, Wanderers had started on their now traditional non-playing route to the final before the shock of actually being forced to kick a ball in anger brought about their demise in the third round. In a refreshing change, the quarter and semi-finals produced only one bye.

As for the final, experience of the big day was plentiful. Nine men had losers' medals from the two previous years. For the Royal Engineers, the season's highest scorers, it proved another day when their sharpshooters could only fire blanks.

The Rawson brothers remain the only pair to have played on opposite sides in an FA Cup final, Oxford's William lining up against Herbert, his elder brother.

1873-1874

IF AT FIRST YOU DON'T SUCCEED . . .

RE:
Merriman ©, Sim, Onslow, Ruck, Von Donop, Wood, Rawson, Stafford, **Renny-Tailyour (1)**, Mein, Wingfield-Stratford

OLD ETONIANS:
Thompson, Benson, Lubbock, Wilson, Kinnaird ©, Stronge, Patton, Farmer, **Bonsor (1)**, Ottaway, Kenyon-Stanley

RE:
Merriman ©, Sim, Onslow, Ruck, Von Donop, Wood, Rawson, **Stafford (1), Renny-Tailyour (1)**, Mein, Wingfield-Stratford

OLD ETONIANS:
Drummond-Moray, Lubbock, Wilson, Kinnaird ©, Stronge, Patton, Farmer, Bonsor, Hammond, Farrer, Kenyon-Slaney

f Wanderers were not the favourites at the start of the season, they certainly were after a 16-0 drubbing of Farningham in the first round with five goals for Kingsford and four for the redoubtable Charles Wollaston.

In the absence of Queen's Park, competing in the inaugural Scottish Cup, it seemed the main threat to Wanderers would again come from the well-organised Royal Engineers. It was something of a shock when Wanderers succumbed instead to Oxford University, the holders. Having already seen off the light blues, Cambridge, 5-0, the Engineers faced Oxford in the semi-final. The Chatham sappers won through after a replay, and faced Old Etonians in the final at Kennington Oval.

After losing in two of the first three finals, Royal Engineers shook off the also-rans tag with their first and only victory. For the first time the final also went to a replay, but goals from Renny-Tailyour, who had scored in the semi-final and the drawn first game against Etonians, and Stafford clinched the game for Royal Engineers. Worthy and deserved winners at last.

Silly name: Lieutenant C. Wingfield-Stratford (Royal Engineers)

1874–1875

Royal Engineers' founder and player, Sir Francis 'The Major' Marindin, faced a dilemma before the final since he was also co-founder of Old Etonians. It is believed that, faced with a conflict of interests, he bowed out gracefully and watched the match from the touchline.

1874–1875

WANDERERS RETURN

WANDERERS:
Greig, Stratford, Lindsay, Chappel-Maddison, Birley, Wollaston, Charles Heron, George Heron, **Edwards (1)**, Kenrick, Hughes

OLD ETONIANS:
Hogg, Welldon, Edward Lyttelton, Thompson, Kinnaird ©, Meysey, Kenyon-Slaney, Alfred Lyttelton, Stugis, **Bonsor (1)**, Allene

WANDERERS:
Greig, Stratford, Lindsay, Chappel-Maddison, Birley, **Wollaston (1)**, Charles Heron, George Heron, Edwards, Kenrick, **Hughes (2)**

OLD ETONIANS:
Hogg, Lubbock, Edward Lyttelton, Farrer, Kinnaird ©, Stronge, Kenyon-Slaney, Alfred Lyttelton, Stugis, Bonsor, Allene

Two sets of brothers played in the final; Alfred and Edward Lyttelton turned out for Old Etonians against Hubert and Frederick Heron for Wanderers.

1875-1876

anderers had strolled to their previous two victories, playing only three games. This time they reached the summit the hard way, winning through after six matches. Their semi-final against Swifts proved to be the crunch with stalwart Charles Wollaston grabbing the winner in an exciting 2-1 victory.

Even the final was a slog. Edwards shot Wanderers into a 35th minute lead, only for Bonsor to peg them back five minutes after half-time. The replay was a different story, Wanderers winning at a canter. The principal factor in this was an injury to Old Etonians captain, the legendary Arthur Kinnaird. He was forced to replace his great friend Quintin Hogg in goal, but was far from mobile. After the reliable Wollaston, Wanderers' only survivor from their 1872 victory, had opened the scoring, Thomas Hughes became the first player to score twice in a final and claim a hat-trick of wins for his club.

The Old Etonians team included five former Wanderers players. Alex Bonsor and Albert Thompson had both won winner's medals in 1872 and 1873.

Alfred Lyttelton was a real Boys Own character. Lyttelton was an England cricket international and would later become President of the MCC. This remarkable all-rounder was also English real tennis champion. Like many others amongst the early Corinthian footballers, he served as an MP (for Warwick). Lyttelton's brother, Edward, also played first-class cricket.

1875-1876

1876

SAME OLD, SAME OLD . . .

1877

WANDERERS:
Denton, Kinnaird, Birley ©, Green, George Heron, Hughes, **Kenrick (1), Lindsay (1)**, Stratford, Wace, Wollaston

OU:
Allington, Bain, Dunnell, Savory, Todd, Waddington, Fernandez, Hills, Otter, Parry ©, Rawson **OG Kinnaird**

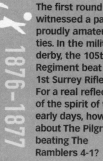

The first round witnessed a pair of proudly amateur ties. In the military derby, the 105th Regiment beat the 1st Surrey Rifles 3-0. For a real reflection of the spirit of those early days, how about The Pilgrims beating The Ramblers 4-1?

1876-1877

T he number of entrants was gradually growing. This season's first round entry numbered a record thirty-seven, although the usual crop of withdrawals reduced the first round to its usual chaos. On the plus side, the increased intake meant that a fourth round could be added before the semi-final.

The most surprising withdrawal was that of the previous year's finalists, Old Etonians. Unlike Manchester United over a hundred years later, we can assume they had not been invited to a World Club Championship.

Wanderers again benefited from a brace of byes and pooped the Varsity party by beating Cambridge University in the semi-final, thus denying them a chance to have a crack at the old enemy. This was to be the closest Cambridge ever came to FA Cup success.

Arthur Kinnaird was back playing for the Wanderers after Old Etonians' failure to compete, and he provided the final's only moment of note. Playing in goal, he caught a hopeful punt, only to be carried over the goal-line by his own momentum. His blushes were spared by Kerrick and Lindsay, whose goals meant Wanderers ran out winners again. Nine of their side had previous Cup final experience; Freddie Green was lining up against his former club, with whom he had won the trophy in 1874.

HIGH FIVES

WANDERERS:
Kirkpatrick, Stratford, Lindsay, **Kinnaird © (1)**,
Green, Wollaston, George Heron, Wylie, Wace,
Denton, **Kenrick (2)**

RE:
Friend, Cowan, Morris, Mayne, Heath, Haynes,
Lindsay, Hedley ©, Bond, Barnet, Ruck

The man in charge of the 1878 Final went by the name of S.R. Bastard. One can only assume the terraces were more genteel and forgiving in those days.

1877-1878

This was by far the most successful year for entrants, with eighteen first-round ties successfully completed and only four teams receiving byes or walkovers. For the first time, the midlands and the north arrived in earnest to supplement the ranks of the military and the public schools. The presence of Sheffield, Notts County, Darwen and Manchester lent a genuinely national feel to the competition.

The winners, though, were as predictable as ever; it would be a few more years before northern teams began make an impact on the competition. Wanderers, including nine of their victorious team from the previous season, won their third consecutive final and their fifth in five appearances.

The Royal Engineers endured tough ties against Upton Park (two replays) and Oxford University, earning the right to have a crack at the Wanderers in a rematch of the first ever final. John Wylie of Wanderers had scored in every previous round but the sappers managed to keep him quiet. Sadly for them, Jarvis Kenrick added two goals to one scored by the mighty Kinnaird and the Engineers were second best again.

After three successive wins, Wanderers were entitled to keep the trophy under the rules, but agreed to return it on the understanding no one else would claim it for 'keeps' at a later date. This would be their last final appearance. As little as three years on they would struggle to raise a team and be forced to withdraw from the competition. 1878 was the last hurrah for the first great FA Cup team.

The Engineers' equaliser in the final was scored by an unidentified player during 'a rush'. The Victorian game featured frequent attacking sorties of this nature; essentially the players would group around the ball and charge en masse at the opposition goal, hoping to force the ball over the line during the ensuing scrimmage. Think 1980s Wimbledon but without the bad behaviour.

1877-1878

TOFFS ON TOP

OLD ETONIANS:
Hawtrey, Christian, Bury, Kinnaird ©, Lubbock,
Clerke (1), Pares, Goodhart, Whitfield,
Chevalier, Beaufoy

CLAPHAM:
Birkett, Ogilvie ©, Field, Bailey, Prinsep,
Rawson, Stanley, Scott, Bevington, Growse,
Keith-Falconer

1878–1879 Darwen's side may
have included the
first two
professionals; James
Love and Fergus
Suter, who joined
from a touring
Partick Thistle side.
Paying players was
still strictly
prohibited.

lthough this was a year in which the public
schools maintained their dominance, the first stirrings of working-class rebellion were also in
evidence. Nottingham Forest, at their first
attempt, became the first present-day league club to
make an impression, but it was Darwen, a Lancashire
mill-town team, who were to provide the cup with one
of its first great romantic stories.

Both were eventually put in their place by the most
famous toffs of all, Old Etonians. Forest reached the
semi-finals and lost only narrowly to the old boys. The
Etonians would not have underestimated Forest after
their encounter with Darwen in the fourth round.
Hampered by the outdated rule that all the last rounds of
the competition be played at Kennington Oval (the rule
changed after this season), Darwen succumbed probably
as much to travel fatigue as to the skills of the Old
Etonians, Kinnaird et al. The first game was drawn 5-5,
Darwen staging an astonishing comeback by scoring four
goals in the last 15 minutes – unsurprisingly the
Etonians declined Darwen's offer to finish the tie in
extra-time. A 2-2 replay followed, with extra-time
included, and the mill team only finally went under in
the third match, losing 6-2 after another trek to London.
They nearly had to scratch the game – their expenses
were only covered after the local townspeople, proud of
the exploits of their team, dug into their own pockets to
pay the fares.

Clapham Rovers had coasted to the final, becoming
the first team outside the 'big four' of Wanderers, Royal
Engineers, Oxford University and Old Etonians to do so.
Even they were no match for the Etonians, a solitary goal
from C.J. Clerke settling the issue.

At 17 years 245 days, Clapham Rovers' James Prinsep
remains the youngest ever finalist.

1878–1879 The first round tie
between
Nottingham Forest
and Notts County is
the oldest between
two current league
clubs.

ROVERS RETURN

QUARTER-FINALS:

Clapham Rov **1** Old Etonians **0**

Nottm Forest* **2** Sheffield **2**

Oxford Univ (1) **1** Royal Engineers (1) **0**

*Nottm Forest

SEMI-FINALS:

Clapham Rov (bye)

Nottm Forest **0** Oxford Univ **1**

at Kennington Oval

FINAL, 10 APRIL 1880, KENNINGTON OVAL

Clapham Rov **1** Oxford Univ **0**

CLAPHAM:
Birkett, Ogilvie ©, Field, Weston, Bailey, Stanley, Brougham, Sparkes, Barry, Ram, **Lloyd-Jones (1)**

OU:
Parr, Wilson, King, Phillips, Rogers, Heygate ©, Childs, Eyre, Crowdy, Hill, John Lubbock

A fter a relatively unblemished set of results, the tournament descended into familiar anarchy in the third round. Only four of the ten 'winning' teams kicked a ball. Sheffield earned the season's bad-boys' crown by refusing to play extra-time after a 2-2 draw with Forest. They were summarily booted out of the competition.

The shape of things to come was provided by the entry of two future giants of the FA Cup, Aston Villa and Blackburn Rovers. Although both were to fall in the third round, fellow league survivors Nottingham Forest were to reach their second successive semi-final. They also beat local rivals Notts County for the second year running, this time 4-0.

It fell to the previous season's beaten finalists, Clapham Rovers, to upset the old guard. In beating Oxford University they became the fifth name on the trophy. This was the last year the two ancient universities entered the FA Cup.

Best team name: Mosquitoes. Perhaps they should have gone for 'Mayflies' as they were snuffed out 7-1 by Hendon in the first round.

1879-1880

Most romantic tie: Hotspur FC v Argonauts. Hotspur have no connection with the current set-up at White Hart Lane. They played most of their matches close to Highbury.

1879-1880

Victorious Clapham Rovers' keeper Reginald Birkett was the first to play football and rugby for England.

1879-1880

1880

LAST OF THE CORINTHIANS

1881

QUARTER-FINALS:

Aston Villa **2** Stafford Road **3**

Grey Friars **0** Old Etonians **4**

Darwen **15** Romford **0**

Old Carthusians **3** Clapham Rov **1**

SEMI-FINALS:

Stafford Road **1** Old Etonians **2**

Darwen **1** Old Carthusians **4**

FINAL, 9 APRIL 1881, KENNINGTON OVAL

Old Carthusians **3** Old Etonians **0**

OLD CARTHUSIANS:
Gillett, Norris, Colvin, Prinsep, Vintcent, Hansell, Richards, **Page (1)**, **Wynyard (1)**, **Parry © (1)**, Todd

OLD ETONIANS:
Rawlinson, Foley, French, Kinnaird ©, Farrer, Macauley, Goodhart, Whitfield, Novelli, Anderson, Chevallier

This was not quite the last hurrah for the public schoolboys, but the final was the last in which two amateur teams participated. This season's cloth-cap upstarts were Darwen, who disposed of Sheffield and Sheffield Wednesday en route to a semi-final defeat by Old Carthusians.

Carthusians were relatively new kids on the block themselves. The former pupils of Charterhouse were playing only their second season of Cup competition, having been dumped out by the fading Wanderers in last year's second round. They were rank outsiders for the final, lining up against previous winners and three-time finalists Old Etonians.

Both sides had qualified for the showdown impressively, each scoring more than twenty goals in the process. Etonians' experience was expected to shade it but the game proved to be a stroll for Carthusians, winners by 3-0 in a one-sided affair.

Best team name: Brigg Britannia. Sadly for them they were stuffed 5-0 by Turton in the first round.

1880–1881

In 1894 Carthusians lifted the FA Amateur Cup, becoming the first club to win both competitions. Only Wimbledon and Royal Engineers have emulated their feat.

1880–1881

Pierce Dix. In modern times one could be forgiven for thinking this might be a body-piercing catalogue. In 1881 it was the name of the Cup final referee.

1880–1881

1881

BLUE BLOODS REFUSE TO GO QUIETLY

1882

OLD ETONIANS:
Rawlinson, French, de Paravicini, Kinnaird ©, Foley, Novelli, Dunn, **Macauley (1)**, Goodhart, Chevallier, Anderson

BLACKBURN:
Howarth, McIntyre, Suter, Freddie Hargreaves ©, Sharples, Jack Hargreaves, Avery, Brown, Strachan, Douglas, Duckworth

n its eleventh season, the FA Cup had evolved into a series of mini-tournaments. The early rounds featured the public schools and gentlemen as before, but the emerging groups featured professional outfits from the midlands and the north.

The battle for northern supremacy began in the semi-final between Blackburn Rovers and Sheffield Wednesday, Rovers triumphing easily in the replay after a tight first match. Rovers were one of four Blackburn teams to enter the Cup; they thumped rivals Blackburn Park Road 9-1, and neither Olympic nor Law made it past the first round.

Old Etonians fought through to the final yet again, with the great Kinnaird once more to the fore. They proved far too experienced for Rovers in the final and one goal scarcely reflected their superiority. With hindsight they would have savoured the moment as it was the last victory for the public schools that had invented the game and its Cup. The rise of the professionals was to be an irresistible one.

Silly Name: Percy de Paravicini (no, not a character from the second series of *Blackadder*, but the Old Etonians' fullback).

1881–1882

This season's goal machine was E.C. Bambridge of Swifts, who netted nine in two games before his team ran up against Old Etonians.

1881–1882

Best Team Name: Esher Leopold. In their only FA Cup match, they were trounced 5-0 by Old Carthusians.

1881–1882

OLYMPIAN HEIGHTS

OLYMPIC:
Hacking, Ward, Warburton ©, Gibson, Astley, Hunter, Dewhurst, **Matthews (1)**, Wilson, **Costley (1)**, Yates

OLD ETONIANS:
Rawlinson, French, de Paravicini, Kinnaird ©, Foley, Bainbridge, Dunn, Macauley, **Goodhart (1)**, Chevallier, Anderson

The symbol of the Cup, and football itself, passing from the public schools to the people, was never more vividly illustrated than in the 1883 final. Olympic's team was fashioned solidly from the working classes. Weaving, spinning, plumbing, metal working, even the unemployed were represented.

The contrast in Old Etonians was not merely social. Ten had previous Cup Final experience and when Harry Goodhart shot them into a first-half lead it seemed that Olympic were doomed to suffer the same fate as local rivals Rovers the previous year.

But Olympic were a well-drilled side; they had even checked into a hotel before the final to ensure their preparation was adequate. In the second half Olympic were transformed. Etonians were hurt not only by an equaliser but by the loss through injury of England forward Arthur Dunn. Extra-time and the extra man were crucial, as Jimmy Costley proved the aptness of his name for the tiring Etonians.

It would be the last appearance in a final by the Old Etonians and the last by their stalwart captain, Arthur Kinnaird.

1882-1883

The Cup proved a less than handsome trophy for one Blackburn fan. 'Is that t'Coop? Why it looks more like a tea kettle?' was one catcall on its presentation. 'Ay, it might do' came the response from captain Sam Warburton, 'But it's very welcome to Lancashire. It'll have a good home and it'll never go back to London.' Prophetic words indeed as this trophy was stolen in 1895 without ever being held again by a southern club.

1882-1883

Arthur Kinnaird remains one of the great figures in FA Cup history. For all the shambolic organisation of many of the early tournaments, Kinnaird's record of five winners' medals in nine finals is hugely impressive. His playing days ended, he became President of the FA from 1890 until his death in 1923. He would have regretted passing away a few weeks before the first Wembley Cup final.

1883

PROFESSIONAL FOUL

1881 1884

BLACKBURN:
Arthur, Suter, Beverley, McIntyre ©, **Forrest (1)**, Jack Hargreaves, Brown, Inglis, **Sowerbutts (1)**, Douglas, Lofthouse

QUEEN'S PARK:
Gillespie, Macdonald, Arnott, Gow, Campbell ©, Allan, Harrower, Smith, Anderson, Watt, **Christie (1)**

Other changes blew in; Nottingham and Birmingham hosted the semi-finals, with Kennington Oval getting only the final. A crowd of 14,000 watched the final.

1883-1884

After simmering for a couple of seasons, the ill-feeling over the still illegal practice of professionalism finally erupted. Accrington and Rossendale were both expelled by the FA but the real showdown occurred in the fourth round. Upton Park, original entrants in 1872 and staunch amateurs, protested after a 1-1 draw with Preston North End. Rather than doff their caps, Preston brazened it out, openly admitting not only their own professionalism but blowing the whistle on a payment policy that was common practice outside London.

Although disqualified, Preston kick-started a debate that resulted in the FA's legalisation of the professional game within eighteen months. Upton Park were well-beaten by eventual winners, Blackburn Rovers, who probably fielded some paid players themselves.

Queen's Park initiated a shock by actually competing in the Cup – having entered every competition to date they had completed only one match in the previous twelve seasons. Heavy scorers with forty-four goals in seven games, Queen's Park gave Blackburn a tough game in the final but were undone by their ignorance of the English rules. Referee Major Marindin applied the English law which demanded three defending players between attacker and goal, not two as in Scotland, thus denying Queen's Park two goals.

Queen's Park's compensation was a walkover in the Scottish Cup final. Vale of Leven refused to turn up after leave of absence due to illness and bereavement was denied.

1883-1884

1884

1885

DEJA-VU

1885

1885

BLACKBURN:
Arthur, Turner, Suter, Haworth, McIntyre,
Forrest (1), Brown © (1), Fecitt, Sowerbutts,
Douglas, Lofthouse

QUEENS PARK:
Gillespie, Arnott, Macleod, Macdonald,
Campbell ©, Sellar, Anderson, McWhammel,
Hamilton, Allan, Gray

1884-1885

This remains the only time in the history of the FA Cup that the same teams have reached the final in successive seasons.

The first year of legalised professionalism provided higher standards and attendances. On the flip side, pantomime and farce were star attractions as never before. The comedy was again provided by the draw. With only nine games in round four, the fifth round was reduced to one fixture and seven byes.

Steamrollering over the farce, Blackburn Rovers' last two fixtures were further proof that the power of the amateur was at an end. Old Carthusians were brushed aside in the semis and despite the respectability of the scoreline, their final victory over Queen's Park was never in doubt. Rovers' power and fitness had told against Queen's Park's superior skills for the second year in succession. No Scottish team would grace the final again but their countrymen would write their own rich history.

Rovers had defended their trophy superbly, drubbing weaker opposition and edging out rivals Blackburn Olympic 3-2 in the second round. This was acknowledged to be the finest game yet played on British soil.

1884-1885

The replay between Queen's Park and Nottingham Forest was played at Merchiston Castle School in Edinburgh, thus making it the only semi-final to be staged outside England. By competing in this game, Forest created the unique record of playing FA Cup ties in all four home countries. As the four have since developed their own competitions, it is likely to prove a unique achievement.

1885

ROVERS' REIGN CONTINUES

1886

BLACKBURN:
Arthur, Turner, Suter, Heyes, McIntyre, Forrest,
Brown ©, Fecitt, Sowerbutts, Strachan, Douglas

WEST BROM:
Roberts, Harry Green, Bell, Horton, Perry,
Timmins, Woodhall, Tom Green, Bayliss ©,
Loach, Bell

BLACKBURN:
Arthur, Turner, Suter, Heyes, McIntyre, Forrest,
Brown © (1), Fecitt, **Sowerbutts (1)**,
Strachan, Douglas

WEST BROM:
Roberts, Harry Green, Bell, Horton, Perry,
Timmins, Woodhall, Tom Green, Bayliss ©,
Loach, Bell

The replay was the first time a final tie had been held outside London. The Racecourse Ground was home to Derbyshire County Cricket Club.

1885-1886

This season's administrative confusion was provided by the new rules governing professionalism. Clubs could no longer just turn up with eleven men as all paid players had to be formally registered. This produced a clutch of disqualifications as some fell foul of the new law. Preston were again amongst them; put out of the competition despite edging Bolton Wanderers 3-2. Wanderers would themselves suffer the same fate along with Burslem Port Vale.

That aside, the Cup's popularity boomed. One hundred and thirty clubs put themselves forward for entry but a well-entrenched Blackburn Rovers ensured that there would no new name on the trophy. Rovers were more seriously tested this season, with one-goal victories against the much-improved Oswaldtwistle and Swifts. West Bromwich Albion nearly exploited their casual approach to the final but, having been offered a second chance, the blue-and-white machine purred to victory. Goals from the powerful forward, Joe Sowerbutts, and Jimmy Brown secured a comfortable 2-0 win in the replay. Brown's goal was a spectacular solo effort, as the Rovers' captain and England international dribbled from the half-way line to score.

27,000 fans watched the two finals including a record 15,000 for the replay.

1885-1886

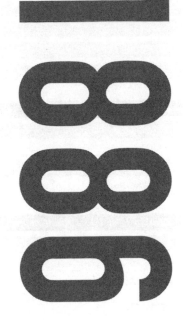

1886

BRUM PUNCH

1887

VILLA:
Warner, Coulton, Simmonds, Yates, Dawson, Burton, Davis, Brown, **Hunter © (1)**, Vaughton, **Hodgetts (1)**

WEST BROM:
Roberts, Harry Green, Aldridge, Horton, Perry, Timmins, Woodhall, Tom Green, Bayliss ©, Paddock, Pearson

For the first and only time, clubs from all over Britain and Ireland were allowed to enter. This produced such bizarre fixtures as Partick Thistle v Cliftonville, whilst Rangers came within 90 minutes of emulating Queen's Park's achievement in reaching the final.

Blackburn Rovers' domination of the competition was ended by a shock defeat at the hands of Renton in the second round. With the holders and favourites out, the West Midlands finally flexed its football muscles. Villa, after eight years, reached their first final following a mixture of one-sided romps and two classics against Wolves and Darwen.

The final was the talk of Birmingham. Albion's experience from the previous year looked to have stood them in good stead and they started as favourites. Form was followed as they dominated the early exchanges but Villa overcame their nerves to beat them with goals from two counter-attacks. After a hotly disputed opener from Derek Hodgetts, the late clincher was scored by Villa legend, Archie Hunter.

Contrary to popular opinion, players of yesteryear were not always gentlemen. Albion's protests after Hodgetts' goal delayed the restart by several minutes.

1886–1887

The Old Carthusians team that reached the sixth round included winger C. Aubrey Smith, who was to find fame between the wars as a Hollywood actor of some note. Smith also played Test cricket for England and later formed an enthusiastic ex-pats team in Hollywood.

1886–1887

BAGGIES' BREAKTHROUGH

WEST BROM:
Roberts, Harry Green, Aldridge, Horton, Perry, Timmins, **Woodhall (1)**, Bassett, **Bayliss ©** **(1)**, Wilson, Pearson

PRESTON:
Mills-Roberts, Howarth, Holmes, Nicholas Ross, Russell, Gordon, Jimmy Ross, Goodall, **Dewhurst (1)**, Drummond, Graham

This season saved all its drama for the final.

Preston had been at the forefront of introducing professionals into the game. They were a well-run club that meticulously prepared their team for key games. Preston had a strong following – their match against Aston Villa drew a record crowd of over 26,000. North End had notched up a preposterous fifty-five goals in seven matches; their 26-0 drubbing of Hyde remains a record. West Bromwich Albion, returning for their third consecutive final, were cast in the role of eternal bridesmaids.

Inspired by diminutive winger, Billy Bassett (no relation to Bertie), Jem Bayliss upset the odds by shooting the underdogs into an eighth-minute lead. Cue the Preston onslaught, which finally broke Albion ten minutes after half-time. A winner for the Lancashire team seemed inevitable but Albion were able to clear their lines. With thirteen minutes remaining West Brom's tall forwards out-jumped the Preston defence and George Woodhall pounced on the knockdown. Proud Preston had been humbled.

Preston's James Ross scored nineteen FA Cup goals in this season, which remains a record. He would have recorded twenty had Everton not been disqualified after their 6-0 defeat by Preston in the second round. The match was declared void.

1887-1888

Arrogant Preston asked the referee if they could be photographed with the trophy before the final to capture as pristine an image as possible. Major Marindin's reply has become folklore: 'Hadn't you better win it first?'

1887-1888

Albion became the first winners to field an all-English XI.

1887-1888

THE INVINCIBLES

PRESTON:
Mills-Roberts, Howarth, Holmes, **Thompson (1)**, Russell, Gordon, **Jimmy Ross (1)**, Goodall, **Dewhurst (1)**, Drummond, Graham

WOLVES:
Baynton, Baugh, Mason, Fletcher, Allen, Lowder, Hunter, Wykes, Brodie ©, Wood, Knight

I n order to bring greater income to the professional game, the Football League had been formed in March 1888 and kicked off its first season in the autumn. As a response to this new-found fixture congestion, the FA restructured the competition. The bigger clubs were exempt from the early stages, which took the form of qualifying rounds, and joined a slimmer field in the first round. Only two further rounds followed until the semi-final. Pity poor Chatham. The Kent club battled through three gruelling second-round matches before edging out Nottingham Forest 3-2. They lost 10-1 at home to West Bromwich Albion in the next round.

Preston were in no mood to repeat the over-confidence of the previous season. Their chairman, William Sudell, had acquired many of the era's finest footballers in his commitment to establish the best team in the country. Although less spectacular than in previous years, North End's efficient progress to a first win was never in doubt as they reached the final without conceding a goal. The final contained none of last year's drama; Preston, with ten of the players who contested the previous year's final, barely gave Wolves a kick.

1888-1889

Not all of the Football League's twelve clubs were exempt until the first round since the FA did not consider all professional teams to be the best in the country. The amateurs of Old Carthusians were deemed worthy and granted a bye to the competition proper.

1888-1889

The first-ever match programme was produced for the final. It cost the princely sum of one penny.

1888-1889

Not content with a first FA Cup win, the 'Invincibles' also coasted to first place in the inaugural football league. They won eighteen of their twenty-two games and drew the other four.

WEDNESDAY WEAK AT THE END

QUARTER FINALS

Sheff Wed (5)(2) **2** Notts County (0)(3) **1**	
Preston **2** Bolton **3**	
Wolves (4) **8** Stoke (0) **0**	
Bootle **0** Blackburn **7**	

SEMI FINALS

Sheffield Wed **2** Bolton **1**
at Villa Park

Wolves **0** Blackburn **1**
at Derby

FINAL, 29 MARCH 1890, KENNINGTON

Blackburn Rovers **6**
Sheffield Wednesday **1**

BLACKBURN:
Horne, James Southworth, Forbes ©, Barton, Dewar, Forrest, **Lofthouse (1)**, Campbell, Jack **Southworth (1)**, **Walton (1)**, **Townley (3)**

SHEFF WED:
Smith, Morley, Brayshaw, Dungworth, Betts, Waller, Ingram, Woolhouse, **Bennett (1)**, Mumford, Cawley

Silliest name: Toodles Woodhouse. How the Wednesday forward made it out of Sheffield alive with this beauty remains one of many conundrums.

1889-1890

1889 was the year that the 'great leveller' showed its colours. There was a shock in each round. In the first, Sheffield United humbled league team Burnley 2-1, having already battled their way through five matches to qualify for the competition proper. They were shown no mercy in the second round, losing 13-0 at Bolton. In the next round it was the city's other team, Sheffield Wednesday, who turned big game hunters with a 2-1 win over Accrington.

Had Ladbrokes existed in 1889, Preston would have been the shortest-priced favourites in history. They would win the league again but their third-round exit to a Bolton team which would finish ninth out of twelve in that competition was a seismic shock, especially as Preston had already beaten Wanderers 6-2 in the league. Wednesday progressed with a win over another league team, thumping Notts County 5-0 and then seeing off Bolton in a semi-final at Villa Park.

Blackburn's march to a fourth Cup victory was no cakewalk either. In a first round thriller, Sunderland were edged out 4-2 after extra-time. The semi-final against Wolves was no less tense.

Non-league Wednesday eventually found their match in the mighty Rovers. Three of the knockout blows were delivered by William Townley, whose hat-trick, the first in a final, underlined the gulf in class.

Biggest farce: Wednesday's third round tie with Notts County. Both teams won a game each, only for each result to be overturned after protests. Wednesday won the decider 2-1, ending up as the first finalists to have 'lost' a match en route.

ROVERS ROUTINE

BLACKBURN:
Pennington, Brandon, Forbes ©, Barton, **Dewar (1)**, Forrest, Lofthouse, Hall, Jack **Southworth (1)**, Walton, **Townley (1)**

NOTTS CO:
Thraves, Ferguson, Hendry, Osborne, Calderhead, Shelton, McGregor, McInnes, **Oswald © (1)**, Locker, Daft

1890-1891

Best team name: Middlesbrough Ironopolis. They were also the most colourful team in their shirts of garish maroon and light green stripes.

1890-1891

This season's mugs: Kidderminster. With their protest upheld after a 3-1 defeat at Darwen, they contrived to lose the replay 13-0.

A fter the thrills and spills of the previous year, the routes to this season's final were more predictable, although Preston's 3-0 first round defeat by Stoke was an upset.

Both semi-finals were classic encounters, with eleven goals producing only one positive result. Blackburn shaded West Brom by one goal at the Victoria Ground, a desperate goalmouth scramble producing their late winner. Such was the confusion that the scorer was never identified.

Sunderland and Notts County shared six goals at Bramall Lane. Jimmy Oswald was to prove the difference in the replay, his brace finally overcoming stout Mackem resistance. Sunderland, newcomers to the league, had provided an early upset by knocking out eventual league champions Everton in the first round.

After that thriller the final was a bitter anti-climax. It should have been the first match to feature goals with nets but the prototypes arrived too late for kick-off and were saved for an international three days later instead. Once again Rovers clamped both hands on the Cup by half-time, having swept to a 3-0 lead. Their fifth success equalled the Wanderers' famous landmark. Blackburn's left-half James Forrest emulated Kinnaird and Wollaston by earning a fifth winner's medal.

THROSTLES ON SONG

VILLA:
Warner, Evans, Cox, Harry Devey, Cowan, Baird, Athersmith, Jack Devey, Dickson ©, Hodgetss, Campbell

WEST BROM:
Reader, Nicholson, McCulloch, **Reynolds (1)**, Perry ©, Groves, Bassett, McLeod, **Nicholls (1)**, Pearson, **Geddes (1)**

The first round was played in such appalling weather that Everton lodged a protest about the state of their Anfield Road pitch. Four games were replayed after complaints but in each case the victorious team triumphed again.

1891–1892

Blackburn Rovers began their attempt at a record-equalling third successive win in some style when England's Jack Southworth netted all four goals in the first-round victory over Derby. West Brom, who would finish bottom of the league, spoilt everything in round two.

For the second season running, the semi-finals were to live in the memory. Villa's game with the new League champions Sunderland promised to be a nail-biter. Villa would have been grateful to play at neutral Bramall Lane as Sunderland had won all thirteen home games in the league at Newcastle Road. A pair each from Devey and Hodgetts provided the champions with a rare bloody nose.

In the other semi-final, after two tight affairs at Molineux, Albion's Alf Geddes moved into overdrive. His hat-trick finally finished off non-league Nottingham Forest, in the midst of a snowstorm at Derby.

The final was a disaster for Villa. Hot favourites before kick-off, they had reckoned without the mercurial Billy Bassett, who unravelled them with a masterful display, just as he had tormented Preston four years previously.

What should have been a post-match bask with the trophy descended into recrimination and acrimony. The third goal was a blockbuster from half-back John Reynolds; Reynolds would anger the Albion board by moving to Villa soon after amid accusations that he had played for a transfer. Reynolds, capped by both Ireland and England, would have the last laugh, playing for Villa in the final in 1895 in a win over . . . Albion, of course.

The Kennington Oval's last final produced its highest attendance. The 32,810 crowd eclipsed last season's record by nearly 10,000.

1891–1892

1892

WOLVES BARE THEIR TEETH

1893

WOLVES:
Rose, Baugh, Swift, Malpass, **Allen** © **(1)**,
Kinsey, Topham, Wykes, Butcher, Griffin, Wood

EVERTON:
Williams, Kelso, Howarth, Boyle, Holt, Stewart,
Latta, Gordon, Maxwell, Chadwick, Milward

A fter last year's final, it became evident that the Kennington Oval had outlived its usefulness. The decline of the southern teams and local distaste for hordes of hobnailed out-of-towners descending upon what was then a genteel district of the capital doubtless sped the momentum for change.

Manchester made sense as an alternative location but the venue at Fallowfield proved a poor choice. Officially 45,000 were shoehorned in, almost doubling the official capacity. A stampede at the gate in scenes that would be repeated 30 years later at the first Wembley final probably added another 20,000.

Champions Sunderland had already fallen to Blackburn; Wolves took full advantage and reached their first final, edging out Rovers in a closely fought semi-final. Everton and Preston had finished second and third in the league with only a point between them. That closeness was evident as they slugged it out in the other semi. Everton finally triumphed in the third game.

Wolves took advantage of an Everton side exhausted by a semi-final that had finished only five days earlier. On the hour Harry Allen surprised keeper Richard Williams with a speculative lob. It proved enough.

1892-1893

The first round tie between Wednesday and Derby County went to a third match without the first two being drawn. A victory for each side had been overturned after protests; Wednesday won the third game 4-2.

1892-1893

Villa's hangover from last season's final disaster continued as they fell at the first hurdle. Their defeat to Second Division Darwen by the odd goal in nine was made all the more painful by the surrender of a 3-1 half-time lead.

LOGAN'S RUN

QUARTER FINALS

Bolton **3**	Liverpool **0**		
Sheff Wed **3**	Aston Villa **2**		
Derby **1**	Blackburn **4**		
Nottm Forest (1) **1**	Notts County (1) **4**		

SEMI FINALS

Bolton **2** Sheffield Wed **1**
at Fallowfield

Blackburn **0** Notts County **1**
at Bramall Lane

FINAL, 31 MARCH 1894, GOODISON PARK

Bolton Wanderers **1** Notts County **4**

BOLTON:
Sutcliffe, Somerville, Jones ©, Gardiner, Paton, Hughes, Tannahill, Wilson, **Cassidy (1)**, Bentley, Dickenson

NOTTS CO:
Toone, Harper, Hendry, Bramley, Calderhead ©, Shelton, **Watson (1)**, Donnelly, **Logan (3)**, Bruce, Daft

The early-round draws threw together many of the league's best sides. The eventual top two, Villa and Sunderland, clashed in the second round. Blackburn had already seen off West Bromwich by this stage.

Second Division Notts County announced their potential by knocking out high-flying Burnley in round one. After a run that had seen them despatch neighbours Nottingham Swifts and, in a major upset, Blackburn in the semi-final, County gave themselves the chance to become the first lower tier team to win the trophy. Another First Division outfit, Bolton, also playing in their first Cup Final, stood in their way.

After last year's stampede, the FA bowed to the inevitable and chose Goodison Park as the venue for the final. The crowd this year was gathered in relative comfort and witnessed a match that belied each club's league placing. Confident County were two goals up by the half-hour and the game was effectively over. Two second-half goals in three minutes from Jimmy Logan completed his hat-trick and the league's oldest club won the only major honour in their long history.

Despite Notts County's inferior league status, their team for the final boasted six internationals including the splendidly named Henry Butler Daft.

1893-1894 The domination by the midlands and north was such that only three southern clubs reached the first round proper. Neither Luton nor Woolwich Arsenal nor Reading progressed further.

1893-1894 Reading won their third qualifying round tie against Southampton St. Mary's courtesy of an escaped convict. Jimmy Stewart was a private in the army who had been confined to barracks on a charge. He was sprung by Reading long enough to play and score the winner. Reading's reward was an 18-0 caning by Preston in the next round.

REVENGE IS SWEET

VILLA:
Wilkes, Spencer, Welford, Reynolds, Jimmy Cowan, Russell, Athersmith, **Chatt (1)**, Jack Devey, Hodgetts, Smith

WEST BROM:
Reader, Williams, Horton, Perry, Higgins, Taggart, Bassett, McLeod, Richards, Hutchinson, Banks

Holders Notts County were dumped out 5-1 by Sheffield Wednesday in the first round, but any notion of a year of surprises had been scotched by the quarter-finals which included a monopoly of First Division teams for the first time.

For the third successive year a new venue hosted the final. Despite the absence of London Cup pedigree the Victorian Disneyland of Crystal Palace was chosen, primarily for the capacity of its natural grass bowl. Despite the novelty of the venue, both finalists were old stagers and had met before at this juncture in 1887 and 1892.

Many of the record 42,000 crowd missed the only goal, a pinball affair in the first minute that ricocheted off various players into the net. The last touch was credited to an unwitting John Devey. The goal remains the quickest goal scored in an FA Cup final. Villa survived 89 minutes of Albion onslaught to win their second final against the old enemy.

Sunderland were knocked out by Aston Villa for the third season in four. Two of these defeats were in semi-finals. These two sides were the giants of the game at the time.

1894–1895

Villa and Albion became the first two teams to contest three finals. It would be 103 years before Arsenal and Newcastle emulated them.

1894–1895

A local shoemaker, William Shillock, was exhibiting the Cup in his shop window, when it was stolen. A £10 reward was offered for information but there were no takers. Villa were fined £25, the money was spent on a replica trophy.

1894–1895

NOT-SO-BLACK WEDNESDAY

SHEFF WED:
Massey, Earp, Langley, Brandon, Crawshaw, Petrie, Brash, Brady, Bell, Davis, **Spikesley (2)**

WOLVES:
Tennant, Baugh, Dunn, Owen, Malpass, Griffiths, Tonks, Henderson, Beats, Wood, **Black (1)**

For the second successive year, the holders fell at the first. Derby, with England goal machine Steve Bloomer at their helm, installed themselves as Cup favourites after winning the tie of the round against Aston Villa. Villa would content themselves with their second league title, while Derby settled for second place. It was a surprise when Derby stumbled against Wolves in the semi-final, losing 2-1 despite Bloomer's fifth goal of the competition.

Sheffield Wednesday had fought their way through a tough draw to face Wolves in the final; Sunderland, Everton and Bolton were all top division sides.

Wednesday began the final as favourites and when Fred Spikesley shot them into a first-minute lead, Wolves' game looked up. David Black's free kick undid the damage seven minutes later only for Spikesley to crash a spectacular volley past a stationary Tennant soon afterwards. The game was not yet 20 minutes old.

Although the action scarcely ebbed in this entertaining final and Wolves' barnstorming style never let up, Wednesday held on. The city that lends its name to the oldest club of all finally had its first trophy.

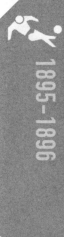

1895–1896

Fred Spikesley was renowned for his spectacular finishes. His second of the match, when he controlled the ball on one foot before volleying in an instant with the other, was hailed as the century's finest. The ball hit the stanchion so hard it rebounded instantly into play and led to a mad scramble before referee Simpson signalled a goal.

1895–1896

Don't be fooled into thinking the notion of a dim footballer was invented by the modern media. Wolves' keeper Tennant remained confused by Spiksley's double. He was convinced the game had finished level and was aghast after the final whistle to discover that there would be no replay.

1896

1897

1887

VILLA AT THE DOUBLE

Preston (1)(0) **2** Aston Villa (1)(0) **3**

Liverpool (1) **1** Nottm Forest (1) **0**

Everton **2** Blackburn **0**

Derby **2** Newton Heath **0**

SEMI FINALS

Aston Villa **3** Liverpool **0**
at Bramall Lane

Everton **3** Derby **2**
at Stoke

FINAL, 14 APRIL 1897, CRYSTAL PALACE

Aston Villa **3** Everton **2**

VILLA:
Whitehouse, Spencer, Reynolds, Evans, Cowan ©, **Crabtree (1)**, Athersmith, Devey, **Campbell (1)**, **Wheldon (1)**, Cowen

EVERTON:
Menham, Meechan, Storrier, **Boyle (1)**, Holt, Stewart, Taylor, **Bell (1)**, Hartley, Chadwick, Millward

For Everton's Bell, Chadwick and Holt, it was their second defeat at Crystal Palace in a week. They had formed part of an England side beaten 2-1 by Scotland the previous Saturday.

1896-1897

The FA Cup's silver anniversary tournament was a season to remember. It produced some of the highest-quality football and reminded everyone how far the bar had been raised by the professional game.

The first round put paid to the minnows as only three teams from outside the First Division reached the last sixteen. Only one, Newton Heath, made further progress, courtesy of a friendly draw that saw them matched against Southampton St. Mary's, the only remaining non-leaguers. This was the first appearance by the side that would become Manchester United in later years.

The third round saw Villa scramble past Preston in a second replay after two stalemates had produced just a single goal for each side. Derby, meanwhile, had purred into the semis, Bloomer helping himself to seven goals in three ties including hat-tricks against Barnsley and Bolton. For the second successive season Derby were thwarted in the semi-finals; their five-goal thriller against Everton seemed the season's high point, but the best was yet to come. In the other semi-final, chances of an all-Merseyside showpiece were ruined by an easy win for Aston Villa over Liverpool at Bramall Lane with a brace from the great Scottish centre-half, Jimmy Cowan.

A record 65,891 souls descended on Crystal Palace for the final, attracted by unprecedented hype. Villa were the best team in the country, Everton the biggest club. Such billing usually ends in anti-climax, but not this time. The customary, cagey opening to such affairs was abandoned as both sides unleashed waves of attack and counter-thrust at breakneck speed.

Having had the 1895 trophy stolen, an understandably paranoid Villa stored its replacement in a bank vault for most of the following year.

1896-1897

Campbell's first-time bullet-shot past Menham gave Villa the lead inside twenty minutes. By the half-hour, however, they were behind, as Richard Boyle's superb free-kick added to Bell's equaliser. Villa threw everything at Everton. Menham's goalkeeping heroics included an amazing double save that had Villa beseeching the referee to award a goal but he could stem the tide for barely seven minutes. First Jimmy Crabtree set up Freddy Wheldon to level then converted Reynolds' cross himself a minute before half-time. Villa were back in front.

The only surprise in the second half was the blank scoresheet. It was the turn of Whitehouse in the Villa goal to demonstrate his gymnastics whilst Reynolds and Athersmith rattled Everton's woodwork. With two minutes left in the game, Edgar Chadwick blazed Everton's best chance high and wide.

Villa had won their second FA Cup trophy in three years. Their joy doubled when they learned that Derby had dropped points in a league match against Burnley that day, thereby confirming that Villa would retain their league title. They had confirmed their status as the dominant side of the 1890s, matching Preston's double-winning achievement of 1889. It would be 64 years before it happened again.

1897

FOREST BRANCH OUT

1898

FOREST:
Allsop, Ritchie, Scott, Forman ©, **McPherson (1)**, Wragg, McInnes, Richards, Benbow, **Capes (2)**, Spouncer

DERBY:
Fryer, Methven, Leiper, Cox, Archie Goodall, Turner, John Goodall, **Bloomer (1)**, Boag, Stevenson, McQueen

1897–1898 The season's glamour was provided by Lucien Boullemier. Not content with scoring a shock winner for Burslem Port Vale against Sheffield United, this son of a ceramic artist was no mean painter himself. Even Queen Victoria sat as one of his models.

S heffield United would win their first league title at the end of the season, so it was a major shock when they were dumped out of the Cup by non-league Burslem Port Vale in a first-round replay.

Southampton have had some glory in the Cup in the later twentieth century but in Victorian times they were still a non-league side. A 4-0 thrashing of Bolton was one of three victories against league opposition in an heroic run which ended with a hard-fought semi-final defeat to Nottingham Forest in a replay at Crystal Palace.

Derby earned their final appearance, beating holders Aston Villa, Wolves, Liverpool and, in the semi-final, Everton – a reversal of the result from the previous year's encounter at the same stage.

Sneaking through the back door were Forest. Victory at West Brom apart, lower or non-league opposition littered their route to the final.

Derby started as favourites – they had beaten Forest 5-0 in a league match only a week before. Come the final whistle though, it was Bloomer and co. who were contemplating their losers' medals. Forest's hero was Arthur Capes, whose two goals halted a stuttering Derby.

1897–1898 Burslem Port Vale would become a league club the following season but would only survive seven years. They would regain league status after eight games of the 1919-20 season when Leeds City were expelled for financial irregularities with the Potteries side, now playing as plain Port Vale, fulfilling City's remaining fixtures. Southampton, despite frequent appearances in the latter stages of the Cup, would have to wait until the league expanded to three divisions in 1920-1921 to gain league status.

1898

BLOOMIN' CURSED

1899

SHEFF UTD:
Foulke, Thickett, Boyle, Johnson, Morren, Needham ©, **Bennett (1)**, **Beers (1)**, Hedley, **Almond (1)**, **Priest (1)**

DERBY:
Fryer, Methven, Staley, Cox, Paterson, May, Arkesden, Bloomer, **Boag (1)**, McDonald, Allen

This was Bloomer's last appearance in a final. Indeed he was probably relieved not to be around when Derby were humiliated by Bury in 1903. With Derby largely a mid-table outfit, the great striker, perhaps the game's first superstar, would retire without a winner's medal of any sort.

1888–1889

As the nineteenth century drew to a close, the FA could reflect with pride on the burgeoning success of a competition whose first final twenty-seven years earlier had attracted only 2,000 spectators. By contrast 73,833 jammed Crystal Palace to witness that season's showpiece.

Southampton provided an upset again by beating Notts County in the first round away from home. Tottenham Hotspur, another non-league side, showed that the capital's teams were improving when they put out Sunderland.

Sheffield United won through to the final only after a marathon semi against Liverpool. A 2-2 draw was followed by a rousing 4-4 at Bolton. The third game at Fallowfield was marred by crowd trouble – as games often were at that highly unsuitable venue – and was abandoned when the light failed, with Liverpool leading 1-0. Sheffield reversed that scoreline in the fourth and decisive encounter at Derby.

Once again, the fall guys in the final were the Rams. Although Sheffield United were defending league champions, their form had largely deserted them and they finished this season only one place above relegation. Mid-table Derby looked to have put last season's disappointment behind them when John Boag gave them the early advantage. The game should have been over early in the second half but the normally deadly Steve Bloomer misfired badly for the second time. It proved a disastrous omen.

On the hour, Walter Bennett headed an equaliser. Less than ten minutes later a shell-shocked Derby were 3-1 down. Priest twisted the knife in the final moments.

Rumours that Derby were cursed by gypsies gained greater currency after their final display. The club was apparently hexed after ordering travellers to leave land that they needed to develop the Baseball Ground.

The final was a fitting stage for the larger-than-life presence of William 'Fatty' Foulke. The Sheffield United keeper, weighing in at more than twenty-two stones, undoubtedly ate all the pies, and all the hot-dogs and doughnuts too.

1888–1889

1899

1900

1899

1900

RIGHT OLD SHAKER-UP

BURY:
Thompson, Darroch, Davidson, Pray, Leeming, Ross, Richards, **Wood (1)**, **McLuckie (2)**, Sagar, **Plant (1)**

SOUTHAMPTON:
Robinson, Meechan, Durber, Meston, Chadwick, Petrie, Turner, Yates, Farrell, Wood, Milward

The early rounds were seriously affected by freezing temperatures, blizzards and rock-hard pitches. The final, by contrast, was played in a heatwave.

1899–1900

This was a fun season for the underdog. The wintry weather provided some 'great levellers', and coupled with some notable early pairings saw an unfamiliar line-up by the semi-finals. The usual suspects, Villa, Derby and the like, had been replaced by three clubs for whom the last four represented uncharted waters.

Southampton, a redoubtable cup side, started their campaign with a stunning 3-0 away win at Everton. Further success against Newcastle and West Brom led them into a semi-final against highly unlikely opponents.

Aston Villa were favourites to win pretty much everything in those days, indeed they would win the league for the fifth time in seven years that season. A quarter-final against a team with its origins in a jam factory works XI, Millwall Athletic, hardly seemed to hold any terrors. The Southern League team thwarted Villa, twice earning hard-fought draws and a third match at Reading. Within twenty minutes, Villa were two down. A goal from Banks and a spectacular solo effort from Millwall's skilful amateur Gettins had rocked the champions. The rest of the game was classic Cup fodder; wave upon wave of Villa attacks against less talented but resolute opponents. Despite conceding ten minutes from time, Millwall hung on for a famous victory. The South London side would have to wait 104 years for a final appearance; Southampton won the semi-final replay 3-0.

In the other semi-final, Forest's experience failed to give them the edge over Bury, who duly lined up against Southern League Southampton.

Despite the Saints' impressive recent record, they were overawed in front of nearly 70,000, the vast majority of whom were rooting for the south's first finalists since Old Etonians in 1883.

Bury pooped the party by taking a three goal lead with the match barely a quarter finished. Time was played out with no further ado and the Lancashire side had their first trophy.

1900

NO RESPECT

1901

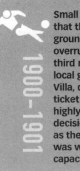

Small Heath, fearful that their tiny ground would be overrun for their third round tie with local giants Aston Villa, declared an all-ticket match. This highly unusual decision backfired as the attendance was well below capacity.

S
outhampton's run the previous season clearly inspired other non-leaguers. Tottenham and Reading won through to the last eight, and copped each other in the draw. Spurs' disrespect for reputations had seen them win 4-2 at Deepdale to oust Preston, before disposing of holders Bury in round two. Three other First Division clubs fell to lowlier opposition in the first round. Newcastle, Blackburn, and Stoke fell to Middlesbrough, Woolwich Arsenal and Small Heath (later Birmingham City) respectively.

The other non-league darlings were Kettering Town, who upset Second Division Chesterfield and probably fancied a trip to Middlesbrough, another division two outfit. A 5-0 hammering brought them sharply down to earth.

Sheffield United's league form had been unimpressive but four prime top division scalps in Sunderland, Everton, Wolves and Villa expedited their passage to Crystal Palace on merit. After this roll call, a bunch of Southern Leaguers would surely present no problem.

The first appearance in the final by a London club in twenty-one years filled the vast Crystal Palace bowl to bursting. The unexpectedly tight thriller turned on one bizarre moment. Tottenham had just taken an unexpected lead in the fifty-first minute, Brown's second overhauling Priest's opener for United. Then Clawley in the Spurs goal fumbled a shot from Bennett but appeared to have spared his blushes by scrambling the ball to safety. The linesman's signal for a corner duly followed but referee Kingscott signalled a goal-kick. Changing his mind, he then confused everyone further by inexplicably signalling a goal before a flabbergasted Clawley could restart, and Bennett duly entered the record books as scorer of United's equaliser.

Justice prevailed in the replay, although Spurs again had to come from behind and left it late before Smith and Brown ensured victory in the final fifteen minutes. London had its winners at last.

At their celebratory dinner, Spurs started a tradition that still endures when they tied ribbons in the club colours to the handles of the trophy.

1901

DASHING BLADES

1902

FINAL, 19 APRIL 1902, CRYSTAL PALACE

Sheffield United **1** Southampton **1**

SHEFF UTD:
Foulke, Thickett, Boyle, Johnson, Wilkinson, Needham ©, Bennett, **Common (1)**, Hedley, Priest, Lipsham

SOUTHAMPTON:
Robinson, Fry, Molyneux, Meston, Bowman, Lee, Arthur Turner, **Wood © (1)**, Brown, Chadwick, Joe Turner

FINAL REPLAY, 26 APRIL 1902, CRYSTAL PALACE

Sheffield United **2** Southampton **1**

SHEFF UTD:
Foulke, Thickett, Boyle, Johnson, Wilkinson, Needham ©, **Barnes (1)**, Common, **Hedley (1)**, Priest, Lipsham

SOUTHAMPTON:
Robinson, Fry, Molyneux, Meston, Bowman, Lee, Arthur Turner, Wood ©, **Brown (1)**, Chadwick, Joe Turner

---

The Cup's most endearing feature is its lack of reverence for reputation. So it proved this season as none of the league's top four survived the first two rounds.

Its respect for tradition was evident in Sheffield United's third final in four seasons. Their captain and playmaker, Ernie 'Nudger' Needham, had vowed to make amends for the previous season's defeat, when he felt his team had 'let the north down'.

Once again, the Blades reached the summit by a difficult route, taking nine games to win a trophy they could have claimed in five. Fred Priest won an epic semi-final saga against Derby, netting the only goal of the second replay.

In the final, after a first half best forgotten, Alf Common livened up proceedings with the opener ten minutes after the break. With the game meandering to a close, Harry Wood levelled with two minutes remaining.

United looked to have repeated their error in a replay which they led for sixty-eight minutes only to be pegged back again. With eleven minutes remaining, Billy Barnes pounced on a parry from Saints' keeper Robinson to fire home the winner.

Southampton's Cup Final team included England international C.B. Fry. Fry was the greatest all-round sportsman of his era, maybe of any era. He was even better known as a cricketer, scoring ninety-four first class hundreds and playing in twenty-six Tests for England. In addition he won a blue for rugby at Oxford, held the world long-jump record, and was a proficient sailor. Fry was also a top scholar, became an excellently lucid writer, and later an MP (in the days when that post retained a degree of respectability.)

The weather brought heavy snow to the first and second rounds. Unlike the rash of postponements that would occur today, only two games were called off.

1901–1902

1902

BURIED

1901

1903

BURY:
Monteith, Lindsay, McEwen, Johnston, Thorpe, **Ross © (1)**, Richards, **Wood (1)**, **Sagar (1)**, **Leeming (2)**, **Plant (1)**

DERBY:
Fryer, Methven, Morris, Warren, Archie Goodall, May, Warrington, York, Boag, Richards, Davis

This was one of the duller years. There were few shocks or classics – only Millwall's defeat of Everton in the quarter-finals. The final is prominent in the record books for one reason only. It was the biggest-ever margin of victory.

Derby's day started badly and just got worse – perhaps the gypsy curse was still working. Their main threat, Steve Bloomer, was already injured and goalkeeper Jack Fryer was crocked shortly after the start of the match. Only when 2-0 down did the Rams bother to replace him with an outfield player. He unwisely returned in goal after the third, only to concede two in the next three minutes.

By now Derby were playing with only nine fit players, with the cramp-ridden Charlie Morris at a virtual standstill. He replaced Fryer in goal after Bury's fifth, the equivalent of leaving the stable door open to ensure the other horse bolts as well. One can only imagine the harrumphing of the venerable Lord Kinnaird as he presented the trophy.

Quiz question:
Who won their only two Cup Finals by an aggregate margin of 10-0?
Answer:
Bury

1902–1903

Surprisingly, only four of the Bury team survived from the win three years previously. Jack Plant, a chubby, but skilful left winger in the John Robertson mould, and inside-forward Willie Wood scored in both finals. The captain George Ross and Billy Richards were the other survivors.

1902–1903

LANCASHIRE HOT-POT

QUARTER FINALS

Sheffield Utd **0** Bolton **2**

Derby **2** Blackburn **1**

Manchester C (0) **3** Middlesbrough (0) **1**

Tottenham (1) **0** Sheffield Wed (1) **2**

SEMI FINALS

Bolton **1** Derby **0**
at Molyneux

Manchester C **3** Sheffield Wed **0**
at Goodison Park

FINAL, 23 APRIL 1904, CRYSTAL PALACE

Manchester City **1** Bolton Wanderers **0**

MAN CITY:
Hillman, McMahon, Burgess, Frost, Hynds, Ashworth, **Meredith (1)**, Livingstone, Gillespie, Turnbull, Booth

BOLTON:
Davies, Brown, Struthers, Clifford, Greenhalgh, Freebairn, Stokes, Marsh, Yenson, White, Taylor

A s the third round loomed, this threatened to be a tournament dominated by the big boys. Six of the eight were from the First Division, with only Tottenham (again) and Second Division Bolton providing the romance.

It was Wanderers who stayed the distance as they shrugged off mediocre league form to surprise Sheffield United at Bramall Lane, then beat Derby in a tense semi-final at Molineux. They were joined in the final by Manchester City, newly promoted to the First Division at Bolton's expense. Surprisingly, given the power of the county's teams, this was the first all-Lancashire final.

Given a fairer wind, Bolton might have won. They were denied not just by Meredith's goal. Yenson broke through the City defence but, in a moment re-enacted by Willie Young and Paul Allen in 1980, he was cruelly tripped with only the keeper to beat. A free kick was rough justice. When White hit a post in the last minute, Wanderers knew their luck was out. City held out and duly collected their first major trophy; Wanderers had at least made amends for a humiliating defeat by Bristol City the previous year.

For the first time since the inaugural season of 1871-72, all twenty-two players were appearing in their first final.

1903–1904

Tottenham's third round tie against Aston Villa was abandoned after the huge crowd at White Hart Lane spilled on to the pitch with Villa leading 1-0. An unimpressed FA fined Spurs £350 and ordered a replay at Villa Park. Tottenham had the last laugh, winning 1-0.

1903–1904

City's Sam Ashworth was one of only three amateurs to have won the Cup since 1900.

1903–1904

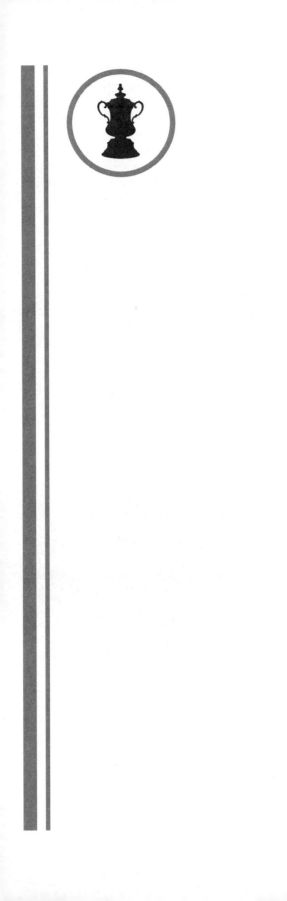

1904

DOUBLE DRAT

1905

VILLA:
George, Spencer ©, Miles, Pearson, Leake, Windmill, Brawn, Garratty, **Hampton (2)**, Bache, Hall

NEWCASTLE:
Lawrence, McCombie, Carr, Gardner, Aitken, McWilliam, Rutherford, Howie, Appleyard, Veitch, Gosnell

1904-1905

Harry Hampton, the final's youngest player, became a legend at Villa. His life ended tragically after being gassed during the Great War. Hampton was a classic old-fashioned centre-forward, a battering ram who thrived on good service from the wing, and terrified opposing goalkeepers – Newcastle's Jimmy Lawrence complained of seeing double after a typically boisterous charge from Hampton.

The big boys flexed their muscles again. For the second successive year, six of the eight quarter-finalists were from the top flight. Once again, one of the interlopers was Bolton, who gained some satisfaction for their final defeat by knocking out their conquerors, Manchester City, in the second round.

Yet non-league Portsmouth had beaten First Division Small Heath in round one and Southampton put paid to Wolves on their way to the last eight for the fifth time in eight seasons.

All the romance soon vanished; the semi-finals were contested by three of the top four in the league, including title winners Newcastle plus last year's champions Sheffield Wednesday.

Newcastle prevailed and arrived at Crystal Palace to face Villa, confident of becoming only the third club to win the Double. Instead, they were caught cold.

A vast crowd, only the second six-figure attendance to date, were thrilled by young Harry Hampton's second-minute header that give Villa the lead. Newcastle, with Bill Appleyard rampant, tried to claw their way back but the longer the game went on the more dangerous Villa looked. Hampton settled a bruising encounter with a tap-in after Lawrence in the Villa goal had brilliantly blocked a drive from Hall. The Geordies' Double dream was in tatters.

1904-1905

Biggest bore: the first round tie between Fulham and Reading produced a solitary goal in three games. For the record, Fulham scored it. The surprise was that anyone stayed awake to notice.

MERSEY BEATS

EVERTON:
Scott, Crelley, Walter Balmer, Makepeace, Taylor, Abbott, Sharp, Bolton, **Young (1)**, Settle, Hardman

NEWCASTLE:
Lawrence, McCombie, Carr, Gardner, Aitken, McWilliam, Rutherford, Howie, Orr, Veitch, Gosnell

The Cup just kept getting bigger. The expansion of the Football League from thirty-six to forty clubs and a proliferation of non-league sides meant a doubling of the competition proper. An extra round was added, which meant the elite clubs now needed six victories to take the trophy.

None of this appeared to hamper Newcastle's inexorable progress to erasing last season's disappointment. Although requiring replays to see off Derby and Birmingham, their free-scoring attack hit twenty en route to the final. They were a terrific side, with the Scots Aitken and McWilliam at the heart of the best midfield in the English game.

Everton had something to prove. Liverpool had won Merseyside's first championship, and were on course for the Double when they met their neighbours in the semi-final at Villa Park. Two goals in a few minutes settled it: a lucky deflection and a tap-in from winger Harold Hardman.

In the final, Everton's defence worked overtime to lock out the Magpies' forwards in a disappointing match. The Scotland centre-forward, Sandy Young, stole it for the Merseysiders in the last quarter of an hour.

1905-1906

Everton fielded two dual football/cricket internationals in the final. Jack Sharp and Harry Makepeace would both play Tests for England at the summer game, although Makepeace had to wait until 1920, when he was thirty-nine years old. Makepeace also won a league title (with Everton in 1915) and a County Championship medal (with Lancashire in 1904).

1905-1906

Harold Hardman was one of only three Cup-winning amateurs since 1900. He also won an Olympic gold medal in 1908 and served as chairman of Manchester United.

WEDNESDAY LICK TOFFEES

EVERTON:
Scott, Bob Balmer, Walter Balmer, Makepeace, Taylor, Abbott, **Sharp (1)**, Bolton, Young, Settle, Hardman

SHEFF WED:
Lyall, Layton, Burton, Brittleton, Crawshaw, Bartlett, Chapman, Bradshaw, Wilson, **Stewart (1)**, **Simpson (1)**

1906-1907

Jack Sharp, scorer of the Final's equaliser, would later join the board at Goodison Park. In 1984 another Sharp scored for Everton in the Cup final. Coincidentally, Graeme's goal against Watford was also scored in the thirty-eighth minute.

Southern League Crystal Palace produced one of the biggest shocks in the Cup's history when they put Newcastle out in the first round. Given no hope before the game, Palace gave it everything and triumphed 1-0 against a complacent and off-colour United. At least Newcastle were able to take consolation from that old cliché and 'concentrate on the league', which they duly won.

Newcastle's early exit suggested the door would be open for the winner of the Everton v Sheffield United tie. After squeezing through this one, Everton then made heavy weather of beating non-league West Ham and Bolton. This set up a tie with the season's heroes, Palace, who had made further progress at the expense of fellow Southern League members, Fulham and Brentford. After another spirited display in a 1-1 draw, Palace finally cracked at Goodison, losing the replay 4-0.

Wednesday's progress was equally arduous and the final was their eighth game in the competition. An inferior side to Everton, they relied heavily on the marksmanship of Jimmy Stewart and Andrew Wilson.

Stewart was on the mark again at Crystal Palace but Sharp's equaliser sent the teams in level at half-time. The second half was nip and tuck before George Simpson wrecked Everton's hopes of defending the trophy with less than two minutes remaining.

1906-1907

Wednesday had last won the Cup in 1896, beating Southampton, Sunderland, Everton and Wolves on the way. They faced all four opponents in 1907.

SURELY THIS TIME?

WOLVES:
Lunn, Jones, Collins, **Hunt (1)**, Wooldridge, Bishop, **Harrison (1)**, Shelton, **Hedley (1)**, Radford, Pedley

NEWCASTLE:
Lawrence, McCracken, Pudan, Gardner, Veitch, McWilliam, Rutherford, **Howie (1)**, Appleyard, Speedie, Wilson

W olverhampton Wanderers had been founder members of the Football League in 1888. They had entered the Cup every year since 1883 but their 1893 victory remained their only major trophy. Prospects looked bleak at the turn of the year as the Black Country club were languishing in the Second Division but they tiptoed through the back door to the final. Bury were their only top flight opposition en route, an easy win over perennial Davids, Southampton, clinching their visit to Crystal Palace.

Waiting were a rampant Newcastle. Although about to renounce their league title to Manchester United, they remained the decade's dominant team. Wolves' best hope seemed to lie with Newcastle's paranoia about the two words 'Crystal' and 'Palace'. Beaten in two finals at the venue and dumped out the previous year by the arena's non-league namesake, stout-hearted Geordies fell to pieces at the mere mention of them.

After forty minutes, all looked calm enough as Newcastle were largely in control. Wolves promptly scored twice before half time and the game was up. Howie's reply with seventeen minutes left proved a false dawn and Harrison administered the coup de grace.

It was a bad year too for Newcastle's fiercest rivals, Sunderland. An easy draw at New Brompton (later Gillingham) in the first round looked like a cakewalk, but a hat-trick from home forward McGibbon wiped out the Wearsiders' early lead.

The final was an added disappointment for Newcastle's Bill Appleyard. He failed to become only the fourth player to score in every round, having already netted eight times.

1907-1908

Wolves could claim their victory relied on divine intervention as their team included one Reverend Kenneth Hunt. Indeed, the sermonising half-back opened the scoring.

1907-1908

UNITED: FIRST OF MANY

QUARTER FINALS

Glossop (0) **0** Bristol C (0) **1**

Derby **3** Nottm Forest **0**

Burnley **2** Manchester Utd **3**

Newcastle (2) **3** Sunderland (2) **0**

SEMI FINALS

Bristol C **2** Derby **1**

at Birmingham after 1-1 at Stamford Bridge

Manchester Utd **1** Newcastle **0**

at Bramall Lane

FINAL, 24 APRIL 1909, CRYSTAL PALACE

Manchester Utd **1** Bristol City **0**

MAN UTD:
Moger, Stacey, Hayes, Duckworth, Roberts ©, Bell, Meredith, Halse, Jimmy Turnbull, **Sandy Turnbull (1)**, Wall

BRISTOL C:
Clay, Annan, Cottle, Hanlin, Wedlock, Spear, Staniforth, Hardy, Gilligan, Burton, Hilton

One of the semi-finals of the 1909 contest was billed as the game of the season. The previous year Manchester United's meteoric rise had culminated in a league title in only their second season in the top flight. Newcastle were about to take back the championship, scaling the heights for the third time in five years. A tense struggle at Bramall Lane saw Newcastle's Double hopes dashed by a solitary goal from Harold Halse.

Earlier United had survived a scare in the fourth round. A blizzard halted their tie at Turf Moor with eighteen minutes to go and Burnley leading 1-0. United scraped through 3-2 in the replayed fixture.

Inevitably, the final that followed the semi's 'Lord Mayor's show' was uneventful. Bristol City were a shadow of the side that had finished as league runners-up two years previously. City couldn't cope with the power of Charlie Roberts and the trickery of Meredith, and once Alec 'Sandy' Turnbull scored midway through the first half, the Bristolians offered little to suggest a comeback. The Cup returned to an ecstatic reception at Manchester Town Hall.

1908-1909
Manchester United were still playing their home fixtures at Bank Street in Clayton. Old Trafford, though, was under construction and opened in February 1910.

1908-1909
This was definitely the highpoint for 'Sandy' Turnbull. He was later banned for life after a match-fixing scandal was uncovered. In 1917 he was killed in the Great War.

1908-1909
As both finalists normally played in red, the FA even-handedly decreed that both should play in neutral colours. Bristol City wore an unfamiliar blue and white strip while United took the field in all white.

1909 1910

AT LAST

NEWCASTLE:
Lawrence, McCracken, Whitson, Veitch ©, Low,
McWilliam, Rutherford (1), Howie, Higgins,
Shepherd, Wilson

BARNSLEY:
Mearns, Downs, Ness, Glendinning, Boyle ©,
Utley, Tufnell (1), Lillycrop, Gadsby, Forman,
Bartrop

NEWCASTLE:
Lawrence, McCracken, Carr, Veitch ©, Low,
McWilliam, Rutherford, Howie, Higgins,
Shepherd (2, 1p), Wilson

BARNSLEY:
Mearns, Downs, Ness, Glendinning, Boyle ©,
Utley, Tufnell, Lillycrop, Gadsby, Forman,
Bartrop

As was customary in all the previous drawn finals, no extra time was played. The tie went directly to a replay..

1909–1910

After three final defeats in the previous five years, Newcastle must have arrived at Crystal Palace weighed down by rabbits' feet and horseshoes. As in their last final, an apparently mediocre Second Division side had come along to make up the numbers.

Newcastle's campaign had almost failed to get off the ground. They were held at non-league Stoke in the first round and only squeezed through 2-1 in the replay. After that neither they nor Barnsley had to contend with much serious opposition as the other big clubs conveniently carved each other up. Non-league Coventry helped by eliminating Preston and Nottingham Forest, both First Division sides, before succumbing to Everton. Barnsley's demolition of Everton in a semi-final replay earned them a crack at the Magpies.

Groundhog Day was in full swing when Harry Tufnell put the Yorkshiremen in front. An increasingly frantic Newcastle huffed and puffed to no avail. With only seven minutes remaining salvation arrived via Jock Rutherford's head. To the Magpies' immense relief, the replay was 200 miles from the accursed Crystal Palace. After a tense first half, two from Albert Shepherd finally laid their ghosts to rest. Greater Cup glory still awaited Newcastle, but no victory would ever be as sweet as this one.

Albert Shepherd's penalty was the first ever in a final. Newcastle had signed Shepherd from Bolton. While still a Wanderer he had scored six playing for the Football League against the Scottish League.

1909–1910

BANTAMS, COCK O'THE NORTH

NEWCASTLE:
Lawrence, McCracken, Whitson, Veitch ©, Low, Willis, Rutherford, Jobey, Stewart, Higgins, Wilson

BRADFORD C:
Mellors, Campbell, Taylor, Robinson, Gildea, McDonald, Logan, Speirs © , O'Rourke, Devine, Thompson

NEWCASTLE:
Lawrence, McCracken, Whitson, Veitch ©, Low, Willis, Rutherford, Jobey, Stewart, Higgins, Wilson

BRADFORD C:
Mellors, Campbell, Taylor, Robinson, Torrance, McDonald, Logan, **Speirs © (1)**, O'Rourke, Devine, Thompson

Teams were competing for a new trophy this season. The FA were concerned that the old cup, which they had failed to copyright, was being devalued by the number of copies on the market. They touted around the country's finest silversmiths for a new design and awarded the fifty guinea contract to Frattorini and Sons of Bradford.

The old trophy found an appropriate and honourable home; it was given to Lord Kinnaird to celebrate his twenty-one years as FA President.

This was one of those seasons when the big boys fell like nine-pins. Sunderland and the two Sheffield teams fell to non-league opposition – Norwich, Darlington and Coventry respectively. First Division Bristol City, finalists only two years before, were beaten by a team from the Birmingham & District League – Crewe Alexandra. This year's champions, Manchester United, having eliminated one of their chief rivals, Aston Villa, were humiliated by non-league West Ham, while Everton were thrashed 5-0 by Second Division Derby.

The last eight contained some unfamiliar names: Bradford City, Chelsea (just starting to establish themselves), and Swindon. Navigating the storm of shocks were Newcastle who survived a replay against non-league Northampton, and then thumped Derby and Chelsea to reach their fifth final in seven years.

Bradford had conceded only one goal en route to their first final, and they were far from rank outsiders; they finished fifth in the First Division, three places above their opponents.

Bradford's defence stayed resolute and Newcastle couldn't breach them in three hours of football. Both games are best forgotten, but the history books will note that this remains the Bantams' only major honour. In its first year, the now familiar big-eared trophy came home to Bradford where it was made.

Two weeks before the final Bradford City and Newcastle met in a league match. In a foretaste of the replay, the Bantams won 1-0.

1910–1911

Crewe's captain in their stunning win at Bristol City was a gentleman by the name of Spittle. A distant antecedent of El Hadji Diouf perhaps?

1910–1911

TYKE TRIUMPH

SEMI FINALS

Barnsley **1** Swindon **0**

at Notts County after 0-0 at Stamford Bridge

West Brom **1** Blackburn **0**

at Hillsborough

FINAL, 20 APRIL 1912, CRYSTAL PALACE

Barnsley **0** West Bromwich Albion **0**

BARNSLEY:
Cooper, Downs, Taylor, Glendinning, Bratley,
Utley, Bartrop, Tufnell, Lillycrop, Travers, Moore

WEST BROM:
Pearson, Cook, Pennington, Baddeley, Buck,
McNeal, Jephcott, Wright, Pailor, Bowser,
Shearman

FINAL REPLAY, 24 APRIL 1912, BRAMALL LANE

Barnsley **1** West Bromwich Albion **0**

BARNSLEY:
Cooper, Downs, Taylor, Glendinning, Bratley,
Utley, Bartrop, **Tufnell (1)**, Lillycrop, Travers,
Moore

WEST BROM:
Pearson, Cook, Pennington, Baddeley, Buck,
McNeal, Jephcott, Wright, Pailor, Bowser,
Shearman

This remains Barnsley's only major trophy. They have never even made it past the sixth round since.

1911–1912

The Cup that cheers became the Cup that bores. Both semi-finals and the final produced goalless games and too many earlier encounters were either sterile affairs or routine thrashings. Relieving the tedium were Manchester United and Blackburn, whose six-goal thriller was a minor classic which Blackburn edged 4-2.

Swindon provided the romance again, progressing to the last eight for the third successive season where they qualified for their second semi-final.

Bradford City had won the title the previous year with an obdurate defence. Barnsley took heed and went a step further. Their cup run took in six goalless games, three of these against the holders who Barnsley beat easily 3-0 in the fourth match. For the second time in three years Barnsley won through to the final as a Second Division club. First Division West Brom may have simply lost the will to live after being forced to a replay after yet another 0-0. Deep into extra-time, with most of the crowd no doubt sleeping peacefully, Harry Tufnell put everyone out of their misery. Draw a veil over this one.

Harry Tufnell scored his second goal in a final, having scored the opener for Barnsley against Newcastle two years earlier.

1911–1912

Not even the final referee, one J.R. Schumacher, could inject some pace into this drab encounter.

1911–1912

1912

HIGH FIVES FOR VILLA

1913

VILLA:
Hardy, Lyons, Weston, **Barber (1)**, Harrop, Leach, Wallace, Halse, Hampton, Stephenson, Bache

SUNDERLAND:
Butler, Gladwin, Ness, Cuggy, Thomson, Low, Mordue, Buchan, Richardson, Holley, Martin

Oldham had to wait seventy-seven years for their next semi-final. Despite two chances in the 1990s, they have so far failed to reach their first final.

1912–1913

This was one of the competition's most eagerly anticipated finals. Both sides were pushing for a Double and both had a handful of top class players. Villa had cruised to the final, enjoying successive 5-0 wins against West Ham, Crystal Palace and Bradford. Harold Halse had seven goals in the competition before the final, Harry Hampton five, and Clem Stephenson, the artful, will-o'-the-wisp inside-forward, had four. A solitary goal from Stephenson saw them through an unexpectedly tough semi-final against Oldham, enjoying a successful decade as a First Division side.

Sunderland had made more laboured progress in spite of the presence of a trio of England internationals Charlie Buchan, the finest midfield player of the era, Frank Cuggy and Jackie Mordue. They needed replays in both the quarter-finals and semis, against Newcastle twice, and Burnley. The replay against Burnley was a humdinger, a decisive goal from inside left George Holley seeing Sunderland home 3-2.

Clem Stephenson dreamed that Villa would win 1-0 with a header from Tommy Barber; he even told Buchan so as they waited for the ball to come back from the crowd. When referee, Mr Adams, awarded Villa only the second penalty in Cup final history, Stephenson's oracular vision seemed awry. At least that was the case until Charlie Wallace nearly hit the corner flag with the penalty.

Villa's goalkeeper Sam Hardy was injured in the second half, but Sunderland could only hit the woodwork while he was off the field. On seventy-five minutes Villa earned a corner. Wallace, who had locked himself in the toilet at half-time after his penalty miss, crossed from the right and Tommy Barber rose to head home. For Villa, and Stephenson, quite literally in his case, it was a dream fulfilled.

Sunderland had their compensation later. A hard-earned draw at Villa sparked a run that saw them clinch the league title by four points from their rivals.

VINTAGE CLARET

BURNLEY:
Sewell, Bamford, Taylor, Halley, Boyle ©,
Watson, Nesbit, Lindley, **Freeman (1)**,
Hodgson, Mosscrop

LIVERPOOL:
Campbell, Longworth, Pursell, Fairfoul,
Ferguson, McKinley, Sheldon, Metcalfe, Miller,
Lacey, Nicholl

W hilst the Cup, like the game itself, continued to spiral in popularity, the finals were often anti-climatic affairs. Burnley and Liverpool, two lower mid-table sides, served up the fifth 1-0 result in six seasons.

As usual the drama had gone before the main act with so many of the big guns misfiring. Eventual champions Blackburn stuttered at home to Manchester City and only two of the league's top nine reached the quarter-finals.

Burnley, having reached their first semi-final the year before, did even better this time. Their route to Crystal Palace was far more arduous than their opponents: Derby, Bolton, Sunderland and Sheffield United were all First Division teams.

Liverpool, a tough semi with Villa notwithstanding, a game won with a brace from left-winger Jimmy Nicholl, had fluked the draw. All their opposition in the earlier rounds had been non-league, a fact that accurately reflects the flatness of that season's competition.

This was the first final for both clubs. It would be a few more decades before Liverpool's dominant days arrived. They had only two previous semis to their name since first entering in 1892.

1913–1914

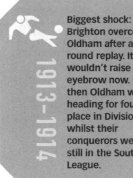

Biggest shock: Brighton overcoming Oldham after a first round replay. It wouldn't raise an eyebrow now. Back then Oldham were heading for fourth place in Division One whilst their conquerors were still in the Southern League.

1913–1914

Burnley's David Taylor had also been a winner with Bradford City in 1911. Conversely, Liverpool's Henry Ness picked up a second loser's medal. He had appeared for Barnsley in 1910.

1913–1914

BLUES GET THE BLUES

CHELSEA:
Molyneux, Bettridge, Harrow, Taylor, Logan, Walker, Ford, Halse, Thomson, Croal, McNeil

SHEFF UTD:
Gough, Cook, English, Surgess, Brelsford, Utley ©, **Simmons (1)**, **Fazackerly (1)**, **Kitchen (1)**, Masterman, Evans

Biggest shock: Swansea Town's first round victory over Blackburn Rovers provided the last instance of the reigning league champions' elimination by a non-league club.

1914–1915

For a nation eight months into the mire and carnage of the First World War, football was proving a worthless distraction. Attendances had halved, and many of the nation's finest players were away on active duty. As its professionals were shipped off to the front, a dark curtain descended that was to last for four years. Lord Derby presented the trophy with the warning that it was time to 'play a sterner game for England'.

The trophy went to Sheffield United. After their purple period incorporating two victories and three finals in four seasons at the turn of the century, they at last returned to centre stage albeit in a different setting. With Crystal Palace requisitioned for war work, attention switched to Old Trafford, opened only five years previously.

The demise of London as host city coincided with only its second finalist. Chelsea's league form had been dismal but they had played out of their skins to topple Newcastle and, most surprisingly, eventual champions Everton in the semi-final.

The final, known as 'the Khaki Final' because the crowd was made up largely of servicemen, proved a step too far. United were well in control throughout, although the scoreline remained tight until two goals in the last six minutes provided a fairer reflection.

Although housed at a proper football venue, this wartime final attracted the lowest attendance, replays excluded, since 1896. Only 49,557 attended.

1914–1915

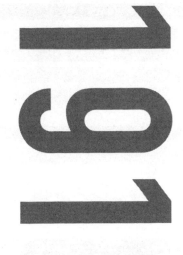

1919

VILLA TAKE A BOW

1920

Huddersfield **2** Liverpool **1**

Bristol C **2** Bradford C **0**

Chelsea **4** Bradford PA **1**

Tottenham **0** Aston Villa **1**

SEMI FINALS

Huddersfield **2** Bristol C **1**
at Stamford Bridge

Chelsea **1** Aston Villa **3**
at Bramall Lane

FINAL, 24 APRIL 1920, STAMFORD BRIDGE

Aston Villa **1** Huddersfield Town **0**
after extra time

VILLA:
Hardy, Smart, Weston, Ducatt ©, Barson, Moss, Wallace, **Kirton (1)**, Walker, Stephenson, Dorrell

HUDDERSFIELD:
Mutch, Wood, Bullock, Slade, Wilson, Watson, Richardson, Mann, Taylor, Swann, Islip

1919–1920

This season's fifteen minutes of fame was reserved for the splendidly-named Thorneycroft's Wanderers. The Hampshire works' club reached the first round for the only time at their first attempt. A heroic draw against high-flying Burnley set the pulses racing, only for the Clarets to snuff out the dream 5-0 at Turf Moor. But just six years later, Thorneycroft's were defunct.

F ive years of footballing drought ended on 10 January 1920, when a nation reeling from the bloodiest conflict in history gratefully embraced the semblance of normality offered by the FA Cup.

The Football League had been expanded, with twenty-two clubs now in each division, a formula that was adhered to for the next seventy-five years. Despite this the Cup lost none of its appeal.

Bristol City accepted the underdog challenge. The finalists of 1909 had lost their top division status five campaigns previously and were plodding along in mid-table. They raised their game sufficiently to embarrass Arsenal and Bradford City, before Huddersfield edged an all Second Division semi-final at Stamford Bridge.

The achievement of Huddersfield in making it that far was even more remarkable. The season had started badly with Leeds City being ejected from the league for making irregular payments. Hard on the heels of that scandal, an FA investigation into Huddersfield's affairs revealed they were, essentially, insolvent. A public appeal and mass transfer of players reduced the debt, and allowed the club to continue competing, which they did with zest, reaching the cup final, and finishing runners-up in their division to a rampant Tottenham.

Stamford Bridge's regular residents Chelsea had won through to the other semi-final. This presented a potential problem for the FA as their stadium was the designated venue for the final, and it would prove embarrassing for one team to be playing on their home ground. Starting as favourites, the FA were surely relieved when Chelsea succumbed to two good goals from Billy Walker, a forward fast achieving cult status at Villa Park.

In the final Villa had the form and pedigree but laboured against game and frustrating opponents. Full-time arrived with the scoresheet still blank. Huddersfield's dam was finally breached by a fluky set piece. Billy Kirton's header from a corner looked accidental, but the record books leave no room for such excuses. Villa had triumphed yet again.

IF THE YEAR ENDS IN 1 . . .

Everton **0** Wolves **1**

Cardiff **1** Chelsea **0**

Tottenham **1** Aston Villa **0**

Hull (0) **0** Preston (0) **1**

SEMI FINALS

Wolves **3** Cardiff **1**
at Old Trafford after 0-0 at Liverpool

Tottenham **2** Preston **1**
at Hillsborough

FINAL, 23 APRIL 1921, STAMFORD BRIDGE

Tottenham Hotspur **1**
Wolverhampton Wanderers **0**

SPURS:
Hunter, Clay, McDonald, Smith, Walters, Grimsdell ©, Banks, Seed, Cantrell, Bliss, **Dimmock (1)**

WOLVES:
George, Woodward, Marshall, Gregory, Hodnett, Riley, Lea, Burrill, Edmonds, Potts, Brooks

1920–1921

Unwisely, the FA still refrained from making the final all-ticket. The near 73,000 crowd proved almost too much for Stamford Bridge, with many watching the game from the running track around the pitch. The FA failed to learn from its mistake, and their pay-on-the-day policy wreaked havoc at the first Wembley final two years later.

S trange as it may now seem, the competition in 1920-21 was the largest it would ever be. The first post-war boom swelled the number of participating clubs to 674, an all-time record.

With all the form clubs either knocking each other out or underestimating less fancied opposition, the draw again provided chinks of light for Second Division sides. Crystal Palace, from the newly constituted Third Division, beat Manchester City 2-0. City would finish runners-up in the First, whilst Palace would win Division Three. The eventual champions, Burnley, were thrashed by Hull, a mid-table Division Two team. Hull made it to the last eight but were beaten there by lowly Preston, who had accounted for a strong Bolton side in the first round.

Continuing the pattern, Cardiff City and Wolves threaded their way through to the last four and gave the second tier three of the four semi-finalists. Cardiff knocked out a strong Sunderland in the first round, while Wolves' outstanding victory at Goodison Park rivalled the surprises sprung by Hull and Crystal Palace. Cardiff, in their first semi-final, were to finish the season by winning promotion. Wolves, four-time finalists, were a pale imitation of pre-war sides. Their victory, although falling short of an upset, raised an eyebrow.

Tottenham's triumph twenty years' previously had been as amateurs from the Southern League. These days they were rubbing shoulders with the elite and their progress to the semi-final was serene, scoring fifteen times in a replay-free run. A 1-0 win over the holders Aston Villa saw them take the top flight's only semi-final place. Two goals from the aptly named Bert Bliss saw off Preston and Spurs marched on to the final as clear favourites.

A downpour reduced the Stamford Bridge surface to a paddy field and gladdened Wolverhampton hearts. Flowing football proved impossible, and the game was reduced to a farcical kick-about. Spurs navigated the swamp just long enough for Jimmy Dimmock to seize on a loose ball and slot a scrappy shot under the keeper from fifteen yards.

ENTER HERBERT

HUDDERSFIELD:
Mutch, Wood, Wadsworth, Slade, Wilson, Watson, Richardson, Mann, Islip, Stephenson, **Smith (1p)**

PRESTON:
Mitchell, Hamilton, Doolan, Duxbury, McCall, Williamson, Rawlings, Jefferies, Roberts, Woodhouse, Quinn

Huddersfield's five FA Cup final appearances were all in the inter-war period. This was their sole victory. They would meet Preston again in a second final sixteen years later where Preston would gain their revenge by the same score.

1921-1922

The competition got off to a bang with an outrageous walloping for Everton at the hands of Crystal Palace. Having eliminated the Toffees the previous season, Palace went one better and inflicted Everton's worst ever cup defeat.

Villa Park was the stage for more drama in the last eight. Notts County, now wearing the 'once proud' mantle in Division Two, appeared to have given their all in an entertaining 2-2 draw at Meadow Lane. This merely served as the hors d'oeuvre as Villa lost 4-3 in the undisputed tie of the season. Chipperfield, the two-goal hero of the first leg, was granted the freedom of Nottingham by scoring the winner.

By the semi-final stage, with other fancied sides falling by the wayside, Spurs looked odds-on to retain the trophy. For the second successive season Preston barred their way to the final. The Lancashire side, languishing in the wrong half of Division One, looked no match for high-flying Tottenham but turned the tables in extra-time, when Billy Roberts maintained his record of scoring in every round.

Preston would face Huddersfield in the final. The Terriers were managed by Herbert Chapman, a disciplinarian and astute tactician. Chapman was suspended by the FA after the disbandment of Leeds City two years before, but he came back to work his magic on Huddersfield. He had bought Clem Stephenson from Aston Villa and built a team around the wiry playmaker. This would be Huddersfield's decade as they won the title three years in succession in 1924, 1925 and 1926 and finished runners-up in 1927 and 1928. They would lose Chapman to Arsenal at the end of the 1924-1925 season but he had launched the club on their golden age.

Everton avenged their humiliating defeat nine years later. They were drawn away at Palace and won by the same 6-0 margin with Dixie Dean bagging four.

1921-1922

1921-1922

Charlton Athletic, Halifax Town and Wigan Borough had ideas above their station. Newly elected to an expanded Football League, they withdrew after refusing to play in the qualifying rounds.

The final, as was becoming customary, was a crushing one-goal disappointment. Billy Smith's penalty was the only incident of note but it was a controversial moment and led to a rule change. Preston were convinced that the England winger was brought down outside the area, and they were probably right. Referee Fowler saw otherwise – or perhaps he thought it was a more fitting punishment than sending off Tom Hamilton for the cynical trip. Smith took the penalty himself, managing to keep his nerve in the face of some bizarre gymnastic manoeuvres from Preston's bespectacled goalkeeper, Mitchell. The FA moved immediately to outlaw attempts by the goalkeeper to distract the penalty kicker.

Stamford Bridge had played host to three of the more uninspiring showpieces. The FA had plans for a change the following year.

1921-1922

This was Clem Stephenson's third FA Cup final and winner's medal. He would play in the 1928 final defeat, but by then both he and the team had their best years behind them.

1922

OPEN ROAD TO WEMBLEY

1923

BOLTON:
Pym, Haworth, Finney, Nuttall, Seddon, Jennings, Butler, **Jack (1)**, **JR Smith (1)**, Joe Smith ©, Vizard

WEST HAM:
Hutton, Henderson, Young, Bishop, Kay ©, Tresadern, Richards, Brown, Watson, Moore, Ruffell

The south had started to make more of an impact. Four London clubs plus Southampton contested the quarter-finals.

1922-1923

The vogue for banana skins continued as none of the league's top nine reached the quarter-finals. Three of them, Everton, Newcastle and Manchester City, perished at the first hurdle.

There appeared to be little threat when the Toffees drew Bradford Park Avenue from the Third Division North at Goodison Park. A 1-1 draw was a major surprise but not seriously heeded. The 'plucky' clichés were put back in the box after the replay and Everton crashed out to 'inferior' opposition for the third year running.

Southampton had enjoyed themselves hugely as a Southern League side at the beginning of the century with many prestigious scalps and two finals on their honours' board. In 1923 they were buried deep in the Second Division. After a stout rearguard action at St. James' Park, they took advantage of Newcastle's growing reputation for travel sickness. Southampton saw off Chelsea too before West Ham ended their run.

City didn't even manage to take their lower division opponents Charlton to a replay. The days of Sam Bartram and Alan Curbishley were a long away off. Charlton were languishing in the bottom half of the Third Division South but added two more First Division victims, Preston and West Brom, before they ran into a determined Bolton and lost 1-0.

Liverpool were unstoppable in the league and won back-to-back championships by six points. But they were dumped out at home in the cup for the second year running, Sheffield United applying the coup de grace this time, although the Reds could at least claim to have lost to a team in the same division. Most of their red-faced peers had to delve deeper for excuses.

Sneaking through the back door to the semis were Second Division Derby and West Ham. Yet only one of their combined total of eight ties tested them against top flight opposition. Derby at least could claim a considerable fourth round victory at White Hart Lane, which made their 5-2 surrender to the Hammers at Stamford Bridge an even greater disappointment.

Bolton's progress was largely courtesy of David Jack, a cultured inside-forward rapidly developing a reputation as one of the league's finest. Wanderers saw off holders Huddersfield in a replay with a goal from Jack, who had also scored the goal to earn the replay. Further 1-0 wins over Charlton and Sheffield United saw Bolton through to their third final. In both games Jack was the scorer.

The authorities learned their lesson, and the final became an all-ticket affair from the following season.

1922–1923

The new Empire Stadium at Wembley waited to host them for its first final. The biggest-ever English ground was to prove not nearly big enough.

With a capacity of 127,000, the FA complacently assumed they could accommodate the final crowd without instigating a ticket-in-advance policy. They were very wrong. The gates closed at 1.45 and the common estimate is that close to 200,000 people were packed inside, with thousands more clamouring to join them. By the time King George V arrived, there were genuine fears that the game would have to be postponed, as the crowd had spilled on to the pitch and every inch of the newly laid turf was covered.

Fortunately, it was a good-natured crowd and the monarch's presence helped calm matters. A team of mounted police gradually, and peacefully, restored order. The most conspicuous presence was Billy, a 13 year-old white horse, and his rider, Constable George Scorey. The press had their hero, and the final has been known ever since as the 'White Horse Final'.

The game kicked off, remarkably only 45 minutes behind schedule. At 3.47 the contest was effectively over, when David Jack (who else?) headed Bolton into the lead. West Ham, even with their England international centre forward Vic Watson, would struggle to break down the obdurate Wanderers defence. When Jack Smith thumped a second soon after half-time, the game was up for the Hammers.

The new stadium was mightily impressive. The chaos surrounding its first major event was wholly down to administrative incompetence and not the inadequacy of the facility. Built on a green-field site adjacent to the then leafy suburb of Wembley, the stadium was the centre-piece of the British Empire Exhibition. Enthusiasm for the project increased noticeably when it was announced that it incorporated a new national football stadium. The FA showed their faith when they contracted to stage the Cup final at the venue for the next twenty-one years. The Duke of York ceremonially cut the turf on 22 January 1922, and the work was completed just in time for the final the following year, at a cost of around £750,000.

West Ham owed five goals in their cup run to one B. Moore. Not Bobby but Billy Moore, an inside forward.

1922–1923

West Ham's compensation was promotion to the top flight for the first time in their history. They only lasted nine years, and remained a Division Two side for almost three decades. But their day would come.

1922–1923

When Smith scored Bolton's second, the ball shot back into play off the crowd packed behind the goal, confusing many (but not the referee) into thinking he had hit the woodwork.

1922–1923

1923

RETURN OF THE OLD GUARD

1924

Manchester C (0) **1** Cardiff (0) **0**

Newcastle **1** Liverpool **0**

West Brom **0** Aston Villa **2**

Swindon (1) **1** Burnley (1) **3**

SEMI FINALS

Manchester **0** Newcastle **2**

at Birmingham

Aston Villa **3** Burnley **0**

at Bramall Lane

FINAL, 26 APRIL 1924, WEMBLEY

Aston Villa **0** Newcastle United **2**

VILLA:
Jackson, Smart, Mort, Moss, Milne, Blackburn,
York, Kirton, Capewell, Walker ©, Dorrell

NEWCASTLE:
Bradley, Hampson, Hudspeth ©, Mooney,
Spencer, Gibson, Low, Cowan, **Harris (1)**,
McDonald, **Seymour (1)**

1923-1924

The final was a repeat of the showpiece of 1905. Newcastle gained perfect revenge for their 2-0 defeat nineteen years earlier. Between them the two sides boasted twelve previous finals.

Only ten times in the history of the FA Cup since the turn of the century have non-league clubs defeated top flight opposition. Corinthians were the last bastion of amateurism in the game; until the year before they had steadfastly refused to play against professional teams. Blackburn were one of the league's founders, and were still good enough to finish in the top half of the First Division. In a match switched to Crystal Palace, Rovers failed to cope with Corinthians' old fashioned cavalry charge tactics and a fifteenth minute goal settled the issue. Five-times winners? You're having a laugh.

Everton's woeful record against lower league opposition continued for a fourth miserable year. A promising Third Division side pitched against one of the league's gentry shouldn't have produced a result like Brighton & Hove Albion's 5-2 victory over Everton. Tommy Cook spat out the Toffees with a hat-trick.

These tremors apart, a quarter-final line-up containing seven First Division clubs was a rare affirmation of superiority. The fly in the ointment was Swindon, who fought gamely against Burnley before falling at Turf Moor.

Newcastle's challenge nearly ground to a halt in the second round. A marathon against Derby ran to a third replay with all four ties crammed into twelve days and the tele-printer apparently jammed after three 2-2 draws. To the credit of both teams, they summoned enough energy in the decider to produce a classic, Newcastle winning through 5-3 with a hat-trick from Neil Harris. They had played 510 minutes of Cup football, scored fifteen goals and had only reached the third round!

Making up for lost time, the Magpies won the next four rounds and the Cup itself without recourse to further replays and without conceding a goal. The final looked like running late until Harris and left-winger Stan Seymour broke Villa's hearts. Contemporary reports have this as one of the better finals with two evenly matched sides only separated in the dying minutes.

1924

NEAR MISS

1925

CARDIFF:
Farquharson, Nelson, Blair, Wake, Keenor ©,
Hardy, Davies, Gill, Nicholson, Beadles, Evans

SHEFF UTD:
Sutcliffe, Cook, Milton, Pantling, King, Green,
Mercer, Boyle, Johnson, Gillespie ©, **Tunstall (1)**

First round. Two Villa forwards helped themselves in their 7-2 win over Port Vale. Len Capewell (4) and a Billy Walker hat-trick completed the rout.

1924-1925

With all due respect to Sheffield United, who by the season's end had put a fourth FA Cup into the Bramall Lane trophy cabinet, this was not a vintage year. Few surprises and a drab final ensured that, while the 1920s may be remembered for the first Wembley final and Cardiff's dramatic win in 1927, highlights of this campaign are restricted to two ties of grinding longevity.

Leyton FC ensured Essex bragging rights over Ilford only after five matches of their third qualifying round tie. That the qualifiers should stretch to a sixth round should have been punishment enough but for the masochists of Barrow and Gillingham, the torture was only just beginning. Five more matches followed before the Cumbrian side finally crawled over the line.

Newcastle started their defence calmly enough, snuffing out Hartlepools quickly at St James' Park. Another home draw, against Second Division high-flyers Leicester, proved a trickier prospect. After a spirited 2-2 draw, the Foxes dumped out the holders 1-0 at Filbert Street.

By the semi-final stage, lower division interest was restricted to Southampton. Even their progress was distinctly unromantic as the Saints had sneaked through without playing a top flight side. A well-drilled Sheffield United were never disturbed.

At least Wembley was in good voice, swelled by a chorus from South Wales. Cardiff, flying the Red Dragon flag for the first time in a final, gave them precious little to sing about. Cardiff were used to disappointment. The previous season they had lost the league title to Huddersfield on goal average by 0.02 of a goal. If goal difference had been used they would have won by dint of scoring one more goal than their rivals. They would have to wait two more years for their great moment.

A disappointing competition ended with another muted finale.

1925

JACK'S FINESSE

1926

BOLTON:
Pym, Haworth, Greenhalgh, Nuttall, Seddon, Jennings, Butler, JR Smith, **Jack (1)**, Joe Smith ©, Vizard

MANCHESTER C:
Goodchild, Cookson, McCloy, Pringle, Cowan, McMullan ©, Austin, Browell, Roberts, Johnson, Hicks

This was the first season of a new format for the FA Cup and established the blueprint that exists today. For the first time, all Football League clubs were exempt from the qualifying rounds, with those from the top two divisions not entering until round three.

A much needed change in the offside law was introduced in an attempt to thwart the sterility of much of the football of recent seasons. The previous rule, which stated that a player became offside if 'fewer than three players' remained between him and the goal, was amended to the current 'fewer than two'. The effect on goalscoring was dramatic. The first round saw two clubs reach double figures. Swindon Town won 10-1 at Farnham, whilst Oldham were demolishing Lytham by the same score.

An even bigger goal-fest was served up at Maine Rd in the fifth round. Manchester City 11-4 Crystal Palace would have had Alan Hansen's granddad shaking his head ruefully for days. Manchester City scored an amazing thirty-one goals en route to Wembley. Frank Roberts (9), Tommy Browell (7) and George Hicks (6) helped themselves. City fans took particular comfort from their semi-final stuffing of United, the first Manchester derby in the Cup for thirty-four years.

Meanwhile, Bolton were making heavy weather of a cushy draw. Despite not meeting a first division side until the final, they edged unconvincingly past Third Division Accrington Stanley and Bournemouth in the early rounds, despatching the latter only after a replay. Goals from England star David Jack proved crucial. They needed a further three games to see off Nottingham Forest before seeing off giant-killing Swansea in a semi-final curiously staged at White Hart Lane.

Once again, the tension of a final dried up the free-flowing attack of earlier rounds. Fittingly, it was Jack, the best player on the pitch, who provided the only significant moment. For City it merely piled on the end-of-season misery. They completed a unique double having been relegated to Division Two.

DESPERATE DAN

THE LAST 16

Arsenal **2**	Liverpool **0**
Wolves **1**	Hull **0**
Millwall **3**	Middlesbrough **2**
Southampton **2**	Newcastle **1**
South Shields (2) **1**	Swansea (2) **2**
Reading **1**	Brentford **0**
Chelsea **2**	Burnley **1**
Bolton **0**	Cardiff **2**

QUARTER FINALS

Arsenal **2**	Wolves **1**
Millwall (0) **0**	Southampton (0) **2**
Swansea **1**	Reading **3**
Chelsea (0) **2**	Cardiff (0) **3**

SEMI FINALS

Arsenal **2** Southampton **1**
at Stamford Bridge

Reading **0** Cardiff **3**
at Molineux

FINAL, 23 APRIL 1927, WEMBLEY

Arsenal **0** Cardiff City **1**

ARSENAL:
Lewis, Parker, Kennedy, Baker, Butler, John, Hulme, Buchan ©, Brain, Blythe, Hoar

CARDIFF:
Farquharson, Nelson, Watson, Keenor ©, Sloan, Hardy, Curtis, Irving, **Ferguson (1)**, Davies, McLachlan

The Den at Cold Blow Lane has been euphemistically described as a 'difficult' place to visit. For difficult, read horrible. Huddersfield, league champions for the last three years, and the first to achieve such a hat-trick of wins, clearly didn't fancy it. The Lions were still baring their teeth in the Third Division but their lifelong crusade to slay the 'southern softies' dragon began here. They chased and harried the more cultured visitors, and by the end of the game had reduced Huddersfield to a shadow of the side still good enough to finish runners-up in the league. No one liked them, but they didn't care.

This reflected the tone of the season's competition. First Division clubs were scalped in abundance. Newcastle should have read the warning signs from an away draw at Southampton in round four. The Saints continued an outstanding giant-killing tradition, a brace from Rowley securing a 2-1 win. West Ham were enjoying their best-ever league season, but a finish of sixth was tarnished with defeat by Third Division Brentford. The Bees had drawn 1-1 in a fourth round tie at Upton Park and completed the upset with a 2-0 win. Everton's annual embarrassment came at Hull – with their recent track record there was scant chance of them avoiding the carnage. The romance ended in the semi-finals. Southampton ran Arsenal close, but Reading were well-beaten by Cardiff.

The final is one of the best–remembered but was far from a classic. Cardiff's continuing achievement in becoming the only non-English club to lift the Cup has long become a quizmaster's cliché. The other point of note was the irony of the misfortune of Dan Lewis, the Arsenal goalkeeper, who fumbled a speculative effort from Ferguson to gift Cardiff their victory. He was a Welsh international. A story survives that his error was blamed on the non-adhesive quality of his shiny new jersey.

1927

ROVERS' RETURN (AND FAREWELL)

1928

BLACKBURN:
Crawford, Hutton, Jones, Healless ©, Rankin,
Campbell, Thornewell, Puddefoot, **Roscamp
(2)**, **McLean (1)**, Rigby

HUDDERSFIELD:
Mercer, Goodall, Barkas, Redfern, Wilson,
Steele, Jackson (1), Kelly, Brown, Stephenson
©, Smith

Following last season's shenanigans, order was most definitely restored. While non-leaguers were gallant, the Football League's lower orders threatened the meekest of rebellions. This was a season for the big boys. Even Everton avoided the ignominy of defeat by a team from a lower division, going out 4-3 to Arsenal in a fourth round minor classic, despite two goals from the prolific Dixie Dean. Dean scored a phenomenal fifty-nine league goals that year as Everton pipped Huddersfield to the title.

Two non-league teams joined Corinthians in the third round. London Caledonians, having registered their first victories in the competition proper for forty-one years, fell to Crewe at Stamford Bridge. Peterborough and Fletton United nearly sprinkled fairy dust at St. Andrews. Birmingham's top division pedigree counted for little but the forerunners to the present-day Posh lost a humdinger by the odd goal in seven.

Romance lovers are advised to turn the page, as the fifth round comprised thirteen teams from Division One, with the oversized 'minnows' of Manchester City, Stoke and Nottingham Forest making up the numbers.

By the semis, Huddersfield had emerged as the form horses. Their tie against Sheffield United proved a battle royal, the Terriers emerging from the second replay as the Cock of the West Riding. Scottish international Alex Jackson was the Terriers' ace, firing the winner at Maine Road.

Facing them at Wembley were a club steeped in Cup tradition. Blackburn Rovers had won through to a record seventh final and could still put out a side with five internationals. Huddersfield, though, had been in the top two in the league for five years and kicked-off as favourites.

They reckoned without James Roscamp, whose first minute launch at Huddersfield's keeper Billy Mercer would probably have brought a red card today. The ball flew from Mercer's grasp into the goal. The goal stood, Huddersfield reeled and were two down at half-time. They rallied briefly in the second half but Jackson's goal merely halved the deficit. Roscamp struck the knockout blow in the closing stages to give Rovers a record sixth trophy.

BOLTON'S ROARING TWENTIES

BOLTON:
Pym, Haworth, Finney, Kean, Seddon ©,
Nuttall, **Butler (1)**, McLelland, **Blackmore (1)**,
Gibson, Cook

PORTSMOUTH:
Gilfillan, Mackie, Bell, Nichol, McIlwaine,
Thackeray, Forward, Smith, Weddle, Watson,
Cook

N o Midland League side had ever gone beyond the third round of the FA Cup. The league comprised strong reserve teams and a few others, like Mansfield Town, trying to build a reputation. A tight game with Wolves was settled with a goal by winger McLachlan, Mansfield's one player with considerable league experience. This defeat put the tin lid on a miserable decade for Wolves. They spent most of it as Second Division strugglers. Mansfield would run out for their first league game three years later.

Reading had joined the league at the start of the decade but were still no better than a bottom-half Division Two side. A great Cup run in 1927 had put them in the spotlight, but they weren't expected to repeat those heroics against Sheffield Wednesday. A 1-0 win against an off-colour Wednesday earned another plum tie against Aston Villa, but Villa proved too strong.

Bolton confirmed their position as the most successful Cup team of the decade with their third final. Unlike their easy draw in 1926, no one could doubt that this one was hard-earned. Apart from a relatively soft tie at home to Oldham in the third round, their other victims were all sides that wouldn't have looked out of place in the shadow of the twin towers.

Liverpool were overwhelmed 5-2 after extra-time in a fourth round replay. Leicester City were sent packing on their own turf and holders Blackburn fell after a replay at Burnden Park. All three sides would finish above Wanderers in the league; Leicester would never finish higher than the second place they achieved that season.

The semi-final draw meant Wanderers would have to overcome both finalists from the previous season to earn their Wembley place. Huddersfield were not the team they had been in the middle of the decade but they were still tricky opposition. Goals from veteran winger Billy Butler, George Gibson and Harold Blackmore saw off the Yorkshiremen 3-1.

Portsmouth's passage to their first final was decidedly less mountainous. They reached the last eight without playing a top division side and only Villa in the semis could be viewed as genuinely difficult opponents.

None of this mattered come the big day but Bolton proved that they were in for the long haul by seeing off dogged opponents with two late goals, Butler and Blackmore were both on target again. Not a vintage year, but at least the most deserving team won.

GUNNERS' OPENING SALVO

ARSENAL:
Preedy, Parker ©, Hapgood, Baker, Seddon, John, Hume, Jack, **Lambert (1)**, **James (1)**, Bastin

HUDDERSFIELD:
Turner, Goodall, Spence, Naylor, Wilson ©, Campbell, Jackson, Kelly, Davies, Raw, Smith

Herbert Chapman had been recruited by Arsenal in 1925. Much to his frustration, though, his team-building had yet to yield any silverware. Classy players like Charlie Buchan, Alex James and David Jack had been brought in, but second place to Chapman's old club Huddersfield was comfortably their best league finish, and they had always met with disappointment in the latter stages of the FA Cup.

Their luck changed in 1930 but it could so easily have been Hull's rather than Herbert's year. The Second Division side belied their mediocre league position to reach the semi-finals. Progress was unspectacular at first, as they worked their way past the past the equally unremarkable Plymouth and Blackpool. In the fifth round, however, they caught fire. A tough draw at Maine Road saw them recover from a goal down to overcome Manchester City following a memorable dribble from Bill Taylor. This was a fine result, as City had obliterated lower league opposition in the previous round, thrashing Swindon 10-1 with five goals from Bobby Marshall. How City fans must have laughed – Swindon had embarrassed a poor Manchester United team the round before.

The sixth round draw was hard on Hull again, but the Tigers roared back from a goal down at Newcastle to equalise through Stan Alexander, his fifth of the competition. In a night of high tension at Boothferry Park, they squeaked through 1-0.

The semi-finals found Hull in exalted company. In terms of league position, Arsenal represented the easiest draw as Huddersfield and champions-in-waiting Sheffield Wednesday completed a formidable line-up. If the Tigers were nervous as they took the field at Elland Road, it didn't show. They tore into Arsenal with Howieson and Duncan shooting them into a two-goal lead with only half-an-hour played. The Gunners regrouped, but sixty-seven minutes had passed before David Jack began the comeback. With Hull only eight minutes from Wembley, Cliff Bastin broke Humberside hearts with the equaliser.

Hull's chance had gone. With Alexander crocked for the replay, they went out tamely to Jack's early goal and their season fell apart. In freefall for the rest of the campaign, they became sucked into a relegation battle in which they succumbed on goal difference. It was a cruel end, more so since they never again came as close as this.

Chapman's team lined up in the final against Huddersfield and as a mark of his contribution to both clubs, they took the field together, a tradition that has flourished. A German airship, the Graf Zeppelin, flew over the ground, as if it knew this was a momentous day. The great silver monster dipped its nose, maybe to Chapman but more probably in acknowledgement of the presence of King George V.

The game resulted in a comfortable victory for Arsenal, with two cracking goals from schemer Alex James and centre-forward Jack Lambert. It was the beginning of a decade of almost continuous success for Arsenal. It was the end of Huddersfield's glory days – they haven't won a major trophy since.

1930

1931

BRUMMIE AFFAIR

BIRMINGHAM:
Hibbs, Liddell, Barkas, Cringan, Morrall, Leslie, Briggs, Crosbie, **Bradford (1)**, Gregg, Curtis

WEST BROM:
Pearson, Shaw, Trentham, Magee, Bill Richardson, Edwards, Glidden ©, Carter, WG **Richardson (2)**, Sandford, Wood

eague form suggested that only Aston Villa could spearhead the second city's challenge but the draw was cruel enough to send them to face the might of Arsenal at Highbury. The tie of the round produced a 2-2 thriller and ensured Villa Park was jammed for the replay. The Gunners simply raised their game further, running out 3-1 winners with two goals from winger Joe Hume. Surprisingly, Arsenal came unstuck at Chelsea in the next round.

This season's darlings were Third Division Exeter, who were drawn at home to Derby in the third round. This Derby team included Jack Bowers, who duly broke the club's goalscoring record that season with thirty-seven in the league. Bowers added two more to his seasonal tally but it wasn't enough as a deeply courageous performance from Exeter saw them triumph 3-2 despite playing most of the second half with ten men. Second Division Bury were beaten 2-1 at Gigg Lane, and then First Division Leeds couldn't cope with the passion of the Devon side, going down 3-1 with something to spare. A battling 1-1 draw in the next round at Roker Park put the Grecians in the hat for the semi-final draw only for Sunderland to end the dream 4-2 in a replay played in front of over 20,000 people shoehorned into Exeter's tiny St James Park ground.

The eventual top four in the Second Division were Everton (surprisingly relegated the year before), West Brom, Tottenham and Wolves. West Brom might have only beaten one top flight side on their way to the final but, after struggling past Charlton in the third round, they put paid to all their major rivals from the second tier. Sandwiched in between was an excellent 1-0 win at Portsmouth, clinched by a goal from WG 'Billy' Richardson.

Joining them in the final were Birmingham City, who had seen off Chelsea and then Sunderland in the semi-final. Two goals from left-winger Ernie Curtis settled the game and set up the first all West Midlands final since 1895.

The prolific Richardson struck first for Albion and his second goal, seconds after Birmingham had equalised, proved decisive.

The oldest surviving FA Cup is displayed at Christie's before its auction on 19th May 2005. Made in 1896 to replace the trophy stolen the previous year, it sold for £478,000.
(Getty Images)

Lord Arthur Fitzgerald Kinnaird (1847–1923). One of the competition's pioneers, he played in a record nine finals and gained five winner's medals. He joined the FA committee aged only 22 and remained its president for 33 years. (Colorsport)

Preston North End, who became football's first Double winners in 1889. In a historic season, 'The Invincibles' won the league without losing a match and kept a clean sheet in every Cup tie. (Empics)

Billy Bassett (1869–1937). The first legend of the professional game, Bassett starred as an Albion player for twelve years, finally hanging up his boots in 1900. He starred in three finals and collected two winner's medals. He remained with Albion as director and chairman, completing fifty years' service with the club. (Colorsport)

Aston Villa show off their trophies after winning the Double in 1897. The FA Cup in the foreground is the trophy auctioned by Christie's in 2005. (Colorsport)

Crystal Palace struggles to contain the vast crowd at the 1901 final. The attendance of 114,815 was a world record at the time, swelled by the rare appearance of a London club. Tottenham and Sheffield United battled out a 2–2 draw, Spurs winning the replay at Burnden Park. (Colorsport)

20th April 1907. Cup final day in Crystal Palace, as crowds make their way to watch Sheffield Wednesday beat Everton 2–1. (Getty Images)

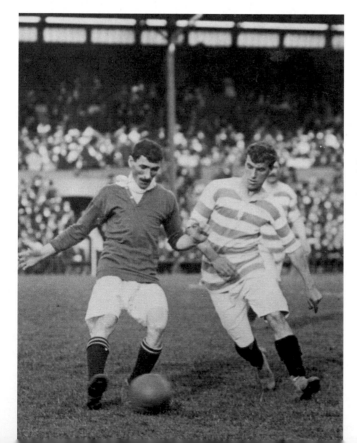

Billy Meredith (1874–1958) shows off his dribbling skills at the 1908 Charity Shield. A star in Manchester for City and United, he won winner's medals with both clubs (1904 and 1909).
He remains the oldest player to play in the competition proper, turning out for a semi-final in 1924 aged 49 years 245 days. (Getty Images)

Old Trafford, 24th April 1915. Soaked spectators watch Sheffield United beat Chelsea 3–0 in a match dubbed the 'Khaki Cup Final' due to the high number of uniformed soldiers in attendance. Many were on leave from the First World War, a conflict that meant the suspension of the FA Cup until 1919/20. (Getty Images)

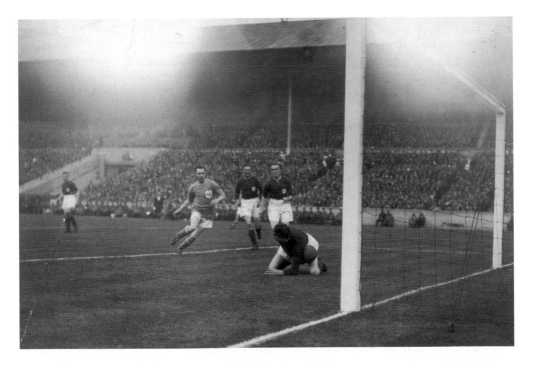

Wembley, 23rd April 1927. Arsenal's keeper Dan Lewis dives over a speculative effort from Cardiff's Hugh Ferguson, handing the Welsh club their only major trophy and ensuring the Cup left England for the only time. (Getty Images)

Wembley, 26th April 1930. The vast Graf Zeppelin pays a courtesy call during the final between Arsenal and Huddersfield. (Getty Images)

One of football's more thankless tasks – proofreading tickets for the 1939 final between Portsmouth and Wolves. (Hulton Archive/Getty Images)

9th March 1946, Burnden Park. Bodies are laid out on the pitch following the crush at Bolton's sixth-round tie with Stoke. Thirty-three spectators died after the terraces became dangerously overcrowded. (Getty Images)

29th January, 1949. Yeovil fans celebrate after the non-League giantkillers claimed their biggest prize, first-division Sunderland. (Getty Images)

The golden age of
Newcastle, who won
three finals in five sea-
sons during the Fifties.
Top: Bobby Cowell
clears off the line dur-
ing the 1951 final v
Blackpool. Middle and
below: Jackie Milburn
in aerial action against
Arsenal in 1952 and
Manchester City in
1955. Cowell and
Milburn, with Bobby
Mitchell, were the only
players to appear in all
three finals.

(Colorsport & Getty Images)

1931

THE CAMERA NEVER LIES

1932

ARSENAL:
Moss, Parker ©, Hapgood, Jones, Roberts, Male, Hulme, Jack, Lambert, Bastin, **John (1)**

NEWCASTLE:
McInroy, Nelson ©, Fairhurst, McKenzie, Davidson, Weaver, Boyd, Richardson, **Allen (2)**, McMenemy, Lang

Everton became the first team to win the league title immediately after gaining promotion. They were able to 'concentrate on the league' after losing a pulsating third round Merseyside derby 2-1.

1931–1932

ucky Arsenal? Not in 1932. After mowing down Darwen, the Gunners fired four past Plymouth before their competition began in earnest. Away victories at Portsmouth and Huddersfield were followed by semi-final success against Manchester City. A formidable trio of wins was achieved without a single goal against.

Newcastle, like many eventual winners, were almost left in the starting blocks. It took five games to see off Blackpool and, embarrassingly, Southport before they clicked into gear. Then Leicester and Watford were emphatically despatched. Their one serious test was Chelsea at Villa Park but with Jack Allen in a rich seam of form they saw off the Londoners 2-1.

Despite the Magpies' record of seven final appearances, they looked a poor bet against Arsenal. Their odds drifted further when outside-left Bob John shot the Gunners into an early lead, but the game turned after thirty-eight minutes in one of Wembley's most notorious moments.

Newcastle's inside-right Jimmy Richardson looked to have run the ball over the goal-line before pulling the ball back to Jack Allen. The normally professional Arsenal defence failed to heed one of the earliest lessons of all. To a man, they stopped but referee Harper's whistle never blew. Allen slotted home, and Newcastle were level.

The Gunners were clearly rattled, their previous fluent football stuttering to a halt. With eighteen minutes left, and the game drifting towards stalemate, the prolific Allen seized his moment to win Newcastle's third Cup.

Newsreel footage clearly showed the ball was over the line and equally clearly gave the lie to Harper's claim to have been eight yards away. To their credit Arsenal accepted the decision with exceptional good grace. It is hard to imagine Mr Wenger's less gentlemanly cohorts doing the same.

The romance of the Cup took a year off. Instead of upsets it was the year of the drubbing. Bath and Northampton ran up nine apiece in the first round surpassing Cardiff's eight and the seven of Aldershot and QPR.

Non-league Crook Town's reward for battling to round three was a 7-0 thrashing at Leicester. The most curious performance was Newcastle's fourth-round saga with lowly Southport. Two insipid performances by the Magpies had resulted in 1-1 draws. The second replay was somewhat more one-sided as six different scorers helped themselves in a 9-0 glut.

The bloodiest slaughter came at Highbury. Non-league Darwen's 'reward' for knocking out third division Colchester was an 11-1 roasting. Bastin got four, Jack three and Hume and Lambert both got two in what remains the Gunners' biggest FA Cup win.

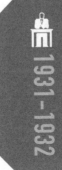

1932

EVERTON SINGIN' DIXIE

1933

EVERTON:
Sagar, Cook, Cresswell, Britton, White, Thomson, Geldard, **Dunn (1)**, **Dean (1)**, Johnson, **Stein (1)**

MANCHESTER C:
Langford, Cann, Dale, Busby, Cowan ©, Bray, Toseland, Marshall, Herd, McMullan, Brook

After a fallow year in 1932, the giant killers roused themselves for a bumper year, including one of the greatest shocks in the competition's history.

Kent part-timers Folkestone started early by beating Newport, who were a rank bad side, and Norwich, who were a more notable prize, to reach the third round for the first time. Folkestone finally fell valiantly, losing 2-0 at First Division Huddersfield.

The same round saw two more top flight clubs fall; Chelsea weren't a good side but should have done better at Third Division Brighton, while a journey of only twenty minutes to Chesterfield shouldn't have left Sheffield Wednesday feeling so travel-sick. Goals from Cook and Bacon were more than Wednesday could stomach in a 4-2 defeat.

And so to Fellows Park, Walsall.

Contemporary reports reveal that Arsenal's defeat was correctly labelled as the most seismic in the competition's history. Even today it stands out as a result that continues to defy all reasonable logic.

Arsenal's pedigree was impressive. The richest club in the country, they led the First Division and were about to embark on a hat-trick of league titles. Walsall were hiding in the Third Division (North). The Gunners were in prime form, recent results included a 9-2 caning of Sheffield United. The Saddlers approached the tie on the back of three draws and a 5-0 defeat.

The only worry for Arsenal was a flu virus and injuries which deprived them of five first-team regulars. Even so, their reserve pool was considerable and a forward line that contained David Jack, Alex James and Cliff Bastin should have provided ample fire power.

Arsenal's undoing was the attitude of the new boys. Rookie centre-forward Charlie Walsh was so nervous that he nearly took the field without socks before being gently reminded by manager Herbert Chapman that his inadvertent dress code may cause more than the odd titter. His confidence in tatters, Walsh was to make a hash of two gilt-edged chances, the second when he took the ball from David Jack's toe when Jack seemed certain to score.

Walsall's tactics were clear from the outset. On a mud-heap of a pitch they conceded ten free kicks in as many minutes. Their roughhouse approach clearly unnerved Arsenal and delighted the home crowd. The longer the game went on the more Walsall gained in confidence. On the hour Alsop eluded the attentions of

As both teams wore blue as a first choice, they were both required to wear neutral colours at Wembley – City lined up in red, Everton in white.

1932-1933

full-back Tommy Black and headed Lee's corner past Moss. If Black's first offence was careless, his second five minutes later was unforgivable. Clearly rattled he hacked at Alsop, conceded a penalty, and left the Walsall centre-forward with a scar he was still proudly displaying fifty years later. Bill Sheppard converted from the spot to score his first goal for the club and give the Saddlers a lead that proved unassailable.

Walsall shut up shop and a bedraggled Arsenal had neither the wit nor will to make inroads. As the Saddlers were chaired from the pitch by a jubilant home crowd, the Gunners trooped off to face a brutal post-mortem from Herbert Chapman. The manager's retribution was swift: Black was transferred to Plymouth within a week and Walsh became a Brentford player by the month's end.

FA Cup success had frequently eluded Chapman. His Huddersfield team that won three successive titles a decade earlier had never made an impression. The Arsenal boss was frustrated that an opportunity to launch the first success-ful Double campaign in thirty-six years had floundered at the first attempt. He never got another chance. A year later he died suddenly and shockingly after a bout of pneumonia.

Once the dust settled from Fellows Park, Everton looked favourites to profit from the First Division's collective *schadenfreude*, and so it proved. They were league champions and in 'Dixie' Dean had a weapon eminently capable of set-tling the sharp-shooting contests that are FA Cup ties. A favourable draw that threw up three consecutive home ties propelled them to the semi-finals on a wave of expectation. Again the balls came out of the hat kindly, pitting Everton against Second Division strugglers West Ham and side-stepping the bigger guns of Manchester City and Derby.

This season's one-hit wonders were Lloyds, a works team from a paper factory in Sittingbourne. Their only appearance in the first round proper was achieved at their first attempt but an 8-1 defeat at Northampton was a dismal ending.

1932-1933

With everything set fair, the Toffees nearly came unstuck but edged past the game Hammers courtesy of Jimmy Dunn's winner. Dean failed to score for the first time in that season's competition.

Everton's firepower always made them the more likely aggressors at Wembley. The controversial selection of Albert Geldard over popular right winger Ted Critchley was proving astute as his crosses were causing City all sorts of trouble. City held on for forty minutes until Langford in goal dropped a cross at Jimmy Stein's feet. Dean's presence had been a key factor in the howler, a mistake which the wretched Langford repeated seven

Despite Dean's winner's medal and his five goals, he was not this season's Cup hot-shot. Derby's England international Jack Bowers racked up eight in County's first four matches.

1932-1933

minutes after the break. This time Dean, who had shown his mortality by missing a sitter in the first half, finished emphatically. Dunn's third made Everton's victory the most emphatic in eighteen years.

For the first time in a first-class match, the players' shirts sported numbers. Everton wore one to eleven, City twelve to twenty-two. Appropriately 'Dixie' Dean became the first British number nine. There was none finer. Dean scored 473 goals in 502 competitive fixtures, including seventeen in sixteen international appearances. Even after a motorcycle accident required him to have silver plates implanted into his skull, Dean's fearlessness and power made him the scourge of every defence in the country. Fittingly for such a great Everton servant, Dean died of a heart attack whilst attending a match against Liverpool at Goodison Park in 1980.

NEARLY MEN FINALLY GET THERE

MANCHESTER C:
Swift, Barnett, Dale, Busby, Cowan ©, Bray, Toseland, Marshall, **Tilson (2)**, Herd, Brook

PORTSMOUTH:
Gilfillan, Mackie, Smith, Nichol, Allen ©, Thackeray, Worrall, Smith, Weddle, Easson, **Rutherford (1)**

arlisle against Cheltenham in 2004-2005 would pit a non-league team against modest league opposition. So it was in December 1933 but the status of the teams was reversed. Carlisle were an uncompromising Third Division (North) outfit; Cheltenham in their second season as a semi-professional team in the Birmingham Combination. The outsiders won 2-1 and the game ended with enraged Carlisle fans invading the pitch to castigate a referee they believed had cost them the game.

After Arsenal's humbling the previous year, the elite were clearly a little wary. Only Huddersfield, league runners-up to the Gunners, were hideously embarrassed, losing 2-0 at home to Northampton. The Cobblers were kicking around the lower reaches of Division Three but added the steel toecaps for this one.

Short on shocks, the excitement of this season was provided by bulging nets. Thrashings were ten-a-penny, with fifteen scores of five goals or better in the competition proper. Tilson of Manchester City and Villa's Astley duelled in their own private competition, the former winning by nine goals to eight. Notable absentees from the goal-fest were holders Everton, 'Dixie' Dean and all. Tottenham put paid to their defence at the first attempt, running out comfortable 3-0 winners at White Hart Lane.

City shrugged off the disappointment of the previous season's defeat by Everton, winning through to the final in fine style. Only once did they meet opposition from outside Division One. Even then, a fourth round trip to Hull was hardly a pushover.

The Cup final referee was to become one of the world's most eminent football officials and the president of FIFA – Stanley Rous.

1933-1934

Both semi-finals tore up the blueprint of tense affairs settled by the old goal. While Portsmouth were dismissing Leicester 4-1 with a hat-trick from Jack Weddle, City demolished Villa 6-1 with four from the prolific Fred Tilson. No foregone conclusion this, as Villa had turned in a monumental performance at Highbury in the previous round. On paper it was a banker for the London club but Astley and Houghton inspired the visitors to a 2-1 win.

At Wembley Pompey seemed set fair to reverse the disappointment of five years earlier. Their left-winger, with the wonderfully old-fashioned name of Septimus Rutherford, gave them the lead midway through the first half and all City attacks had been successfully repelled as the game entered its final quarter-hour. The Wembley injury hoodoo, so much a feature of later years, chose this moment to intervene. Captain and centre-half Jim Allen was led off with concussion and Portsmouth cracked. The predatory Tilson sensing a kill struck twice. Cruel for Pompey but their wounds were to be healed by the end of the decade.

1934

SHEFFIELD'S SWANSONG

1935

SHEFF WED:
Brown, Nibloe, Catlin, Sharp, Millership, Burrows, **Hooper (1)**, Surtees, **Palethorpe (1)**, Starling ©, **Rimmer (2)**

WEST BROM:
Pearson, Shaw, Trentham, Murphy, Bill Richardson, Edwards, Glidden ©, Carter, WG Richardson, **Sandford (1)**, **Boyes (1)**

n the 1930s, Arsenal were the team to beat. Like the all-conquering Liverpool of the seventies and eighties, the Cup was often an unsettling experience for them as opponents raised their game for the big occasion.

A quarter-final at Hillsborough against a Wednesday team who were to finish third in the league behind the Gunners and Sunderland promised to be one of the season's titanic ties. Over 70,000 raised the roof as Ellis Rimmer hit the winner in a 2-1 victory.

Vying with them for performance of the season were Bolton. Second Division Wanderers faced the unenviable prospect of a trip to Goodison Park. Everton scored for fun; they had beaten Grimsby 6-3 and Sunderland 6-4. A free-scoring side themselves, Bolton rightly saw attack as the best form of defence. They carried the game to Everton, and the tactics paid off with a 2-1 triumph.

Division Two's second representatives in the semi-finals were Burnley. The Clarets route was far less heroic, a weak Birmingham providing their only top level scalp. A rampant Wednesday were always too good for them. Bolton gave West Brom a far tighter contest; Albion needed a replay and face-saving goals from the ubiquitous Billy Richardson before edging past opponents who would join them in Division One the following season.

Jackie Palethorpe put Albion on the back foot after barely two minutes at Wembley but they battled back and Wally Boyes drew them level with less than a quarter of the game played. From then on it settled down and, with twenty minutes remaining, there was still nothing to choose between the teams. Suddenly, the match caught fire.

Outside-right Mark Hooper's goal might have been the winner in any normal year but his effort served only to galvanise Albion. They were level for the second time with a thunderous drive from Ted Sandford and the game entered the final five minutes seemingly destined for extra-time. Ellis Rimmer decided otherwise. The Owls' outside-left, a scorer in every round, left his best until last. Two in the last five minutes was tough on Albion, who had slugged it out toe-to-toe with their conquerors, only to be counted out at the death.

1935

DRAKE PROVIDES HEAVY ARTILLERY

1936

ARSENAL:
Wilson, Male, Hapgood, Crayston, Roberts, Copping, Hulme, Bowden, **Drake (1)**, James ©, Bastin

SHEFF UTD:
Smith, Hooper ©, Wilkinson, Jackson, Johnson, McPherson, Barton, Barclay, Dodds, Pickering, Williams

Arsenal relinquished the league title after three years and Sunderland ended up runaway winners by eight points. Therefore their defeat at Port Vale, a very ordinary Second Division side, qualifies as a jaw-dropper. At least they didn't lose to Margate – that distinction was left to QPR and Crystal Palace in the first two rounds.

The fairytales were brief. Margate fell at Blackpool in the next round, while Port Vale got a 4-0 clattering by Grimsby and ended up being relegated.

This was a shaky season for the form clubs. By the quarter-finals, the Gunners were the only team remaining from the top half of Divison One. Grimsby, enjoying a rare spell among the league's elite, reached the last eight for the first time, while Middlesbrough appeared in their first quarter-final since 1888. Other relative novices included Fulham with only their second appearance in twenty-eight years, and Barnsley with their first since 1912.

Having seen off Manchester City, Grimsby continued their march into virgin territory with victory over Middlesbrough. With two Second Division teams in the semi-finals, they looked odds-on to reach Wembley. Alas, they drew Arsenal and went out at Leeds Road to a single goal from Cliff Bastin.

In the other semi-final at Molineux, Sheffield United won the Division Two bragging rights over Fulham but became the longest-priced bet in a final for many a year. Arsenal may have failed to win the title for the first time in four seasons, but a team containing Hapgood, James, Bastin and Ted Drake, the goal-scoring machine, looked far superior. Earlier that season Drake had scored all Arsenal's goals in a 7-0 thrashing of Aston Villa. A cartilage injury had then kept him out for a long period and the final was only his second game back.

In the event, the final proved tighter than most expected, although the Gunners failed to spark and the game produced few quality moments. With fifteen minutes remaining Drake finally seized on Bastin's cross to fire Arsenal ahead. The determined Blades almost struck back immediately, Barton eluding Hapgood to cross perfectly for Jock Dodds. The centre-forward's header crashed off the bar and United's chance had gone. It was a relieved Arsenal team that collected their second Cup.

CARTER THE UNSTOPPABLE

PRESTON:
Burns, Gallimore, Beattie, Shankly, Tremelling ©, Milne, Dougal, Beresford, **Frank O'Donnell (1)**, Fagan, Hugh O'Donnell

SUNDERLAND:
Mapson, Gorman, Hall, Thomson, Johnston, McNab, Duns, **Carter © (1)**, **Gurney (1)**, Gallacher, **Burbanks (1)**

T he last time Blackburn Rovers had played Accrington Stanley in the Cup was in 1909 when Rovers had cruised to a 7-1 victory. Times were harder at Ewood Park in 1937; they had lost their status as a top division club for the first time and Stanley were in a decent run of form, especially their centre forward Bob Mortimer. A 2-2 draw at Ewood saw Stanley bring their neighbours back to tiny Peel Park. A stunning fight-back resulted in a 3-1 win; Mortimer scored twice in each game and Rovers snapped him up at the end of the season.

After the strong showing the previous season by the Second Division, Millwall of the Third Division (South) flew the flag for the league's basement. Cold Blow Lane was never the away ground of choice and it certainly spooked the First Division this season. Chelsea and Derby had already shown little stomach for the fight. Manchester City, en route to a first league title, should have been made of sterner stuff but veteran striker Dave Mangnall's double finished them off. They became the first Third Division team to reach the semi-finals, but their obstacle to Wembley looked tough – defending league champions Sunderland.

Mangnall had already scored nine in the competition, including four against Aldershot in the first round. After ten minutes he shot the Lions in front and another shock looked on the cards. A rattled Sunderland regrouped and equalised on the half-hour through Bobby Gurney. The second half was one-way traffic, and it was no surprise when Patsy Gallacher headed the winner.

Their opponents in the final were a Preston side appearing at Wembley for the first time. They owed their place to the prolific Frank O'Donnell, whose ten in five games included a goal in every round.

As half-time approached, O'Donnell proved unstoppable again and Preston's talisman looked to have struck a decisive blow. Raich Carter, the finest player on the pitch, proved that the truly great save their best for the big stage. In the second half, the England maestro dictated play completely and it was fitting that he converted what proved to be the match-winning second. For Sunderland, one of the competition's bridesmaids, their first Cup couldn't come soon enough.

MUTCH ADO ABOUT SOMETHING

HUDDERSFIELD:
Hesford, Craig, Mountford, Willingham, Young ©, Boot, Hulme, Isaac, Macfadyen, Barclay, Beasley

PRESTON:
Holdcroft, Gallimore, Andy Beattie, Shankly, Smith ©, Batey, Watmough, **Mutch (1p)**, Maxwell, Bobby Beattie, Hugh O'Donnell

For a while it looked as if Third Division York might emulate Millwall's exploits of the previous year and get to the semi-finals. They were in the draw, having held Huddersfield to 0-0 at Bootham Crescent. West Brom and Middlesbrough, both top flight clubs, had already succumbed at York's ground. Huddersfield had too much experience in the replay and won through 2-1.

By the quarter-finals most of the clubs in the top half of the table had fallen, so Huddersfield, Sunderland and Preston all fancied their chances, especially when Aston Villa, suffering a two-year sojourn in Division Two, put out reigning champions Manchester City.

Teams from Lancashire, South Yorkshire, the north-east and the midlands had formed the backbone of football in the nineteenth century. They had taken the game from its polite amateur origins, blazing a professional trail that improved standards and shaped the country's great competitions. After the war many of them provided only fleeting glimpses of former glories as Manchester, Merseyside and London came to the fore. Preston North End were one of the about to be dispossessed.

Deepdale fans must now be heartily sick of the 'once proud' tag. This was the last season that ended with a prestigious trophy and it came from a victory that at times hung by the slenderest of threads.

Their success was based on mean defence. No team in Division One conceded fewer goals and their FA Cup run was in a similarly miserly vein with only one goal against, scored by Aston Villa in the semi-final. Six goals came from George Mutch but none came more dramatically than the one in the final.

With a minute to go in extra-time, almost two hours of forgettable football looked to be grinding towards a first replay since 1912. As Preston launched their final attack, Huddersfield's captain Alf Young upended Mutch on the edge of the box. Referee Thompson saw it differently and awarded a penalty. Mutch was injured in the challenge but was given the ball to place on the spot. Apparently still dazed, his hopeful punt sped dead-centre, before finding the net off the underside of the bar.

The same two sides had contested the 1922 final, with Huddersfield triumphing after a questionable penalty decision. Perhaps justice was done.

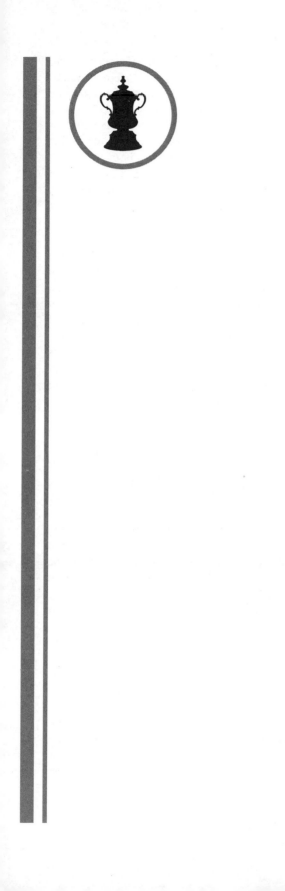

SPATS AND CHIMES

H ow times change. When Cardiff won the Cup twelve seasons previously, they were an established First Division side whilst Charlton were mid-table in the third. The Charlton of 1939 were destined to finish third in Division One, their highest ever position. Cardiff were now in freefall, dining off former glories two leagues below. The gloom returned at Newcastle in the fourth round but at least they enjoyed one last hurrah by beating their more exalted opponents with the only goal of the game.

Cheeky young pups indeed. The upstart Essex boys of Chelmsford had only been formed for a matter of months. In their first season they reached the fourth round. Second Division Southampton should have been warned by Chelmsford's 3-1 crushing of Darlington, a decent Division Three side. Saints had caused plenty of upsets themselves over the years but this was a case of the biter bit. Two-goal hero Coulter enjoyed the freedom of Essex after starring in a 4-1 rout. But then it was back to the bruising reality of a 6-0 hammering by Birmingham in the next round. There's been nothing like it in Chelmsford since.

While the semi-professionals became the darlings of the general public, the league's big boys administered some merciless bullyings. Grimsby hit Tranmere for six, Spurs put seven past Watford and Everton caned Doncaster with eight strokes. The Toffees were heading towards a fifth league title, hotly pursued by Wolves who were dishing out some stiff punishment of their own courtesy of head boy Dennis Westcott. Their meeting would have made a worthy final but the draw decreed they should battle it out in the sixth round at Molineux. Westcott rose to the challenge and bagged both in Wolves' 2-0 win.

Portsmouth's progress had been infinitely quieter and easier. Their first real challenge was against holders Preston in the quarter-finals, a game settled by a single goal from centre-forward Jock Anderson. At Highbury they despatched Huddersfield, the other finalists from last season. Again it was Anderson who grabbed the winner.

In the other semi-final Wolves looked irresistible. Grimsby, a sturdy First Division outfit, were simply swept aside, Westcott helping himself to four in a 5-0 win. Westcott was aiming to join the select band of players who had scored in every round. The final looked a mismatch despite Portsmouth's First Division parity.

Before the 1888 final hot favourites Preston had asked

1938-1939

Grimsby's 5-0 pasting in the semi-final must have comprehensively traumatised the club. They have never been beyond the fifth round since.

referee Mandarin whether they could be photographed with the Cup, thus presenting a pristine image for the camera. His prescient reply, 'Hadn't you better win it first?' became part of football history after opponents West Brom beat them 2-1. Wolves had obviously not done their research.

Half a century on, the same suggestion was made, although admittedly not by the team themselves. Even so, such was the pre-match talk that it was felt that Wolves simply had to turn up to win it.

Most of the first half-hour was a non-event. There was little hint of what was to follow as many favourites needed time to settle and find their feet. When Bert Barlow opened the scoring for Portsmouth it was a painful blow; Barlow had been on the Molineux staff until two months before when he was deemed surplus to requirements. It wasn't yet half-time, and there was plenty of time for Wolves to regroup and mount a counter attack.

One minute after the interval they were dead and buried. Anderson and Cliff Parker had stunned the favourites and there could be no dispute that Portsmouth were full value for the lead. Wolves' inept display bore no relation to any league performance in the previous eight months. They boasted the First Division's most parsimonious defence and in Stan Cullis possessed the country's most commanding centre-half. Yet for all that Pompey made them look like a pub team. Even Dicky Dorsett's strike for Wolves failed to convince as they never threatened to peg back their opponents. Cliff Parker's header for his second and Portsmouth's fourth meant that Wolves spent the last twenty minutes chasing shadows.

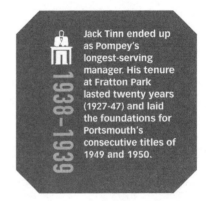

1938-1939

Jack Tinn ended up as Pompey's longest-serving manager. His tenure at Fratton Park lasted twenty years (1927-47) and laid the foundations for Portsmouth's consecutive titles of 1949 and 1950.

Pompey manager Jack Tinn had always claimed his spats were lucky. This result, though, owed nothing to luck.

1938-1939

When both teams were asked to sign a souvenir programme before the match, Wolves signatures were unrecognisable and virtually illegible. Living up to their billing as favourites had evidently created a pressure all its own.

In some of the press reports, Wolves' defeat was blamed on a pre-match dietary supplement allegedly containing monkey glands, which were widely believed at the time to improve stamina. This was strongly denied by the players, who dismissed the story as nothing more than a publicity stunt dreamed up by flamboyant boss Major Frank Buckley.

Pompey unwittingly became the longest holders of the Cup in the competition's history. With the professional game suspended for the duration of the War, the next final didn't take place for another seven years. Portsmouth kept the trophy safe, despite the bombing raids aimed at the local harbour.

1945

1945/6

BACK IN THE SWING

1946

CHARLTON:
Bartram, Phipps, Shreeve, **Bert Turner (1)**, Oakes, Johnson, Fell, Brown, Arthur Turner, Welsh ©, Duffy

DERBY:
Woodley, Nicholas ©, Howe, Bullions, Leuty, Musson, Harrison, Carter, **Stamps (2)**, **Doherty (1)**, Duncan OG (**Bert Turner**)

Although the war was over, the country was still some way from running smoothly again. There were no Football League fixtures this season just regional sections, so the only national competition was the FA Cup. To extend the appeal of the competition and increase revenue the FA decreed that every round before the semi-final would be played over two legs.

It was unclear who the strong sides would prove to be since the war had left many teams short of players with such large number of them either dead or still enlisted.

Derby, with the still canny Raich Carter pulling the strings alongside the Northern Ireland inside forward Peter Doherty, won through to the semi-final and were the clear favourites. Their best result was a thrilling 4-3 win away at Villa in the sixth round. After a tense opening 1-1 draw, they would prove more than a match for Birmingham, winning the replay 4-0 with two goals apiece for Doherty and the powerful centre forward, Jack Stamps.

Charlton faced Bolton in the other semi-final. The Addicks had centre-forward Arthur Turner and free-scoring winger Chris Duffy in fine form and had sauntered past Preston and Brentford. Bolton's progress had been marred by events off the pitch. After an impressive 5-0 win over Liverpool in the fourth round, Bolton followed it up with an equally satisfying away win at Stoke in the first leg of the fifth round.

A huge crowd turned up to see the second leg, both to encourage Wanderers in their pursuit of cup glory and to witness the wizardry of Stoke's Stanley Matthews. A crowd of 65,419 were officially admitted but there were 20,000 more outside. It was the restlessness of the

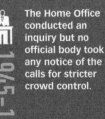

The Home Office conducted an inquiry but no official body took any notice of the calls for stricter crowd control.

1945-1946

crowd outside that caused the problem, coupled with the antiquated grounds and poor security. When some of the supporters who had been shut out started pulling down the fence around the ground and forced their way into an already packed Railway Embankment, panic predictably ensued. The crowd was forced forward and hundreds were hurt as they were crushed underfoot or squashed against railings. Thirty three people died in what was at the time the worst disaster in British football.

Irrelevantly, Bolton won through but were too shell-shocked to give Charlton a game in the semi-final.

A joyous final reminded people of the good things football could offer a country trying to forget the misery of six years of war. The score was 1-1 at full time with Charlton's Bert Turner accounting for both goals. Turner became the first player to score for both sides in a final when he made amends for a deflected own-goal by banging in an equaliser a few minutes later. Derby upped the ante in extra-time, and Carter and Doherty ran rings round a tiring Charlton. Two strikes from Stamps and one from Doherty settled the game by a flattering 4-1.

SEED OF VICTORY

CHARLTON:
Bartram, Croker, Shreeve, Whittaker, Phipps, Johnson, Hurst, Dawson, Robinson, Welsh ©, **Duffy (1)**

BURNLEY:
Strong, Woodruff, Mather, Attwell, Brown ©, Bray, Chew, Morris, Harrison, Potts, Kippax

As the country gradually returned to normal, so did the FA Cup. The two-legged ties were dropped now the league was up and running again and the Cup returned to its traditional winner takes all format. Those looking for early light relief were found wanting. Not a single league side fell to non-league opposition, while the third round was entirely made up of teams from the top four divisions.

Second Division Burnley made sure the big boys didn't have it all their own way in the third round. The Clarets hammered Aston Villa 5-1 with Billy Morris and Ray Harrison bagging two apiece. Coventry were easily seen off in round four, and a Harrison hat-trick ended Luton's hopes after the Hatters had battled out a 0-0 draw at Kenilworth Road.

Burnley's season was now in full swing. Their successful promotion challenge was entering the home straight and they had the chance to pit their wits against more First Division opposition in the sixth round. They held Middlesbrough to a 1-1 draw at Ayresome Park thanks to a strike from Billy Morris, who was on the mark again with the only goal of the replay at Turf Moor.

Burnley's test in the semi-final was the toughest of all. Liverpool were on their way to the title and had already knocked out holders Derby. At Ewood Park, the teams played out a tense, dour contest which, after 120 minutes of largely chanceless football, had failed to produce a goal. At Maine Road a fortnight later, the game was just as tight, but Ray Harrison finally won it for Burnley. For a club with such a long pedigree, this was only the Clarets' second final and their first since 1914. They owed much of their success to a watertight defence, which had conceded a mere twenty-nine league

1946-1947

Charlton manager Jimmy Seed, who had won a winner's medal as a player with Tottenham in 1921, broke the lid of the Cup when he dropped it getting out of a taxi. He arranged a silversmith to repair the trophy at his own expense to cover his embarrassment.

goals, easily the stingiest of all league clubs. Their eight-game route to Wembley had produced a goals-against tally of just two.

Charlton, after forty years without a whiff of glory, reached their second final in a row. Only two of their six ties were against top-level opposition, but a sixth round win against a decent Preston side deserved great credit. Yet the Addicks finished their league season in an undistinguished nineteenth place and only the weakness of Leeds and Brentford prevented them from being distracted by a prolonged relegation battle.

As Charlton were one of the First Division's more goal-shy teams and Burnley owed their success to prudent defending, a classic final was always going to be too much to hope for. After Harry Potts struck the bar early on, the game descended into a ritual of toothless Charlton attacking against a Burnley side playing the forerunner of *catenaccio*. As the game ground into extra-time, the biggest talking-point had been the replacement of the match ball, which had burst for the second final running. With six minutes of extra-time remaining Charlton finally found a way through. Robinson crossed a ball which Welsh headed on to Chris Duffy who rifled the ball past Strong. The cheers were of relief more than joy. To have to sit through a replay would have been torture. Not that Charlton cared now. They had won their first trophy, a feat they are still to replicate in any competition.

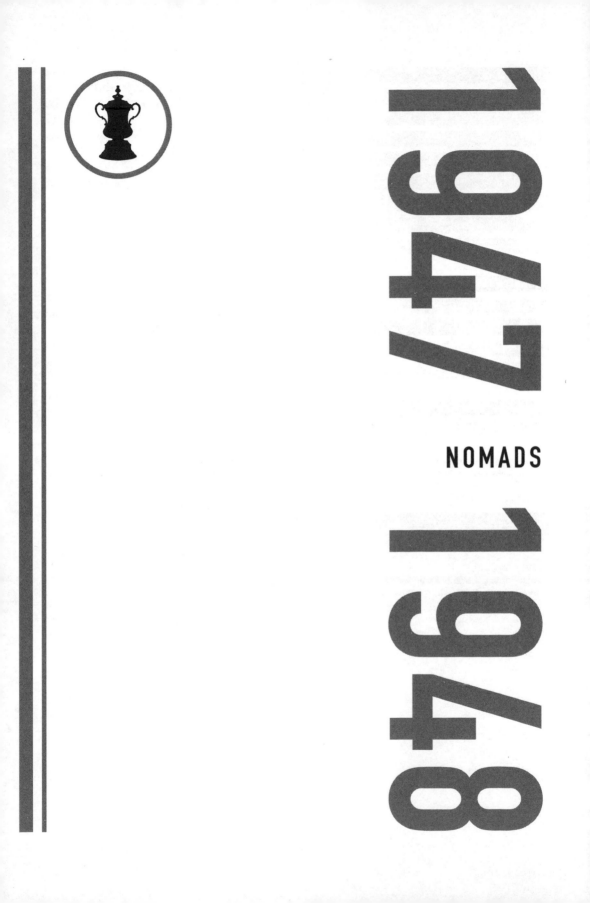

NOMADS

1947

1947

1948

1876

Meagre post-war resources had been ploughed into rejuvenating top-class football and the professional game. The trickle-down effect had yet to occur, so that non-league teams, if not quite extinct, were a luxury in some areas. By and large the ones that took part got thrashed.

What a glorious exception, then, Colchester made in 1948. Seeing off Wrexham, one of the better Third Division sides, earned them a crack at First Division Huddersfield. Colchester were only formed in 1937 but they had ambition. They had acquired the veteran Arthur Turner, a Cup finalist in 1946 with Charlton, and had other players with league experience. Huddersfield had a winner from the same final in Peter Doherty, bought from Derby, and were hot favourites. A fiercely committed performance from Colchester saw them dominate their opponents and Curry's winner, twenty minutes from the end gave them their just desserts. By now the Layer Road outfit were firm media favourites, who enjoyed the sound-bites of the coach Ted Fenton, a no-nonsense sort with no respect for reputation and a cute line in mystical tactics. After seeing off Second Division Bradford PA with two more goals from Curry, Colchester faced Blackpool. Much was made of an innovative 'M' formation, to counter Blackpool's forwards, including Stanley Matthews who had been recruited from Stoke that season. Maybe the 'M' ultimately stood for Munro, McIntosh and Mortensen, who shared Blackpool's goals in a 5-0 thumping?

Colchester would be elected to the Football League two years later. A glamorous date with Leeds and history beckoned some twenty-three years further on.

What the occasional mismatches did throw up in these early rounds were some prodigious goalscoring feats, none more so than at South Shields. They overwhelmed Radcliffe Welfare United 13-0 in the preliminary round where Chris Marron wrote his own entry in the record books with ten goals. Nobody has scored more in any one match, and Marron stood in splendid isolation for fifty-five years until the feat was equalled in 2002.

When the competition started in earnest, Notts County's Lawton and Sewell were forced to carve up the match ball after hat-tricks in the same game against Horsham. Although County were only a Third Division side, they had managed to persuade England international Lawton to sign for them for an astronomical £20,000. Bristol City were faced with an even bigger conundrum after their first round tie against Dartford. Their 9-2 victory contained hat-tricks from three players:

Clark, Townsend and Williams. City equalled the nine goals they had scored in the previous season's campaign against Hayes when Don Clark had netted four.

A surprise was provided by Crewe in the third round as First Division Sheffield United were toppled 3-1 at Gresty Road. Derby heeded the warning to win 3-0 at the same venue in the next round.

Second Division Fulham enjoyed a run that took them to the quarter-finals. Arthur Stevens' hat-trick in their fourth round tie against Bristol Rovers earned him the award of an overcoat promised by Fulham director Tommy Trinder, although rumour has it that the celebrity comic failed to cough up. He definitely failed to see the funny side after Fulham's sixth round tie against Blackpool. The Tangerines were cutting a swathe through the tournament, scything through Leeds, Chester and Colchester by an aggregate of 13-0. Fulham kept the score down to two but found Stan Mortensen too hot to handle.

The England centre-forward continued his streak with a semi-final hat-trick against Tottenham. Blackpool's 3-1 win in extra time had seen them through to their first final.

Manchester United earned their passage to Wembley the hard way. The potential tie of the third round proved just that as Aston Villa and Manchester United squared up at Villa Park. United found themselves a goal down in thirteen seconds, a shock which they clearly regarded as effrontery. By half-time they were 5-1 up, only for Villa to roar back after the break with three in reply. Stan Pearson finished the avalanche with his second, United's sixth and the game's tenth goal. United were managed by a tyro Scot called Busby. An intelligent and observant player, Busby was already showing an acute appreciation of tactics and positional attributes; his captain, Johnny Carey, was a decent inside forward he had turned into an outstanding full-back.

After their epic against Villa, they faced Liverpool, Charlton, Preston and Derby – all top-division clubs. What made United's task all the harder was that Old Trafford was unusable following wartime bomb damage meaning that all home games had to be played at Maine Road. This arrangement worked for league games but when both were drawn at home in the fourth and fifth rounds, United had to look elsewhere. Nowadays, the demands of television mean that one single round can be

Bob Curry of Colchester had thought his playing days were over when he was badly wounded at Dunkirk. He recovered to show some of the same spirit.

1947-1948

All Colchester's victims played in red; Blackpool wore tangerine.

1947-1948

Manchester United's road to the final was witnessed by over 300,000 spectators, an aggregate record that still stands.

1947-1948

staggered over four days. In 1948 the notion that a week-end fixture could kick off at a time other than 3pm on Saturday afternoon amounted to sacrilege. While City kicked off as usual at Maine Road, United played 'home' ties against Liverpool and Charlton at Goodison Park and Leeds Road respectively. All venues came alike to Stan Pearson. He followed his brace at Villa Park with two against Preston and all three in the semi-final against Derby.

Both sides had scored eighteen times in five games on the way to Wembley; the final was a mouthwatering prospect. Unlike so many, it lived up to its billing.

After twelve minutes Blackpool drew first blood. Mortensen broke free of United's defence and advanced on Robinson only to be upended by Chilton. Under modern rules, the centre half would have been sent off. But in 1948 it was all part of the rough and tumble. The controversy lay in the award of a penalty, which owed everything to Mortensen's momentum that had sent him sprawling inside the box after the initial contact had been made a yard outside the area. Eddie Shimwell fluffed the spot-kick, but Crompton dived over the ball and Blackpool were one up.

United levelled just before the half-hour. Delaney's lob forward seemed nothing more than speculative, but dithering between Hayward and Robinson let in Rowley for the equaliser. Parity lasted only five minutes. Matthews found Kelly with a free-kick, and the half-back's incisive pass put Mortensen through to fire home. Blackpool's centre-forward had scored in every round, the eighth player to do so.

United pressed hard in the second half, but ran up against a Blackpool defence whose reputation for parsimony looked justified. Teams ran by Busby never gave up; Morris's quickly-taken free kick caught the Tangerines off guard, and Rowley's diving header levelled the scores for the second time.

The game was in the balance. With ten minutes remaining Mortensen looked well placed to win it for Blackpool but Crompton made a crucial save. United reaped an immediate dividend as they broke upfield for Anderson to score a third, his shot flying in off a post. United were ahead for the first time and sealed the game in slightly fortunate fashion three minutes later. John Anderson's shot was deflected off Kelly's head leaving Robinson stranded. It was a cruel finish for Blackpool but they had played a full part in Wembley's finest final to date.

For Matt Busby, it was his first trophy and heralded United's first golden age. Their only previous FA Cup victory had been in 1909 and the last of their two league titles was won in 1911. By winning in 1948 they became the first side to win the Cup having faced only top division opposition.

WOLVES EAT FOXES

LEICESTER:
Bradley, Jelly, Scott, Walter Harrison, Plummer ©, King, **Griffiths (1)**, Lee, Jim Harrison, Chisholm, Adam

WOLVES:
Williams, Pritchard, Springthorpe, Crook, Shorthouse, Wright ©, Hancocks, **Smyth (1)**, **Pye (2)**, Dunn, Mullen

F orget a mundane final topping off a competition with few thrills in the latter stages. This was the year Yeovil and their famous sloping pitch stamped themselves on the FA Cup. When Yeovil were finally promoted from the Conference in 2003, their FA Cup legacy was twenty league victories, the most by a non-league club. No shock reverberated more than scalp number six in January 1949.

Yeovil should have just been enjoying the day. The fourth round represented a unique experience, and a 3-1 win against Second Division Bury in the previous round was prestigious enough. Their prospects against the power of Sunderland were hardly improved by the loss of regular keeper Stan Hall just days before the big game.

Sunderland were not only a leading First Divison club, they were also the country's biggest spenders. Their maverick inside-forward Len Shackleton had been signed from Newcastle for £20,500 (think £20m today). By contrast, their part-time opposition enjoyed a wage bill of just £100 per week.

Yeovil were well prepared for the match by their eloquent player-manager, Alec Stock. Stock was so much the heart of the club that reports suggest he even cut the grass. With a crowd of 17,000 roaring them on, they started brightly. Sunderland's distaste for the less than salubrious surroundings and the sloping pitch seemed apparent as Yeovil dominated the opening exchanges. On twenty-eight minutes, Blizzard's free-kick found Wright, who put through to Stock. The player-manager turned and struck a left-foot drive past the diving Mapson. It was Stock's first goal of the season.

Having been served with a wake-up call, Sunderland stirred. Despite their superior technique and greater possession, Yeovil kept them at bay for nearly an hour. With fifteen minutes of normal time remaining, stand-in keeper Dyke made his first mistake. He flapped at Ramsden's long, deep cross leaving Robinson with an open goal.

A side with less tenacity may have folded, but Yeovil held firm to take the game into extra-time. By now conditions were becoming hairy and the fog that began to envelop Huish added to Sunderland's discomfort. The closer they came to a replay, the more it seemed to dull their ambition here. It was an attitude that cost them dear.

On 104 minutes, Shackleton's aimless pass was seized upon by Yeovil's inside-forward Ray Wright. His pass put Eric Bryant in the clear and the recipient fired calmly past Mapson for the winner.

That was the game's last moment of calm; the final

1948-1949

Alec Stock commented later on the press's exaggeration of the slope at Yeovil's Huish Park, suggesting that 'everyone must have had the idea we played on the North face of the Eiger.'

few minutes were chaotic. Sunderland threw everything at the home defence, who punted away at will. A pitch invasion seconds from the end, led by supporters who mistook a blast from the referee for the final whistle, added to the confusion. When the end eventually came, it signalled one of the Cup's greatest upsets.

Yeovil's efforts were handsomely rewarded as they were drawn away to Manchester United in the fifth round. United were still a club in exile so the tie took place at Maine Road. Six special trains were chartered to transport fans from Somerset and such was the interest in the tie that the crowd shattered several attendance records. The gates were shut with 81,565 inside and thousands of disappointed fans locked out. This remains the largest crowd for an FA Cup tie, finals excepted.

On the pitch, Yeovil got the hiding they were expected to receive from Sunderland. Jack Rowley scored five as United carried out the 8-0 demolition that inflicted the Somerset club's record defeat.

Yeovil walked away with heads held high and gate receipts that eclipsed their entire income from the previous season.

While Yeovil finally proved that the non-leaguers were not simply cannon fodder, Second Division Bradford Park Avenue demonstrated that their run to the sixth round two years earlier had been no fluke. At St James' Park, they stunned title-chasing Newcastle with a

1948-1949

Stock was later the boss at several league clubs, including Bournemouth, Luton, QPR and Fulham. Stock is also rumoured to be an inspiration for the Paul Whitehouse creation Ron Manager. He would return to the FA Cup spotlight with Fulham in the 1975 final.

2-0 victory. The fourth round handed them the tallest of orders as holders Manchester United awaited them at Maine Rd. The tie should have been a mismatch but it took United three games and 360 minutes to win through. Bizarrely, with the teams locked together in extra-time of the second replay, United ran riot. With Burke and Rowley each scoring twice, they overwhelmed their plucky opponents 5-0.

Although Bradford Park Avenue failed to spring a surprise, Third Division strugglers Newport claimed a real scalp. After a 3-3 thriller at home, it seemed as though Park Avenue had forfeited their best chance. At Leeds Road Eddie Carr's two goals shocked Huddersfield as the First Division side crumbled 3-1. Newport, after their heroics at Huddersfield, faced the most daunting of journeys in the fifth round. Fratton Park was about to witness its greatest days, as Portsmouth were en route to the first of successive league titles. Amazingly, Newport

1948-1949

After their Wembley defeat, Leicester remained in grave danger of becoming the first finalists to be relegated to the Third Division. Their Cup run had caused such a backlog of fixtures that they were forced to play three times in four days within a week of the final. They escaped by a point.

led 2-1 in the second half, with goals from Bobby Harper and that man Eddie Carr, but Jack Froggatt's winner in extra-time sneaked Portsmouth home. Pompey benefited from post-war austerity measures which meant that replays had been decreed as unwelcome, resource-sapping extras. The FA had deemed that extra-time should apply after ninety minutes in all drawn matches, rather than just replays. Portsmouth were spared a tricky visit to Newport and given an extra half hour to win the tie on their own turf.

The sixth round produced a mouth-watering prospect as Portsmouth hosted Derby. Both teams were title rivals and eventually filled two of the top three places. Pompey won it 2-1 and were installed as clear favourites after drawing Second Division strugglers Leicester in the semi-finals. Leicester had already seen off First Division opposition in Birmingham and Preston, and had won through an extraordinary fifth round tie against Luton. A 5-5 draw at Luton featured four goals from inside forward Jack Lee. Such a scoreline might have preceded an anti-climactic replay but not on this occasion, Leicester winning 5-3 with two more from Lee. Lee may have been scoring the goals but the team's guile was supplied by the other inside-forward, a young unknown called Don Revie. Portsmouth should have had too much for the Foxes but they blew it in spectacular fashion as two goals from Revie upset the form book and earned the midlands team a 3-1 win.

Manchester United and Wolves battled out the other semi-final. United had overcome a partisan, club-record crowd of 55,000 at Boothferry Park to edge out Third Division Hull. The Tigers' fortunes had been revived by the appointment of an old Cup hero, Raich Carter, as player-manager. Away wins against Second Division Blackburn and Grimsby and, even better, top flight Stoke were all good preparation for taking on the holders but a solitary goal from Stan Pearson saw United home.

One goal had also been enough to win Wolves a Black Country derby against West Brom. At Hillsborough in the semi-final, Sammy Smyth earned Wolves a 1-1 draw and ended United's hopes of retaining the trophy with the only goal in the replay at Goodison Park.

Wolves had been founder members of the Football League but the trophy cabinet at Molineux bore little testament to such long traditions. They had yet to win the Championship and the most recent of their two FA Cup victories was a forty-one-year-old memory. Their last visit to Wembley had been a huge embarrassment. In 1939, they had started as red-hot favourites against Portsmouth only for their big day to end with a 4-1 defeat.

The captain on that day, Stan Cullis, was now manager at Molineux. Under his regime of iron discipline and uncompromising pragmatism, Wolves' golden age was about to unfold. This victory was the curtain-raiser.

Despite their defeat of Portsmouth, Leicester's task at Wembley looked an uphill one. Their league form was dreadful, a final position of nineteenth in Division Two representing their worst-ever finish. When they were deprived of Don Revie's services, whose mystery nosebleeds had failed to clear up, Wolves looked to be holding all the aces. So it proved as Wanderers swept into a 2-0 lead by half-time. Creditably, Leicester went for broke in the second-half and scored within two minutes from Mal Griffiths. Wolves quelled any thoughts of rebellion midway through the half, when Sammy Smyth waltzed through the Leicester defence to end the contest.

1949

REDS SHOT DOWN

1950

THE LAST 16

Arsenal **2** Burnley **0**

Leeds **3** Cardiff **1**

Chesterfield (1) **0** Chelsea (1) **3**

Man United (3) **3** Portsmouth (3) **1**

Stockport **1** Liverpool **2**

Wolves (0) **0** Blackpool (0) **1**

Derby **4** Northampton **2**

Everton **1** Tottenham **0**

QUARTER FINALS

Arsenal **1** Leeds **0**

Chelsea **2** Man United **0**

Liverpool **2** Blackpool **1**

Derby **1** Everton **2**

SEMI FINALS

Arsenal **1** Chelsea **0**

at White Hart Lane after 2-2 at WHL

Liverpool **2** Everton **0**

at Maine Road

FINAL, 29 APRIL 1950, WEMBLEY

Arsenal **2** Liverpool **0**

ARSENAL:
Swindin, Scott, Barnes, Forbes, Leslie
Compton, Mercer ©, Cox, Logie, Goring, **Lewis**
(2), Denis Compton

LIVERPOOL:
Sidlow, Lambert, Spicer, Taylor ©, Hughes,
Jones, Payne, Barron, Stubbins, Fagan, Liddell

O ne of last year's heroes made an early mark on this season's competition. Eddie Carr had been the toast of Newport but was offloaded to Bradford City. At Valley Parade he simply carried on where he had left off. Fleetwood were clobbered 9-0 in the first round with Carr netting four. The Bantams' Bill Price tucked in with a hat-trick.

Yeovil were again the only non-leaguers to catch the eye. Their 3-1 defeat of Gillingham was the sole surprise of the first two rounds, although after their derring-do against Sunderland last season, one assumed the locals simply took this in their stride.

Joining Yeovil in the third round were Weymouth, whose journey abruptly ended with an away draw to Manchester United. Jack Rowley once again played the bully with two more.

Jackie Milburn warmed up his shooting boots with a hat-trick in a 7-2 defeat of Oldham, but Newcastle blew their fancied status by losing 3-0 to an ordinary Chelsea. Another celebrated forward in fine form was Derby's Jack Stamps. Two hat-tricks saw off Manchester City and Bury, but Derby were undone by Everton in the sixth round.

The tie of the fifth round lived up to expectations. Manchester United, back at Old Trafford, shared six goals with champions Portsmouth. In the replay at Fratton Park, goals from Delaney, Downie and Mitten powered United to a 3-1 win. Having done the hard work, United surprisingly lost 2-0 at Stamford Bridge. Chelsea's second goal came from emerging centre-forward Roy Bentley, who nearly pulled off another surprise in their semi-final. Against a technically superior Arsenal at White Hart Lane, two goals from Bentley in the first twenty-five minutes rattled the Gunners, but the game turned on an incident just before half-time. A corner from right-winger Freddie Cox was carried on the breeze and over the line before keeper Harry Medhurst could claw the ball to safety. With fifteen minutes left, Arsenal won another corner. Before Denis Compton shaped to take it, he motioned for brother Leslie to move up from centre-half. Captain Joe Mercer waved him back but his instruction was ignored to good effect. Leslie headed home his brother's corner and the Gunners escaped with a replay.

The second match was a typically tense semi-final. It seemed destined for a second replay when, in the four-teenth minute of extra time, Freddie Cox scored Arsenal's winner. Credit for Cox's goal was claimed by his wife

Eileen, who had apparently dreamt of it in the days before the replay.

The other semi-final threw up another derby, Liverpool and Everton battling it out at Maine Road. The game was decided by goals from two of Anfield's biggest legends; Bob Paisley, later to become Liverpool's most successful manager, and Billy Liddell, one of the club's most celebrated forwards.

Liverpool had reached Wembley without leaving the north west. They had won away ties at Blackburn and Stockport and played their semi-final at Maine Road. Even more curiously, Arsenal's journey to Wembley was the longest of their run. They enjoyed four home draws then both semi-final matches were at White Hart Lane.

As both teams played in red, the rules demanded that both teams change their strips. Liverpool took the field in what was to become a familiar away kit of white shirts and black shorts. Arsenal invited chants of 'Are you Wolves in disguise?' after electing to play in old gold.

The most crucial moment occurred when Gunners' manager Tom Whittaker kept faith with Reg Lewis. The Arsenal forward's phlegmatic approach had often been frowned on by management and he was frequently dropped. His selection owed much to a lobbying campaign from Joe Mercer. Whittaker's decision was repaid handsomely after seventeen minutes when Lewis latched on to an incisive pass from Jimmy Logie to slot home.

Another Arsenal legend had already decided that this game was to be his last. Denis Compton was a national sporting legend, an international footballer and cricketer of the highest class. The increasing demands on his time, and his suspect knee, meant that something had to give. Arsenal's loss was English cricket's gain as Compton was able to prolong his sporting career by several years. This being the Brylcreem Boy, Compton's exit contained a typical slice of drama. At half-time he was exhausted and had to be revived with a glass of brandy. Although it was a remedy that would be frowned on by today's coaches, in 1950 it was just the job. Compton's deep cross was flicked on by Cox for Lewis to pick his spot again.

Joe Mercer's advice had been vindicated and enabled the veteran Gunners' captain to lift the Cup for the first and only time. He nearly left Wembley with a loser's medal, after being mistakenly handed one by the Queen.

1950

'WOR' JACKIE

1951

THE LAST 16

Birmingham **2** Bristol City **0**

Man United **1** Arsenal **0**

Blackpool **2** Mansfield **0**

Chelsea (1) **0** Fulham (1) **3**

Stoke **2** Newcastle **4**

Bristol Rovers **3** Hull **0**

Sunderland **3** Norwich **0**

Wolves **2** Huddersfield **0**

QUARTER FINALS

Birmingham **1** Man United **0**

Blackpool **1** Fulham **0**

Newcastle (0) **3** Bristol Rovers (0) **1**

Sunderland (1) **1** Wolves (1) **3**

SEMI FINALS

Birmingham **1** Blackpool **2**

at Goodison Park after 0-0 at Maine Road

Newcastle **2** Wolves **1**

at Huddersfield after 0-0 at Hillsborough

FINAL, 28 APRIL 1951, WEMBLEY

Newcastle Utd **2** Blackpool **0**

NEWCASTLE:
Fairbrother, Cowell, Corbett, Harvey ©,
Brennan, Crowe, Walker, Taylor, **Milburn (2)**,
George Robledo, Mitchell

BLACKPOOL:
Farm, Shimwell, Garrett, Johnston ©, Hayward,
Kelly, Matthews, Mudie, Mortensen, Slater,
Perry

The lifeblood of the FA Cup is provided by clubs at the grassroots. Persistence, based more on hope than expectation, fuels the eternal belief that this just might be their year. In the 1951 competition, a brief moment arrived for two such clubs.

The marvellously-named Cleator Moor Celt from West Cumbria had been formed in 1908 and are still going strong. They can bask forever in their solitary first round appearance. Although outclassed 5-0 by Tranmere, they can take their place in FA Cup history.

Linbury Colliery are a works team with an even longer tradition. Formed in 1892, they have outlived the colliery itself, which was closed in 1987. The team, now named Linbury Colliery Welfare, still competes in the Notts Alliance League. They hosted Gillingham in their first round tie. The 4-1 defeat seems irrelevant. This was another occasion where taking part was more important than the winning.

Norwich's better days were ahead of them – they had only enjoyed five years in Division Two in their history, and it would be another decade before they hit those heights again. They reached the fifth round of the Cup for the first time in 1951 by way of a momentous victory over Liverpool in the third round. Football passion was beginning to stir in East Anglia.

Liverpool weren't the only top division side to fall by the wayside in the third round:

Everton, Middlesbrough and Portsmouth all travelled to Second Division grounds (Hull, Leeds and Luton respectively), failed to score, and went out.

Holders Arsenal also failed to cover themselves in glory. Held by Third Division Carlisle at Highbury, they relied on two goals from Reg Lewis in the replay to win 4-1. The Gunners laboured against another side from that division in the fourth round. Northampton were nervously seen off 3-2 with another brace from Lewis. With Arsenal in such stuttering form, Manchester United picked them off in round five with a single goal from Stan Pearson.

When United drew Birmingham, one of only two quarter-final teams from outside Division One, progress to the last four looked assured. The 50,000 crammed into St Andrews witnessed a dream start from the home side, Higgins shooting them in front after just twenty-two seconds. For the remaining eighty-nine minutes, United did everything but score. Birmingham, with a combination of heroism and good luck, held out for a famous victory.

The other surprise of the sixth round came at Newcastle. With Jackie Milburn in irresistible form, the Magpies faced Bristol Rovers, the season's surprise package. Rovers had already seen off two of the third round Davids, Hull and Luton. Against the odds, Rovers held out for a goalless draw at St James' Park. In the replay at Eastville, 'Wor Jackie' was back on song and the Toon, despite conceding an early goal, ran out comfortable 3-1 winners.

They were joined in the last four by Wolves and Blackpool. Wolves had won a hard-fought derby against Villa in round four and seen off Sunderland in a replay in the last eight. Blackpool had enjoyed an untroubled run after beating Charlton in a third round replay, avoiding top division opposition in every subsequent round.

The semi-finals proved the absurdity of the rose-tinted memory of some older fans that all games in the fifties finished 5-4. Both were scoreless but with Stan Mortensen and Milburn again on target in the replays, Blackpool and Newcastle took their places at Wembley.

Much of the ballyhoo before the final centred around Stanley Matthews who, at thirty-six, was running out of time to land a major honour. Newcastle, too, were hungry for success. This was a club whose proud FA Cup tradition was a receding memory. The most recent of their seven finals was in 1932.

The teams looked evenly matched as Blackpool, whose third-placed league finish was their highest at that point, had finished the campaign only one point ahead of the Geordies. Both teams had a potent centre-forward and it seemed as though the respective form of Mortensen and Milburn would be crucial.

After a scoreless first half, it was Milburn who drew first blood. His run to accept Robledo's pass left Blackpool's ponderous offside trap looking foolish, and the Magpies' talisman ran unchecked to place the ball past Farm. This was his seventh goal of the competition and Milburn joined the select band of those who had scored in every round.

Milburn's second, five minutes later, has passed into Wembley legend. Milburn played a short pass to Ernie Taylor, who wrong-footed the Blackpool defence with a smart back-heeled return. Milburn's bullet twenty-five yarder left Scotland keeper George Farm a spectator. It was a goal fit for a final, maybe the finest ever goal on that stage. It heralded Newcastle's next golden age.

1951

HOLDING ON

1952

THE LAST 16

Luton **3** Swindon **1**

Leyton Orient **0** Arsenal **3**

Southend **1** Sheffield Utd **2**

Leeds (1)(1) **1** Chelsea (1)(1) **5**

Portsmouth **4** Doncaster **0**

Swansea **0** Newcastle **1**

Blackburn **1** West Brom **0**

Burnley **2** Liverpool **0**

QUARTER FINALS

Luton **2** Arsenal **3**

Sheffield Utd **0** Chelsea **1**

Portsmouth **2** Newcastle **4**

Blackburn **3** Burnley **1**

SEMI FINALS

Arsenal **3** Chelsea **0**
at White Hart Lane after 1-1 at WHL

Newcastle **2** Blackburn **1**
at Elland Road after 0-0 at Hillsborough

FINAL, 3 MAY 1952, WEMBLEY

Newcastle Utd **1** Arsenal **0**

NEWCASTLE:
Simpson, Cowell, McMichael, Harvey ©,
Brennan, Ted Robledo, Walker, Foulkes,
Milburn, **George Robledo (1)**, Mitchell

ARSENAL:
Swindin, Barnes, Smith, Forbes, Daniel, Mercer
©, Cox, Logie, Holton, Lishman, Roper

I n the first round, cup ties arrived like buses in East London. Three turned up within a few hundred yards as Leyton, Leyton Orient and Leytonstone were all drawn at home. They all won, although it was the league side who endured a struggle. Leyton Orient took three ties to overcome Gorleston from the Eastern Counties League and only sneaked home by the odd goal in nine. Leytonstone produced a rare moment of giant-killing by knocking out Shrewsbury. Buxton Town were the other non-league headline grabbers, overcoming third tier Aldershot 4-3.

In the third round, three ties upset the form book. Leyton Orient held Everton, then won the replay 3-1 at Goodison Park. The Toffees were suffering a rare spell in the Second Division but should have dealt better with a team that finished eighteenth in the Third Division (South). Buoyed by their success, the Os won at another Second Division ground in the next round as Birmingham City were put out 1-0. Their sternest examination was yet to come, and they fell at home to Arsenal in the fifth round. Doug Lishman scored twice for the Gunners in a 3-0 stroll.

Bradford Park Avenue powered through the first three rounds by beating fellow Yorkshire clubs: York City, Bradford City and Sheffield Wednesday were knocked out before they faced more local opposition at Elland Road. Leeds took the Tyke bragging rights with a 2-0 victory.

The shock of the season came at Old Trafford. Matt Busby, having already won the Cup four years earlier, had developed a side that threatened to win the league in 1949 and 1951. On both occasions they had finished as runners-up, but this season they went the distance and brought home United's first title since the First World War. The great 'Busby Babes' side was taking shape but it fell apart on 12 January. Visitors in the third round were Hull City, whose final league placing of eighteenth in Division Two suggested a team not at the peak of form. It made their 2-0 win all the more remarkable. Ken Harrison and Sid Gerrie inflicted the damage but the Tigers' joy was short-lived. They lost 2-0 at Blackburn in the next round.

The more famous battle between Chelsea and Leeds was yet to come, but their tie in 1952 produced a marathon. The Blues' hero was an unlikely one, an eighteen-year-old still doing national service. Bobby Smith had to be drafted at a day's notice from his barracks at Aldershot to play in the first match. He obviously left in a hurry as he turned up at Elland Road without his boots. Wearing a borrowed pair, he scored the equaliser in a 1-1 draw. Chelsea came from behind for a second time in the replay and were rescued by a strike from Jimmy D'Arcy two minutes from time. In the second replay, Smith again rose to the fore, this time in spectacular fashion. The youngster, still wearing the 'wrong' boots, fired a hat-trick as the Blues overpowered Leeds 5-1. Five days later Roy Bentley scored the only goal at Bramall Lane putting Chelsea through to their second semi-final in three years.

Arsenal, after breezing through their first three ties, wobbled at Luton in the sixth round. At half-time they trailed 1-0 but a switch in formation worked wonders. Freddie Cox scored twice and the Gunners prevailed 3-2. Chelsea must have heard the news with foreboding as Cox had ended their Wembley hopes with a late semi-final winner in 1950. West London hearts sank when the same man shot the Gunners in front but the Blues were rescued by a second-half equaliser from Billy Gray. It only delayed the outset of Groundhog Day. Another semi-final replay – opposition Arsenal; venue White Hart Lane; scorer Freddie Cox: this time he managed two as the Gunners coasted home 3-0.

Holders Newcastle were determined to keep a grip on their trophy. Early progress was smooth, the only surprise being a tally of nine goals in three matches without a single contribution from Jackie Milburn. Bobby Mitchell and George Robledo were the Magpies' early sharpshooters. Milburn finally sparked with a hat-trick in the sixth round victory over Portsmouth before Newcastle laboured against Second Division opposition in the semi-final. At Hillsborough, Blackburn ground out a 0-0 draw before this season's double act of Mitchell and Robledo saw the Geordies through to Wembley.

The final promised to be a tight affair. Newcastle and Arsenal, the winners from the two previous seasons, were set to lock horns. The game began with neither side gaining the advantage, but Arsenal suffered a blow after thirty-five minutes. Right-back Wally Barnes tore knee ligaments and with no substitutes the Gunners ploughed on with only ten fit men. Three Arsenal players were already carrying injuries so this

The trophy was presented by Winston Churchill, the only time the PM has presented the Cup in its history.

was a major setback. Barnes' misfortune was the first in a sequence that saw nine of the next fourteen finals over-shadowed by serious injury. The run became known as the 'Wembley hoodoo' and was blamed on the unfamil-iar lush and clinging turf.

Arsenal, to their credit, remained disciplined, with the ageing Joe Mercer turning in an outstanding, com-mitted performance. They may have won the game with eleven minutes left when Lishman met Cox's corner only to see his header clip the bar. Victory turned to defeat six minutes later when, with two more Arsenal players felled by injury, Mitchell crossed for George Robledo whose header hit the post and dropped over the line. Arsenal still summoned enough energy for Alex Forbes to rattle the crossbar but the Cup was destined for Newcastle. The Magpies became the first club that century to retain the trophy.

The final's referee was Arthur Ellis, the first to become a minor celebrity in his own right. As the rule then applied that a referee could only officiate at one final, this was his only appearance. His more notorious claim to fame was his misfortune in 'taking charge' of the spiteful World Cup match between Hungary and Brazil in 1954. He lost control, as many would have done, and it probably cost him the chance to referee the final. That honour went to another Englishman Bill Ling, who had overseen Newcastle's cup triumph in 1951. The Magpies' third win of the decade was presided over by Reg Leafe, another World Cup referee.

THE MORTENSEN FINAL

THE LAST 16

Burnley **0** Arsenal **2**

Blackpool **(1) 2** Southampton **(1) 1**

Chelsea **0** Birmingham **4**

Halifax **0** Tottenham **3**

Rotherham **1** Aston Villa **3**

Everton **2** Man United **1**

Plymouth **0** Gateshead **1**

Luton **0** Bolton **1**

QUARTER FINALS

Arsenal **1** Blackpool **2**

Birmingham **(1)(2) 0** Tottenham **(1)(2) 1**

Aston Villa **0** Everton **1**

Gateshead **0** Bolton **1**

SEMI FINALS

Blackpool **2** Tottenham **1**
at Villa Park

Everton **3** Bolton **4**
at Maine Road

FINAL, 2 MAY 1953, WEMBLEY

Blackpool **4** Bolton **3**

BLACKPOOL:
Farm, Shimwell, Garrett, Fenton, Johnston ©,
Robinson, Matthews, Taylor, **Mortensen (3)**,
Mudie, **Perry (1)**

BOLTON:
Hanson, Ball, Banks, Wheeler, Barass, **Bell (1)**,
Holden, **Moir © (1)**, **Lofthouse (1)**, Hassall,
Langton

Although remembered principally for the classic final, 1953 was a good year all round for Cup exploits.

The fun started in the third round when Gateshead were drawn against First Division Liverpool. A sterling defensive performance from the Tyneside team, on a cold day with fog swirling around Redheugh Park, saw them edge out their supposed betters one-nil. Even a mysteriously disallowed goal failed to thwart the determined Geordies. Gateshead went on to win at Second Division Hull and Plymouth, before being edged out by eventual finalists Bolton in the sixth round.

On the same day at the other end of the country, Stockport County of the same Division Three (North) faced a tricky tie at Isthmian league Walthamstow Avenue. Not since Corinthians in 1929 had an amateur team reached the fourth round of the cup but two first half goals from inside forward Dick Lucas suggested that was about to change. The A's withstood a pounding in the second-half and hung on for a 2-1 win. In the next round, when Walthamstow earned a splendid draw at Old Trafford, it seemed that Manchester United could also face the ignominy of defeat by the amateur side. Moving the replay to Highbury perhaps did Walthamstow no favours as they were walloped 5-2. Not that it was to be a vintage year for United. They would lose to Second Division Everton in the next round.

It was Everton who carried the flag forward for the lower division clubs, following up the defeat of Manchester United with an excellent 1-0 win at Aston Villa. Again Bolton proved too high a hurdle for the underdogs. Everton couldn't handle the power of England centre forward Nat Lofthouse, who had scored in every round, and added two in a thrilling 4-3 win at Maine Road.

Holders Newcastle had suffered an embarrassing home defeat to Rotherham in the fourth round and the other strong teams had picked each off, so it was left to mid-table teams to make up final.

While Bolton had had a relatively easy time of it – they reached the final without encountering top-flight opposition – Blackpool had endured a rough passage. All their ties had been won by a single goal margin and they accounted for the season's eventual champions Arsenal, as well as Sheffield Wednesday and Tottenham in a tight semi-final. Their toughest tie had been against second division Southampton who had forced a replay at The Dell before succumbing.

Walthamstow enjoyed one or two more successes against league opposition in the 1950s, most notably a 4-0 second replay win against QPR in 1954. Their last appearance in the competition proper was in 1968.

1952-1953

And so to the final, one of the most famous games of football ever played.

Myth and misunderstanding exist about this match. It certainly wasn't the titanic tussle between two super-powers that some later versions contend. Bolton and Blackpool were decent, honest First Division sides – Bolton lifted by the goalscoring prowess of Nat Lofthouse, Blackpool by the predatory instincts of Stan Mortensen and the ageing twinkle of Stanley Matthews' toes. Both sides remained in the top flight for the whole of the fifties, without ever threatening to win the title – the best either managed was Blackpool's second place in 1956, eleven points behind runaway winners Manchester United.

When Blackpool reached the Cup final in 1951, many felt it was Matthews' last chance for a winner's medal. Blackpool lost, but here was the maestro again, at thirty-eight, turning up for what was surely a last hurrah.

The fates seemed to be against Matthews when George Farm, in the great tradition of Scottish goalkeepers, made a hash of a half-hearted Lofthouse strike. Bolton 1-0 up inside a minute and the Lion of Vienna had joined the select band who scored in every round. Bolton lost the services of left-half Eric Ball with barely twenty minutes gone; He would return to hobble about on the left side of attack, little more than a passenger. The extra man gave Blackpool some space but they were making little impression on Bolton's defence despite some pretty approach play. Bolton broke dangerously and Lofthouse hit the post on one counter-attack.

Gateshead would not be a league club much longer after failing to be re-elected in 1960. Coronation year was, by some distance, their most glorious year in the cup.

1952-1953

The breakthrough for the Tangerines came with a large slice of fortune. Mortensen's speculative shot took a wicked deflection off Hassall and left goalkeeper Hanson stranded. The respite lasted four minutes for Blackpool. Langton, switching wings, put in a swerving cross and Moir's merest flick at the near side of goal took it beyond Farm. Moments later Doug Holden crashed a shot off the Blackpool bar; Bolton were on top.

The Trotters continued to press after the interval. Holden got clear of his marker and crossed invitingly. The man on the end of the cross was the injured Bell. Maybe Blackpool thought him too hurt to bother marking because he was all alone when he thumped a header beyond Farm. With only half an hour to go, it looked all over for Blackpool and Matthews.

Blackpool's Ernie Taylor played in FA Cup finals for three clubs, winning in 1951 and 1953 with Newcastle and Blackpool respectively, but finishing on the losing side with Manchester United in 1958 – against Bolton.

1952-1953

If there was hope, it was that Wanderers were visibly tiring and Ralph Banks, the left-back, was looking increasingly exposed without Bell as cover. Matthews was going through the left side of Wanderers' defence with

1952-1953

Stan Mortensen, despite a prodigious scoring record in the FA Cup, had not managed a goal in this season's competition before the final.

ease. One particularly inviting cross was met with a scuffed shot from Mortensen: the badly positioned Hanson watched it dribble over the line, and Blackpool had a lifeline.

Blackpool had latched on to Bolton's weak spot and the whole team fed Matthews every time they got possession. A yard of pace was gone from his heyday but the shimmies and feints were still potent and Banks, cramped and exhausted, had no answer. One weaving run after another produced a cross, usually drilled across the area, occasionally flighted. But there was no finish. Mudie and Perry both missed good chances and time was running out. Lofthouse, too, was hobbling now, and Bolton had no outlet. Penned on the edge of their area, they conceded a free-kick in a promising position three minutes from time. A thumping drive from Mortensen brought the scores level.

Time still for one last drama. Matthews, again, waltzed down the right, almost to the by-line, and cut the ball back for the queue of Blackpool forwards. It was Bill Perry who reached the ball and side-footed it into a gaping net. Matthews had his medal. He was chaired from the field by his team-mates while the Bolton players applauded.

Blackpool's Ernie Taylor played in FA Cup finals for three clubs, winning in 1951 and 1953 with Newcastle and Blackpool respectively, but finishing on the losing side with Manchester United in 1958 — against Bolton.

1952-1953

Like so many finals then, the absence of substitutes counted harshly against one team. Had they been able to replace Bell and Banks, Bolton would surely not have caved in so dramatically in the last quarter. In fairness, Blackpool had also suffered, having lost Allan Brown, their talented inside forward, when he broke his leg scoring the decisive goal against Arsenal in the last eight.

FINNEY DISAPPOINTED

THE LAST 16

Norwich **1**	Leicester **2**	
Preston **6**	Ipswich **1**	
Sheffield Wed **3**	Everton **1**	
Bolton (0) **2**	Portsmouth (0) **1**	
West Brom **3**	Newcastle **2**	
Hull (1) **0**	Tottenham (1) **2**	
Leyton Orient **3**	Doncaster **1**	
Port Vale **2**	Blackpool **0**	

QUARTER FINALS

Leicester (1)(2) **1**	Preston (1)(2) **3**
Sheffield Wed (1) **2**	Bolton (1) **0**
West Brom **3**	Tottenham **0**
Leyton Orient **0**	Port Vale **1**

SEMI FINALS

Preston **2**	Sheffield Wed **0**

at Maine Road

West Brom **2**	Port Vale **1**

at Villa Park

FINAL, 1 MAY 1954, WEMBLEY

West Bromwich Albion **3**	
Preston North End **2**	

WEST BROM:
Sanders, Kennedy, Millard ©, Dudley, Dugdale, Barlow, **Griffin (1)**, Ryan, **Allen (2,1p)**, Nicholls, Lee

PRESTON:
Thompson, Cunningham, Walton, Docherty, Marston, Forbes, Finney ©, Foster, **Wayman (1)**, Baxter, **Morrison (1)**

T he previous season Crystal Palace had been knocked out of the Cup by non-league Finchley. Presumably they travelled to Great Yarmouth in the first round in November, 1953 with no thoughts of complacency. In which case one can only assume they were outplayed, as Rackham's sixth minute goal proved decisive, and Yarmouth recorded their only victory over a league side. The East Anglian club deserve credit for declining to play the tie at Carrow Road, preferring to construct temporary stands from the town's plentiful supply of fish crates!

It was a good year for East Anglian clubs. Ipswich secured promotion to Division Two and went past the third round of the Cup for the first time in their history. They proved they were worth a place in the higher division, beating Birmingham and Oldham, both Divison Two sides, before getting thumped 6-1 by Preston.

Norwich drew Arsenal in the fourth round at Highbury. A penalty in the second minute seemed a godsend but it was saved and Arsenal took the lead soon after. Undeterred, City came back, and two goals from Tom Johnston gave them a memorable win against the reigning league champions.

Other good sides fell early, too. Burnley beat Manchester United 5-3, Huddersfield got thumped at West Ham, and Stan Cullis's Wolves were surprisingly beaten by local rivals Birmingham.

By the fifth round, only West Brom, and last year's finalists, Blackpool and Bolton, remained of teams in the top half of the table. Blackpool joined the casualties at this stage, falling to Third Division Port Vale in the season's big upset. Vale were romping away with their league and had already seen off Cardiff at a snowbound Ninian Park so they were no soft touches. They had a mean defence and hadn't conceded a home goal for nearly six months.

Stanley Matthews was returning to his hometown – not that there was ever any love lost between Stoke and Port Vale – and it all added to a fevered atmosphere at Vale Park. Matthews had a bit of a stinker, as did all the Blackpool forwards who never got to grips with the tough Vale half-backs. By contrast, inside forwards Leake and Griffiths were giving Blackpool no end of trouble and when the former scored twice in ten minutes it was all over.

When Vale drew Leyton Orient in the sixth round, it meant a Third Division side would make the semi-finals

Tom Finney was great crowd favourite. Not as outrageously skilful as Matthews, Finney was in some ways a more complete footballer. He had a much better scoring record than his England colleague, and varied his game more. Thirty goals in seventy-six internationals is a good haul for a winger. That shooting prowess led to Preston moving him to centre forward in 1956-1957 and he rewarded them, as ever, by scoring twenty goals as Preston finished third. Finney was made Footballer of the Year for the second time.

Finney resisted all offers to leave Preston, including a mouth-watering proposal from Serie A's Palermo. When he retired in 1960, he was cheered to the rafters by a packed Deepdale. He later became president of the club and remains a figure of great honour in the town.

for the first time since the war. Orient failed to breach Vale's resolute defence and the Potteries side were in uncharted territory.

The semi-final against West Brom was played in front of a crowd in excess of 68,000 at Villa Park. Unfazed, Vale took the lead; Leake, who had scored in every round since the third, was again the scorer. They were always combative and very much in the game, even when West Brom equalised. The match was settled by a debatable refereeing decision late on. Ronnie Allen converted the spot-kick, and Vale's resistance was finally broken.

Facing Albion in the final were Preston, who had cruised through the early rounds and only really met resistance from Leicester, a tie which went to a replay in the sixth round. The sentimental attention this year was focused on Tom Finney. Like Matthews the year before, Finney was an icon whose loyalty to his home club had denied him a winner's medal of any sort.

Unlike 1953, the final was a muted affair despite a 3-2 scoreline. Ronnie Allen scored another crucial penalty to bring the scores level with twenty minutes to go and Frank Griffin sealed the Cup for Albion with three minutes remaining. Finney had a quiet game by his elevated standards. His chance had gone.

1954 1955

BLACK AND WHITE CUP

NEWCASTLE:
Simpson, Cowell, Batty, Scoular ©, Stokoe, Casey, White, **Milburn (1)**, Keeble, **Hannah (1)**, **Mitchell (1)**

MANCHESTER CITY:
Trautmann, Meadows, Little, Barnes, Ewing, Paul ©, **Johnstone (1)**, Hayes, Revie, Spurdle, Fagan

The First Round opened with one of the Cup's most emotional matches. Accrington Stanley's 7-1 whacking of Cresswell Colliery sounds a tie shorn of all romance but the recent history of this Derbyshire mine had ensured an extraordinary occasion. In 1950, a fire at the colliery claimed eighty lives in one of the industry's worst-ever disasters. That the club could recover sufficiently to win a place in the competition proper within four years was nothing short of miraculous.

In London, Wathamstow Avenue continued their own brand of heroics. The Isthmian League side had knocked out three league sides in the last two years as well as earning a famous draw with Manchester United. Drawn at Loftus Road in the first round, QPR looked to have put the upstarts firmly in their place by half-time. Rangers led 2-0, but Stan Anderson and Len Julians took the tie to a replay. On the following Thursday afternoon, 10,500 crammed into Green Pond Road in E17 but hopes were deflated as QPR again sped into a two-goal lead. Walthamstow had another sting in the tail, this time in the guise of striker Johnny Bee. His two goals sent the contest to a second replay at Highbury. If Rangers were hoping that their professionalism and fitness would prevail, they were in for a rude awakening. On a mud-heap, the match remained scoreless until half-time but the tempo rose dramatically after the break. Julians, Paris and Anderson netted three times in six minutes for Walthamstow and, with the confidence of Rangers' debutant keeper Alan Silver in ribbons, Anderson added his second and Avenue's fourth eighteen minutes from time.

Bishop Auckland were another non-league club with a fine cup tradition. The Northern League side were to the Amateur Cup what Newcastle were to the professional version. They travelled to Crystal Palace in the second round and won 4-2, then held Second Dvision Ipswich to a 2-2 draw at Portman Road. The Bishops belied their amateur status by thumping Ipswich 3-0 in a replay played in the midst of a blizzard. An unlucky draw against Third Division York in round four was to prove the end of the line. The Minstermen won 3-1 to pick up the giant-killing baton in fine style.

York had caused a major surprise in round three by winning 2-0 away at Blackpool. After negotiating the Bishop Auckland banana skin, they earned a sixth round draw at home to Tottenham. They eased home by 3-1 after a disappointing Spurs showing, then won a sixth round tie at Notts County with a goal from a man named

The third round tie between Bury and Stoke created a record for the competition proper. In all it lasted for five matches and nearly nine and a half hours. Stoke eventually won the fourth replay 3-2.

1954-1955

Arthur Bottom. His seventh goal of the campaign ensured that York followed in Port Vale's footsteps from the previous season in reaching the semi-finals as a Third Division club.

By now York were the nation's favourite. The 'Minster Marvels', as they now were, lined up at Hillsborough against a Newcastle team attempting to reach their third final in five years. York were unlucky to fall behind after thirteen minutes to Vic Keeble's strike but their enterprise was rewarded twenty minutes later when the formidable Bottom netted his thirty-third goal of the campaign. Sadly for York, it was their last in the FA Cup this season. Although they earned the distinction of becoming the only Third Division side to force a semi-final replay, Newcastle ran out 2-0 winners at Roker Park to become the first side to reach ten FA Cup finals.

Newcastle would have faced Sunderland at Wembley had Roy Clarke not spoiled the Tyne-Wear party with the only goal in the other semi-final at Villa Park. This earned Manchester City their first final appearance in twenty-two years and the Maine Road faithful had every reason to be optimistic. City's league finish of seventh was their highest since winning promotion four years earlier and in deep-lying centre-forward Don Revie they possessed the Footballer of the Year. Newcastle, and one man in particular, were to prove there was no substitute for experience.

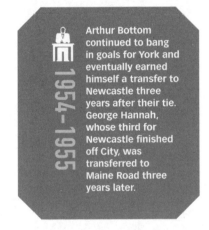

Arthur Bottom continued to bang in goals for York and eventually earned himself a transfer to Newcastle three years after their tie. George Hannah, whose third for Newcastle finished off City, was transferred to Maine Road three years later.

1954-1955

Jackie Milburn had already joked before the final that it felt like a home tie, and so comfortable was he in the surroundings that it took just forty-five seconds for the Magpies' centre-forward to head them in front. Milburn's campaign thus far had been nothing to write home about, with just one goal in Newcastle's nine ties. Now he had written himself into history with Wembley's fastest Cup final goal, a record he held until 1997. When the injury hoodoo claimed right-back Jimmy Meadows inside twenty minutes, things looked desperate for City. To their credit, their ten men hauled them level just before the break when Bobby Johnstone's diving header converted a cross from Joe Hayes.

That City lost was due in part to keeper Bert Trautmann. The German, a former prisoner of war, had won over fans after initial hostility, but he tested their new-found faith after fifty-three minutes. Anticipating a cross from winger Bobby Mitchell, who had advanced to the goal-line after fine work on the left, he left a tantalising

For Newcastle's Scottish goalie Ronnie Simpson, this was not the most prestigious medal that he would win. Twelve years later, he was in the Celtic goal for their memorable European Cup triumph in Lisbon.

1954-1955

1954–1955

Newcastle's centre-half was Bob Stokoe, who achieved immortality eighteen years later at rivals Sunderland by managing them to their famous Cup triumph against Leeds.

gap at his near post. Mitchell's low shot exploited it to the full and Newcastle were back in front.

Seven minutes later, the contest was over. This time, Mitchell turned from scorer to provider, laying on a chance that George Hannah buried past Trautmann. Newcastle were now the undisputed Cup kings. They had not only equalled Blackburn and Villa's record of six wins but were unbeaten in four Wembley finals.

1954–1955

The match against York was another bleak FA Cup moment for Alf Ramsey, who was given a torrid afternoon by winger Billy Fenton. Spurs' manager Arthur Rowe resigned soon after the match. The new boss, Jimmy Anderson, decided Ramsey's time was up. Before long he was player-manager at Ipswich and later led them to the League Championship. The rest, as they say, is history.

1954–1955

Only three men played in all three of Newcastle's victorious Fifties' finals: Bobby Cowell, Jackie Milburn and Bobby Mitchell.

1955

CITY BY A NECK

1956

Strikers had a field day in the first round. Lovell's Athletic, the works side from Newport, travelled to Leyton Orient hoping for a repeat of their victory a decade earlier against Bournemouth. This time, however, the Welsh toffee makers were chewed up and spat out by Ron Heckman, who hit five in a 7-1 thrashing. Heckman's performance was matched by Southport's George Bromilow as Ashton United were overwhelmed 6-1. Brighton were the day's top scorers, putting eight past Newport County. Peter Harburn with four and a hat-trick from Denis Foreman completed a miserable day for the Welsh town.

The next round saw one of the Cup's most extraordinary scorelines. Derby had fallen from grace since their Cup final victory in 1946 and had been relegated from Division Two the previous season. Nonetheless they came into their home tie with Boston United full of confidence as the league's top scorers and fresh from a 6-2 thrashing of Darlington. Cute tactics and an inspired performance from Boston saw them win by an astonishing 6-1 margin, with Geoff Hazledine the hat-trick hero.

The surprise package of the third round was Bedford Town. Having beaten Watford 3-2 in the previous round, a tie at Highbury seemed a purely financial reward. Remarkably, though, the Gunners were held 2-2 before squeaking through the replay 2-1. If Arsenal were somewhat embarrassed, Manchester United were thoroughly humiliated.

The Busby Babes were a team coming of age. Their league season was proving a cakewalk and they were to wrap up the championship by eleven points. A trip to Bristol Rovers in the third round could have been politely viewed as 'tricky'. Rovers were a decent Second Division side but nothing could have prepared United for what awaited them. In front of nearly 36,000 at Eastville, Rovers triumphed 4-0 with two goals from Alfie Biggs, another from Barrie Meyer and a penalty from Geoff Bradford to leave United stunned. Rovers even fielded a stand-in keeper making his Cup debut but Ron Nicholls, like most of the fans, remained an overjoyed spectator.

Another eye-catching scoreline from the third round was Birmingham's 7-1 win at Torquay. An Eddy Brown hat-trick and a Peter Murphy double set Blues on their way and finally saw them emerge from the shadow cast across the city by Villa. The Brown and Murphy double act was to serve the team well, scoring thirteen goals en route to Wembley. Murphy scored the only goal at the

Hawthorns in round five and the pair bagged a goal each at Highbury as Arsenal came to grief 3-1. Both were on target again at Hillsborough in the semi-final as Sunderland tripped at the last hurdle before Wembley for the second successive season. Birmingham had reached the final without playing a single tie at home.

Meanwhile, Manchester City were determined to put the disappointment of last year's Wembley visit behind them. Unlike Birmingham, theirs was a three-pronged goal attack with Bobby Johnstone, Joe Hayes and Jack Dyson scoring all their goals en route to the final. City's main weapon, though, lay just behind their forward line. Don Revie was billed as a centre-forward and wore the number nine shirt. English football's rigid 2-3-5 system dictated that he should take his position at the head of the attack. Revie had other ideas. Having seen how the deep-lying Hidegkuti had been used to devastating effect for Hungary against England in 1953, Revie assumed a similar role. It brought such success that the system was dubbed 'The Revie Plan' It also won City the Cup although this final is not remembered for Revie's outstanding performance alone.

For Bert Trautmann the final proved an opportunity to exorcise the demons of the previous year when his mistake had allowed Bobby Mitchell to grab Newcastle's match-winning second goal. His moment arrived fifteen minutes from the end when, with City 3-1 up, he rushed from his line and dived fearlessly at the feet of Peter Murphy. Trautmann looked in agony from the resulting collision and required treatment for what was assumed to be concussion. He emerged after a couple

of minutes with the magic sponge apparently unscathed. His goal remained intact for the rest of the game, which is more than can be said for his neck. It was diagnosed as broken four days later.

Trautmann's heroics overshadowed a good performance from City. They took the lead after three minutes when Revie's intuitive back-heel gave Joe Hayes the opportunity to pick his spot past England international Gil Merrick. On the quarter-hour, Noel Kinsey put Birmingham on level terms by firing in off the post. This opened up the game, which developed into one of free-flowing entertainment, but it took another fifty minutes before the next goal. Wing-half Ken Barnes put Jack Dyson clear and he easily slipped the ball past Merrick. Five minutes later, City wrapped up their first Cup since 1934 when Dyson touched on Trautmann's punt for Bobby Johnstone to complete the scoring.

1955-1956

City's Ken Barnes is father of another Maine Road favourite, Peter. The latter's performances on the left wing earned him the first of twenty-two England caps in 1977.

1955-1956

Chelsea and Burnley slugged out an epic battle in the fourth round. The Clarets were finally counted out in the fourth replay by goals from Ron Tindall and Jim Lewis. Chelsea's victory took its toll, as they were knocked out 1–0 by Everton three days later.

1955-1956

Don Revie only just made the team for the final. He had been in contractual dispute with City for much of the season. An attack of boils for Bill Spurdle left a gap that Revie was selected to fill.

1956

PATIENCE GETS ITS REWARD

1957

THE LAST 16

Huddersfield 1	Burnley 2	
Aston Villa 2	Bristol City 1	
Blackpool (0) 1	West Brom (0) 2	
Preston (3) 1	Arsenal (3) 2	
Bournemouth 3	Tottenham 1	
Manchester Utd 1	Everton 0	
Millwall 1	Birmingham 4	
Barnsley 1	Nottm Forest 2	

QUARTER FINALS

Burnley (1) 0	Aston Villa (1) 2
West Brom (2) 2	Arsenal (2) 1
Bournemouth 1	Manchester Utd 2
Birmingham (0) 1	Nottm Forest (0) 0

SEMI FINALS

Aston Villa 1 West Brom 0

at St Andrews after 2-2 at Molineux

Manchester Utd 2 Birmingham 0

at Hillsborough

FINAL, 4 MAY 1957, WEMBLEY

Aston Villa 2 Manchester United 1

VILLA:
Sims, Lynn, Aldis, Crowther, Dugdale, Saward, Smith, Sewell, Myerscough, Dixon ©,
McParland (2)

MAN UTD:
Wood, Foulkes, Byrne ©, Colman, Blanchflower, Edwards, Berry, Whelan, **Taylor (1)**, Charlton, Pegg

Matt Busby's hugely talented Manchester United had just won back-to-back league titles. With an average age of under twenty-five, they weren't even at their peak. It seemed inevitable that they would be the first club this century to win the elusive Double. Their FA Cup final opponents Aston Villa had finished mid-table in the league and certainly couldn't boast the gilded roster of internationals that United could muster.

Once again the Cup swung on an injury, this time to a goalkeeper, the most specialist position on the field. United's keeper Roy Wood was flattened by Villa winger Peter McParland inside the first five minutes. Although Wood returned after half an hour, he couldn't go back in goal but hobbled about on the left wing, barely more than a passenger. With Jackie Blanchflower deputising, United kept their discipline and the massively talented Duncan Edwards filled in at centre-half.

It took Villa an hour to beat Blanchflower but when they did so they repeated the dose five minutes later. The scorer on both occasions was the villain of the first half, McParland. United launched everything into attack and when Tommy Taylor gave them a lifeline with a bullet header seven minutes from time, they threw caution to the wind and put Wood back in goal. Villa held on and United's Double dream was over.

Villa had earned the right to a crack at United. A tough draw had seen them play either First or decent Second Division opposition throughout the competition. They had needed replays to see off Luton, Burnley and, in the semi-final, West Brom. Bill Myerscough had scored the only goal in that replay at St Andrews, but it was another double from McParland that earned a 2-2 draw at Molineux.

United, meanwhile, had waltzed through an easy draw. Only Everton in round five had provided a tight contest which was settled by a goal from Duncan Edwards. The next round had brought United up against the season's giant-killers Bournemouth, who were bidding to become the Third Division's third consecutive representatives in the semi-finals.

Warming up with an 8-0 win against Burton Albion, the Cherries had slipped past Swindon and Accrington before coming up against Stan Cullis's Wolves. The mighty fell to the only goal of a physical game. Tottenham were next at Dean Court where Bournemouth had a good home record. An opener from the combative Ollie Norris was soon equalised but Bournemouth continued to be positive and ran out 3-1 winners. Both top flight sides complained of Bournemouth's rough-house style, proving sour grapes are not a post-Millennium invention. A claim by Norris that no one could win at Dean Court proved a red rag to a Mancunian bull as Johnny Berry's double saw off the upstarts.

Other shocks had already livened up the trophy: Newcastle had survived a classic replay with Manchester City, winning 5-4 at Maine Road, only to fall 2-1 in the next round to Third Division Millwall. The Dockers' striker Stan Anslow, a converted full-back, was the hero, scoring both goals.

The previous round saw Rhyl take a rare bow. The club's only ever sally into round four was courtesy of a tremendous 3-1 away win at Notts County. Supported by 1,500 travelling fans including their own band, the Cheshire League side had a day out to remember.

UNFINISHED SYMPHONY

BOLTON WANDERERS:
Hopkinson, Banks, Hartle, Hennin, Higgins, Edwards, Birch, Stevens, **Lofthouse** © **2**, Parry, Holden

MANCHESTER UNITED:
Gregg, Foulkcs ©, Greaves, Goodwin, Cope, Crowther, Dawson, Taylor, Charlton, Viollet, Webster

The 1958 FA Cup became a tale of one team's efforts to wrest some small comfort from a season marred by tragedy. The Munich air crash on 6 February and its aftermath overshadowed the whole football world for the rest of the season.

Leaving Belgrade for home after reaching the semi-finals of the European Cup, the plane carrying the young United team and staff, plus a few journalists, crashed at Munich in atrocious conditions after attempting to take off following a break for refuelling. Geoff Bent, Roger Byrne, Eddie Colman, Mark Jones, David Pegg, Tommy Taylor and Billy Whelan all died in the crash; the great Duncan Edwards never came out of a coma and died soon after. Johnny Berry and Jackie Blanchflower never played again. The heart was ripped out of what might have been the best club side England had ever seen.

Less than two weeks later, United were lining up in a fifth round FA Cup tie against Sheffield Wednesday. Spare a thought for Wednesday, who were on a hiding to nothing, but the whole nation cheered when United pulled off a remarkable 3-0 win. Shay Brennan, a reserve full-back playing on the left wing, scored twice and Alex Dawson, also playing out of position, scored the other. United had quickly brought in one or two experienced pros after the crash and Ernie Taylor, picked up cheap from Blackpool, repaid their faith with a goal in the next round at West Brom. Another one from Dawson earned United a draw and they won the replay with a goal from Welsh international, Colin Webster.

Semi-final opponents Fulham would have enjoyed neutral sympathy in any other year. The Cottagers hadn't faced a top side, beating off teams mostly from their own division. Fulham's trump card was their tricky inside-forward Jimmy Hill, who had scored in every round so far. Hill scored again as the first game at Villa Park was drawn 2-2 with Bobby Charlton, moved now from sideshow to main attraction, scoring both United goals. At Highbury for the replay, United always dominated and Dawson helped himself to hat-trick in a 5-3 win.

Every game brought up a new swell of emotion for the team. Their league form had naturally disintegrated since they hammered Cup final opponents Bolton 7-2 in January. And Bolton were not the opposition of choice. They were a tough, well-drilled side and had the redoubtable Nat Lofthouse at centre-forward.

The old warhorse made an immediate impact, scoring after three minutes. Despite the excellence of young

1957-1958

An intriguing fifth round tie saw the Bristol clubs meet at Ashton Gate. It was their third meeting in the cup and the first time Rovers triumphed, in a 4-3 thriller. Rovers were unable to prevent another Division Two side, Fulham, from reaching the semi-finals.

Ron Cope at the back and occasional surges from Charlton that had the crowd on its feet, Bolton were in control. Their rugged full-backs snuffed out United's young wingers and Dennis Viollet was clearly unfit for such an important game – maybe United should have stuck with Dawson at centre forward. Charlton rattled the timber with one of his trademark thunderbolts but it would have been against the run of play. Much is made of the second goal; Harry Gregg fumbled a cross and as he turned to collect the ball was steamrollered by Lofthouse, man and ball ending up in the back of the net. Today it would have been a red card for Nat and a free-kick for Man U; even in 1958 most observers thought the goal should have been disallowed.

This debate conceals the fact that the better team on the day won. The question of whether the 'Babes' would have won the Double can never be answered. Yes, they were the best team in the country before the disaster but Bolton were not cannon fodder.

This win, their fourth, signalled the start of Wanderers' descent into the wilderness; it would take more than forty years for them to reach a Cup semi-final again.

For United it was just another beginning as Busby, semi-recovered but a spectator only at Wembley, began to rebuild his broken dream.

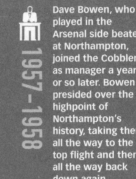

1957-1958

Dave Bowen, who played in the Arsenal side beaten at Northampton, joined the Cobblers as manager a year or so later. Bowen presided over the highpoint of Northampton's history, taking them all the way to the top flight and then all the way back down again.

1957-1958

Bolton full-bank Tommy Banks was the brother of Ralph, who had been unlucky enough to face Stanley Matthews in the 1953 Cup final. One wonders what Stanley would have made of Tommy; to say Banks was from the old-style, uncompromising mould would be an understatement. He won the first of six England caps two weeks after the final.

Scunthorpe, Darlington, Northampton Town. Not exactly games to get the First Division elite quaking in their boots.

Darlington were, frankly, rubbish. Pottering along for a decade in the lower reaches of the Third Division (North), they had only ever twice been beyond the third round. Chelsea had won the league in 1955 and were comfortably mid-table. True, they had no Cup pedigree but a home draw against Darlington looked a formality. Darlington's Ronnie Harbertson had scored in every round and he opened the scoring at Stamford Bridge. The game finished 3-3 and Darlington's chance seemed to have gone. The replay at Feethams was a disaster for the Londoners, Chelsea losing 4-1 with Harbertson again amongst the scorers. A different class of striker, Wolves' Jimmy Murray, scored a hat-trick in the next round as Darlo were routed 6-1.

It was a bad year for the big London sides. Arsenal,

1957-1958

too, fell to lowly opposition, losing 3-1 at Northampton. Reports show a very complacent Arsenal performance against hard-working opponents. All the goals came from set pieces, exploiting a weakness in the air in Arsenal's defence. Like Darlington, Northampton found their next round opponents forewarned and too hot and went down 3-1 to Liverpool at Anfield.

Scunthorpe were better than either Darlington or Northampton; they were runaway leaders of the northern section. Newcastle, by contrast, were no longer a power-house, and their home form was shocking. They had still managed to hammer Plymouth 6-1 in round three and would expect to get past Scunthorpe. The game was nearly called off but volunteers managed to clear the pitch of snow, leaving it a mixture of slush and mud, a perfect leveller. Except the game wasn't evenly balanced. Despite equalising Haigh's opener, Newcastle never got going in the awful conditions and Scunthorpe ran out worthy 3-1 winners. Liverpool again played party-poopers, winning 1-0 at Scunthorpe in round five.

Liverpool themselves would fall victim to the last giant-killing act of the season, when goals from Clayton and Macleod completed a splendid double for Blackburn Rovers, who had knocked out Everton in the fourth round. Not that these were major upsets as Rovers were promoted back to Division One that season.

Whilst the others dropped around them, Bolton chugged on towards their date with unpopularity. Wins over Preston, York – only after the Third Division side forced a replay – and Stoke took them into a sixth round tie with Wolves. With the demise of Busby's team, Wolves were easily the best side in the country. After twice taking the lead, the second time with an artful free-kick from Ray Parry, Bolton had their backs to the wall. They rode their luck. Wolves pounded the woodwork and there were innumerable goalmouth scrambles. With Parry concussed and off the pitch for the last minutes, the Trotters' goal came under siege. Wanderers held on to meet Blackburn in the semi-final.

Blackburn must have thought they had a chance when Nat Lofthouse was declared unfit. His stand-in Ralph Gubbins was a good player but he wasn't one of the all-time greats. When Rovers took the lead, it looked ominous for Bolton but Gubbins stood tall and notched two good goals to take his team to a Wembley final in which he knew he wouldn't play.

FOREST END THE WAIT

NOTTM FOR:
Thomson, Whare, McDonald, Whitefoot, McKinlay, Burkitt ©, **Dwight (1)**, Quigley, **Wilson (1)**, Gray, Imlach

LUTON:
Baynham, McNally, Hawkes, Groves, Owen ©, **Pacey (1)**, Bingham, Brown, Morton, Cummins, Gregory

As the fifties drew to a close, many would later recall the decade as a golden age. Tales of the 'Matthews Final', Newcastle and Milburn, and Lofthouse and Bolton helped shape the pageantry of the FA Cup. This season barely gets a mention due to the presence of two less fashionable teams in the final; hardly fair, as the competition contained romance and excitement like any other.

The first round shocks were traditional ones: Crewe lost and Yeovil won. South Shields provided a miserable afternoon for 'the Alex', dishing out a 5-0 drubbing while Southend became yet another league victim for Yeovil.

The genuine novelties were Tooting & Mitcham United and Worcester City. Both were in virgin territory when they reached the third round with victories over Northampton and Millwall. The Lions proved particularly toothless, going down 5-2 at Worcester. In the third round, both non-leaguers covered themselves in glory against tough opposition. At home to Nottingham Forest, Tooting & Mitcham led 2-0 at half-time through Grainger and Murphy but were pegged back by an own goal and a dodgy penalty. Forest, having had the early scare that many eventual winners endure, made no mistake with a 3-0 victory in the replay.

For Liverpool, there would be no second chance. The Reds may have been enjoying a rare spell in Division Two but a trip to St George's Lane to take on Worcester should have provided easy pickings. The Liverpool side included Ronnie Moran who, as a member of the legendary Anfield boot room, would witness many glory days over the next four decades. This was not one of them. Liverpool crashed out 2-1, the winner arriving via the outstretched leg of defender White, who diverted a cross from Worcester legend Harry Knowles into his own net.

Although Worcester lost 2-0 at home to Sheffield United in the fourth round, the torch was being carried with distinction by Norwich. The Third Division side caused a sensation in round three when, on a snowbound Carrow Road, they despatched Manchester United 3-0. Hero of the hour was two-goal Terry Bly, whose speed and balance on the tricky surface embarrassed many of his supposed betters. This may have been post-Munich Manchester United but they were still good enough to finish runners-up in the league. Bly netted twice again in the fourth round as Cardiff were beaten 3-2, then scored the only goal in a fifth round replay against Spurs.

This was a Tottenham side that was coalescing into the Double winners of two years hence, but this was a poor season for them and they found Norwich more than a handful. The Canaries would have settled the tie at White Hart Lane had Cliff Jones not forced home a last-gasp equaliser.

Norwich travelled to Bramall Lane next, where Second Division Sheffield United looked to have gained the upper-hand early in the second half. The Blades were already one up when Canaries' keeper Ken Nethercott dislocated his shoulder. He continued in great pain and Norwich held firm, grabbing a deserved equaliser through Bobby Brennan. Back at Carrow Road, the Terry Bly show was in full swing. He scored twice and another by Brennan saw Norwich home 3-2 and into their first semi-final.

The last four saw only one team who could boast an FA Cup pedigree. Aston Villa, with a record seven victories, were attempting to reach their second final in three years. Opponents Nottingham Forest had never played at Wembley and were seeking their first final appearance of the century. They achieved it with a single goal from John Quigley. At White Hart Lane, Luton and Norwich couldn't boast a semi-final between them and can-celled each other out with goals from Brown and Brennan. In the replay at St Andrews, Billy Bingham's fifty-sixth minute goal finally won it for Luton. The result was hard on Norwich, who had outplayed Luton for most of the game. Norwich, after becoming the only Third Division side to reach a semi-final replay,

suffered a double disappointment. Their Cup exploits had caused an enormous fixture pile-up which cost them dear. A promising promotion challenge faded and they ended the season in fourth place.

The final, despite the clubs' First Division status, had an unfamiliar ring. Neither side had much league form: Forest's mediocre thirteenth place was four places higher than their opponents. After fifteen minutes, Forest looked to have the match sewn up. They started fluently and had most of the ball. Roy Dwight converted Imlach's cross after ten minutes and Gray's centre was headed home by Tommy Wilson soon after. With just over half an hour played, Luton got a break . . . literally. Dwight was stretchered off with a fractured leg and the Hatters, with a numerical advantage, took the initiative. Just after the hour, Hawkes' pass put through Dave Pacey to halve the deficit but Forest clung on to take their first Cup since 1898.

1959 1959

SAVAGED BY WOLVES

1960 1960

BLACKBURN:
Leyland, Bray, Whelan, Clayton©, Woods,
McGrath, Bimpson, Dobing, Dougan, Douglas,
McLeod

WOLVES:
Finlayson, Showell, Harris, Clamp, Slater ©,
Flowers, **Deeley (2)**, Stobart, Murray,
Broadbent, Horne: **OG McGrath**

Much like the preceding year, 1960 is often overlooked when the FA Cup is discussed. Reminiscences tend to leapfrog from Nat Lofthouse and a post-Munich Manchester United in 1958 to Spurs' Double-winning exploits of 1961. If the neglect of 1959 is rather harsh, to ignore 1960 seems more justified.

The final was one of the most artless and drab ever played. Wolves were a stereotype of their former selves. Stan Cullis's teams had always been hard, with an emphasis on the physical rather than the beautiful game. To give them their due, it was a successful formula that brought them three league titles. But the 1960 team, now shorn of the great Billy Wright, just looked boorish.

The final was effectively settled in the five minutes before half time. Firstly, Rovers centre-half Mick McGrath turned Stobart's cross past his own keeper Harry Leyland. Blackburn were reduced to ten men two minutes later when Dave Whelan broke his leg in a collision with Wolves' Norman Deeley. Although Whelan's misfortune was accidental, Wolves' roughhouse tactics were threatening to kick Rovers out of the game.

Events continued in similar vein after the break. Midway through the half, Deeley converted Horne's cross to banish lingering thoughts of a Rovers revival. Then, two minutes from time, Deeley grabbed his second, reacting first after Stobart's shot had hit the post. Wolves' display had proved so unpalatable that most neutrals jeered them on their lap of honour. The same fans would have been pleased that a more entertaining Burnley had deprived them of the championship on the last Saturday of the league season. The thought of this team becoming the century's first Double winners was not a palatable one.

If most from outside the Black Country were prepared to consign this season to history's footnotes, Millwall must have wished to expunge all record of it. After their humiliation at Worcester the year before, the de-clawed Lions crashed out in the first round again. Their opponents were Bath City, who followed a 3-1 home victory with a 1-0 success at Notts County. The fledgling Fourth Division, in only its second year, was giving a poor account of itself but Bath's next opponents were to prove a step-up in class. Second Division Brighton brought their journey to an end with a 1-0 win.

After Norwich's run to the semis last year, Norfolk provided further romance with the antics of King's Lynn.

The Southern League side put out Aldershot 3-1 but failed a tough assignment at Reading in the second round, losing 4-2. In a good third round, Bradford City's 3-0 defeat of Everton was one of three results that raised more than an eyebrow. Bradford's hero was two-goal Alf Stokes; Stokes scored ten in this season's competition. The other Third Division side to beat top-flight opposition did so in even more emphatic style. Southampton won 5-1 at Manchester City with Derek Reeves scoring four times. City were a struggling side, who only clung on to their First Division status by a single point, but this was still humiliation.

Arsenal were the third round's other victims, losing 2-0 to Second Division Rotherham. The tie went to a third match played at Hillsborough. Millers' hero Keith Kettleborough set them on their way but Rotherham's exit bizarrely came at Highbury. Their fourth round opponents were Brighton, and again the tie needed a second replay. An exhausted Rotherham, having played six Cup matches alone in five weeks, folded 6-0.

Peterborough of the Midland League achieved another in a line of league scalps going way back into the fifties. A ding-dong battle with Ipswich ended 3-2 for the Posh, so named because their 30,000 capacity stadium put many league facilities to shame. Peterborough's reward was election to Division Four at the end of the season replacing Gateshead.

The game that really lingered in the memory came in the fourth round. Crewe Alexandra, whose inglorious Cup history consisted chiefly of providing a league scalp to 'lesser' clubs, had fought valiantly to hold Tottenham 2-2 at Gresty Road. The Fourth Division side scored twice again at White Hart Lane four days later but the positives ended there. Spurs' 13-2 triumph represented a club record victory. For Crewe, the defeat was their worst ever and both records remain to this day. Three players scored hat-tricks; Les Allen (five), Bobby Smith (four) and Cliff Jones (three) presented Spurs with their only headache – the award of the match ball.

From the fifth round on most of the fancied sides slipped away. Spurs were surprisingly beaten 3-1 at home by Blackburn, who then had the satisfaction of defeating local rivals and champions-elect Burnley in the quarter-finals. Rovers again ignored their league form in the semi-finals when they defeated the highly-fancied Sheffield Wednesday. The Owls had won at Old Trafford in the fifth round and put paid to the hopes of city rivals United at Bramall Lane. Young hotshot Derek Dougan

Blackburn's centre forward Derek Dougan requested a transfer on Cup final day. Good move for team morale.

1959-1960

The press dubbed it the 'dustbin final', presumably a reference to the detritus from the stands that was hurled at the Wolves players as they took their lap of honour.

1959-1960

This was it for Wolves and the Old Gold now looks a bit tarnished. Four losing semi-finals are all they have managed since and they have spent almost as long in the second tier of the league as the top one.

1959-1960

scored twice at Maine Road and Blackburn were in the Cup final for the eighth time.

Wolves, too, battled past mostly top flight opposition to meet them. Newcastle gave them a scare but a 4-2 replay win saw them through the third round. Second Division Charlton were narrowly despatched, Luton were thrashed 4-1 and Leicester beaten with a lucky deflection. The 1-0 semi-final win against Villa was almost as soporific as the final, Norman Deeley scoring the crucial goal.

The most lasting postscript concerns the fate of Blackburn's Dave Whelan. He never fully recovered from his Wembley leg fracture and he was entitled to claim an insurance settlement by way of compensation for his enforced retirement. He invested the money shrewdly, buying a market stall which grew into a thriving supermarket business. It made Whelan a millionaire when he sold his stake to the Morrison's supermarket chain. He subsequently diversified into sports retailing which has reaped an even bigger dividend. His company is JJB, a business worth hundreds of millions pounds. Whelan has also purchased stakes in Wigan Warriors rugby league club and Wigan Athletic Football Club. Both play at his JJB stadium, now a Premier League venue since the football team's promotion. All in all it has not turned out to be such an unhappy ending to Dave Whelan's Cup final misfortune.

1960

1961

OLD BILL NICKS THE DOUBLE

1961

1960

THE LAST 16

Newcastle **3** Stoke **1**

Sheffield Utd **2** Blackburn **1**

Birmingham (1) **1** Leicester (1) **2**

Barnsley **1** Luton **0**

Norwich **0** Sunderland **1**

Aston Villa **0** Tottenham **2**

Leyton Orient **0** Sheffield Wed **2**

Burnley **4** Swansea **0**

QUARTER FINALS

Newcastle **1** Sheffield Utd **3**

Leicester (0) **2** Barnsley (0) **1**

Sunderland (1) **0** Tottenham (1) **5**

Sheffield Wed (0) **0** Burnley (0) **2**

SEMI FINALS

Sheffield Utd **0** Leicester **2**

*at St Andrews after 0-0 at Elland Road
and 0-0 at County Ground*

Tottenham **3** Burnley **0**

at Villa Park

FINAL, 6 MAY 1961, WEMBLEY

Tottenham Hotspur **2** Leicester City **0**

TOTTENHAM
Brown, Baker, Henry, Blanchflower ©, Norman, Mackay, Jones, White, **Smith (1)**, Allen, **Dyson (1)**

LEICESTER:
Banks, Chalmers, Norman, McLintock, King, Appleton, Riley, Walsh ©, McIlmoyle, Keyworth, Cheesebrough

When Bill Nicholson died in 2004, there were genuine and heartfelt tributes at White Hart Lane. Tottenham are now regarded as a club starved of success since they have gone without a major trophy since 1991. A similar view prevailed in 1960-1961. A league triumph in 1951 seemed distant; Spurs had become nearly men, adept at reaching semi-finals and, occasionally, the upper reaches of the table, but never bringing home the bacon.

During the 1958-1959 season Bill Nicholson was appointed as manager. A dour, almost curmudgeonly figure, Nicholson was a great talent-spotter and a great nurturer of that talent.

Within three years he had built a formidable side; good enough to end the previous season on a high by beating Wolves in their last league game and denying them the opportunity to win the Double. Spurs themselves had finished a point behind in third place. The captain and fulcrum of the team was Danny Blanchflower. Blanchflower was one of those mysterious players; not apparently blessed with amazing talent, he always seemed to take the right option, never wasting the ball and able to play the game at the pace he wanted. If Blanchflower was the head, the heart was Dave Mackay. The most uncompromising of players, he was a manager's dream; a totally committed player who could put the fear of God into opponents but could play as well. With a powerful centre forward in Bobby Smith and good wingers, Tottenham were a threat to everyone.

By the time the FA Cup started Tottenham were sprinting clear at the top of the league. They had lost only one game (to Sheffield Wednesday) and were scoring for fun.

Division Two Charlton put up a good fight in the third round, only going down by the odd goal in five. Crewe were thumped 5-1 in the next round, carved up by Spurs' five different goal-scorers, but at least the Railwaymen had improved on their 13-2 thrashing of the previous season.

An excellent Tottenham performance at Villa Park saw them outclass their hosts and win 2-0 but a trip to Sunderland proved more demanding. When Spurs went 1-0 up early on, it looked like another routine win but Second Division Sunderland proved tenacious opponents and Spurs made the mistake of relaxing. A deserved equaliser earned Sunderland a replay at White Hart Lane but Tottenham had learnt their lesson. They notched up five again in the replay with four different scorers this time.

1960–1961

The forward line contributed a remarkable ninety-one goals in the league for Tottenham: Bobby Smith (28), Les Allen (23), and double figures for Cliff Jones (15), John White (12) and Terry Dyson (12). Only left-back Ron Henry of the regular outfield players failed to find the goal.

Their semi-final against reigning champions Burnley should have been a classic. The omens, however, were against Spurs as their allotted venue was Villa Park where they had lost three semi-finals since the war. All the pre-match promise of an absorbing encounter was misplaced as the teams scrapped it out in a poor game in tough conditions, which Spurs comfortably won 3-0. After Cliff Jones' opener, Tottenham survived a few squeaky moments as Burnley pressed hard but two second half goals from Bobby Smith put Spurs totally in control.

With six weeks to go to the final, Tottenham concentrated their efforts back on the league where a minor recent wobble had seen their lead cut. A run of three wins put them back on track and the title was eventually clinched with a 2-1 win over Sheffield Wednesday, their nearest rivals.

Their Cup final opponents were Leicester, an honest but unspectacular First Division side. They were well-organised and hard-working with a young Frank McLintock at half-back and a genius, Gordon Banks, in goal. They had needed replays to get through the last three rounds, and only finished off Sheffield United in the third match after two goalless draws. Goals from Jimmy Walsh and Ken Leek settled it. Leek's goals had been instrumental in the Cup run but Leicester would miss him in the final.

Tottenham were a better side than Leicester, and may well have won the final in any circumstances despite the weight of expectation and consequent nerves. Yet again, any judgment on the final must take account of a crucial injury, and, with no substitutes, the handicap that placed on one team. Leicester's right back Len Chalmers was this year's victim; after a collision with Les Allen, Chalmers spent the match a limping passenger on the wing, and left the field for good after seventy minutes. His colleagues defended stoutly but when Bobby Smith gave Spurs the lead, the game was over. Terry Dyson added a second soon after and Tottenham had their Double.

1960–1961

This year saw the inaugural League Cup. The first final, played over two legs, was contested by Aston Villa and Second Division Rotherham. Rotherham had beaten Leicester at Filbert Street en route, but generally had a favourable draw, meeting Third Division Shrewsbury in the semis. Villa squeezed past Burnley but the tie had needed a third match after two draws as no one had dreamed up away goals in 1961.

SPURS KEEP POSSESSION

BURNLEY:
Blacklaw, Angus, Elder, Adamson ©,
Cummings, Miller, Connelly, McIlroy, Pointer,
Robson (1), Harris

TOTTENHAM
Brown, Baker, Henry, Blanchflower © (1p),
Norman, Mackay, Medwin, White, **Smith (1)**,
Greaves (1), Jones

n the first round, the Cup refused to play ball. Only Gateshead, with a 3-2 win at Tranmere, sprang a surprise. The tournament woke up in round two and it was King's Lynn who nudged it into life. The Norfolk non-leaguers had reached the second round for the fourth successive season but a trip to Coventry looked a tough prospect. The Linnets were really on song as goals from Mick Wright and Mick Johnson gave them a famous victory.

For Coventry the defeat proved a blessing in disguise. Manager Billy Frith was immediately shown the door and replaced by Jimmy Hill. The bearded tyro went through Highfield Road like a dose of salts and in less than six years Coventry were a First Division club.

King's Lynn's first-ever third round tie was a lucrative one. Nearly 45,000 turned up at Goodison Park but Everton strolled to a 4-0 win. The other two non-league sides must have looked on in envy. Morecambe had earned their place with a fine victory at Chester, while Weymouth had knocked out Third Division Newport.

In a cruel twist the two were drawn against each other. Despite the record crowd of 9,234 at Christie Park, the expectations of the home fans became a millstone for Morecambe, Weymouth winning the tie with the only goal. A trip to Deepdale proved a more fitting draw, but Weymouth's big day at Preston was snuffed out almost immediately. With the game only fourteen minutes old a blanket of fog enveloped the ground and the referee had little option but to abandon the game. They tried again forty-eight hours later, but a Monday kick-off removed a little gloss from the occasion. Preston won 2-0 and the non-leaguers left disappointed.

Weymouth weren't the only club rueing the fickle nature of football. Newcastle, winners three times in early Fifties, were a club in decline. They had lost their First Division status and were drifting in the Second. The Cup could have provided a welcome diversion and a home draw against Third Division Peterborough appeared a gentle springboard to launch a decent run. They reckoned without goal ace Terry Bly – the man who had spearheaded Norwich's campaign to the semi-finals three seasons earlier. Bly had slammed a record fifty-two goals in the previous season, when the league's 'newbies' had won the Fourth Division at the first time of asking. Geordie gloom deepened when Bly scored the only goal of the game at St James's Park. Sadly for the Posh, they lost 3-1 at Sheffield United in round four.

Liverpool began in fine style with a 4-3 win over

Chelsea at Anfield. In other years, this would have been the tie of the round. In 1962 Liverpool were a Second Division club, albeit one en route to promotion as champions. Chelsea were well on the way to replacing them and finished the season rock bottom of the First Division. Scotland international Ian St John scored twice for Liverpool and a young striker called Roger Hunt was on the mark as well. St John repeated the dose as the Reds won at Oldham in the next round. This led Liverpool to a three-game marathon against Preston, where they were undone by a single goal from a promising winger called Peter Thompson. Bill Shankly was sufficiently impressed to sign Thompson for the start of the following season. He quickly developed into one of Liverpool's most reliable players, winning two league titles during his Anfield career.

Stealing up on the blind side were Fulham. The Cottagers were no great shakes in the league, indeed only the weakness of Cardiff and Chelsea helped them to maintain their First Division status. The luck of the draw had seen them past Hartlepools, Walsall and Port Vale before they finally met First Division opposition in the quarter-finals. Cook won them the tie with the only goal at Ewood Park and Fulham had reached their fourth semi-final. Their three previous ties had ended in defeat and the opposition at Villa Park could hardly be tougher.

Burnley were one of the most technically astute teams in the country and were to finish the league season as runners-up. When Graham Leggatt put Fulham in front it looked as though they might have cracked their semi-final jinx, but John Connelly levelled for the Clarets. Two goals from Jimmy Robson sank Fulham in the replay, leaving them with the record that no club wants. Fulham's fourth semi-final failure was the most by any team that had yet to reach a final.

Tottenham were aided in the defence of their trophy by the arrival of Jimmy Greaves. The former Chelsea prodigy had failed to settle in Milan and returned to London for a record fee of £99,999. The curious price-tag had been imposed by Spurs' boss Bill Nicholson since he wanted to avoid what would have been the first British six-figure fee from weighing on Greaves' shoulders. Whatever the price, it made no difference to the laconic striker. His seven Cup goals were instrumental in Tottenham's return to Wembley.

Spurs' route to the final had been a stylish one. Only Plymouth, their fourth round opponents, played outside the First Division. Spurs had mown through the second city and its neighbours, beating Birmingham, West Brom and Villa before meeting Manchester United in a semi-final at Hillsborough.

United had made impressive progress; victories against Bolton, Arsenal, Sheffield Wednesday (after a replay) and Preston (after a replay) came with only two goals conceded. United weren't ready; Matt Busby was still building his third great team, and they were outclassed by Tottenham's sweet football, losing 3-1.

With two fine ball-playing teams at Wembley, the final was as accomplished as the previous year's had been artless. So interesting was the tactical battle that the match was dubbed 'the chessboard final.' Spurs' first move after three minutes was a deadly one. Bobby Smith's header sent Greaves on a run and he demonstrated his class by stopping, checking back and outsmarting a ring of defenders. His turn and shot outfoxed Blacklaw in the Burnley goal to put Spurs one up.

Burnley refused to panic and continued to play patient, cultured football. They gained a deserved reward five minutes after half-time. Gordon Harris's cross was met by Jimmy Robson, who beat Bill Brown at the near post. But after doggedly sticking to their task, Burnley suddenly switched off. It cost them dear and within a minute they were chasing the game again. John White's cross found Bobby Smith, who turned and fired home.

The goal knocked the stuffing out of Burnley and the Lancastrians finally surrendered ten minutes from time. Terry Medwin's goal-bound shot was handled on the line by Tommy Cummings. The punishment on this occasion fitted the crime. Danny Blanchflower's penalty sent Blacklaw the wrong way, and Spurs had retained the Cup.

1962

DIG THE NEW BREED

1963

MAN UTD:
Gaskell, Dunne, Cantwell ©, Crerand, Foulkes, Setters, Giles, Quixall, **Herd (2)**, **Law (1)**, Charlton

LEICESTER:
Banks, Sjoberg, Norman, McLintock, King, Appleton ©, Riley, Cross, **Keyworth (1)**, Gibson, Stringfellow

F or the second successive season, the Cup came in like a lamb. In the first two rounds only one non-league club upset opposition from Divisions Three and Four. Gravesend and Northfleet put themselves on the map with a 3-2 win against Exeter.

Mansfield Town livened up an ordinary start, but despite scoring twenty-three goals, they won only two games. Roy Chapman and Ivan Hollett both grabbed hat-tricks in a 9-2 defeat of Hounslow after the first game had finished 3-3. Crystal Palace, after holding their own in a 2-2 draw, were put to the sword 7-2 in the second round. The goal-fest continued in round three but Mansfield succumbed by the odd goal in five to Ipswich.

By the third round, the Cup and the country had been plunged into chaos. One of the coldest winters on record reduced the sporting calendar to a monotonous list of postponements. Only three of the thirty-two ties kicked off as scheduled on 5 January. Sixty-six days later, Middlesbrough beat Blackburn 3-1 to complete the round. The match took place on 11 March, two days after the original date for the quarter-finals.

Lincoln City's tie with Coventry suffered seventeen postponements, while Birmingham's match with Bury was cancelled fourteen times, abandoned once and finally took place on 5 March. After a delay of exactly two months, the match predictably finished as a draw.

The freakish weather threw up some strange results. Spurs, after nearly three years without a Cup defeat, crashed 3-0 to Burnley on a frozen pitch at White Hart Lane. The Clarets gained revenge for their Wembley defeat the previous May in a game which meant that the two sides had met each other in successive ties.

Gravesend and Northfleet, in the third round for the first time thanks to beating Wycombe, took advantage of the levelling conditions with a 1-0 win at Carlisle. Tony Sitford, who later managed the club, scored the only goal with a thirty-yard thunderbolt to take the Kent non-leaguers into the fourth round for the first time. A record 12,000 crowd packed Stonebridge Park to see Gravesend take on Sunderland, and they proved equal to the task, emerging with a 1-1 draw. Their campaign ended with a 5-2 defeat in the replay but they had the satisfaction of creating a new record. Having embarked on their Cup trail on 8 September, Gravesend bowed out at Roker Park on 18 February, five months and ten days later. This remains the longest single run in the competition's history.

Another remarkable but unenviable record fell in

the third round. By beating Stoke City 3-1, Leeds registered their first FA Cup victory in eleven years. Their previous victory had been in February 1952, which heralded the Cup's longest-ever losing streak. Flushed with success, Leeds won 2-0 at Middlesbrough in round four, then resumed normal service with a 3-0 defeat at Nottingham Forest.

Manchester United finally got to start their third round tie with Huddersfield on 4 March. They made up for lost time by reaching Wembley just fifty-four days later, the quickest-ever run on record. Huddersfield were swept aside 5-0 with Denis Law scoring a hat-trick. A week later, Albert Quixall's goal was enough to beat Aston Villa. Five days on and United were in the quarter-finals after Quixall and Law had ensured a 2-1 win over Chelsea. Before the month was out Coventry had been seen off 3-1 with a brace from Bobby Charlton. Having wiped off the backlog, United waited the regulation four weeks before meeting this season's surprise package at Villa Park in the semi-final.

Southampton have often reserved their finest Cup moments when playing outside the top division. This year was no exception, as they made the semi-finals for the first time since 1927. Pick of their ties was a sixth round clash with First Division Nottingham Forest. After Terry Paine had earned them a 1-1 draw at the City Ground, the two teams battled out a 3-3 thriller at the Dell. The second replay at White Hart Lane was much anticipated, but even the most die-hard Saint could hardly have dared to predict the outcome. Southampton romped home 5-0, with two each for Burnside and O'Brien. At Villa Park they stuck gamely to the task, but a single goal from Denis Law saw United to Wembley.

In the final, United would meet Leicester, who were hoping for third time lucky after Wembley defeats in

1949 and 1961. They had an easier route; their only top flight opposition in the earlier rounds were Leyton Orient and Ipswich, both struggling near the foot of the table. A semi-final against Liverpool was a tougher proposition, but Gordon Banks was a formidable barrier and another clean sheet saw Leicester go through with a goal from left-winger Mike Stringfellow. The Foxes

1962-1963

finished fourth in the league, their highest position since 1929, and they started as favourites against a United side who finished only three points above relegated neighbours City.

It was United who drew first blood. Just before the half-hour Crerand found Law, who swivelled and shot past Gordon Banks. United doubled their lead twelve minutes into the second-half, when David Herd fastened on to a rebound once Charlton's shot had been parried by Banks. Leicester were experiencing that sinking Wembley feeling once again, but gave themselves hope with ten minutes left after Ken Keyworth had flung himself at a McLintock cross. It was a flicker that was snuffed out five minutes later after a rare error from Gordon Banks. The Leicester keeper, who was to achieve immortality at the same ground three years later as part of England's World Cup-winning side, dropped a cross from Johnny Giles, and Herd grabbed his second. The team dubbed a 'ragged rabble' in the press had won United their first trophy since Munich. For Bill Foulkes and Bobby Charlton, who had played in the Busby Babes' last final in 1957 and the emotional post-Munich encounter with Bolton a year later, this was a poignant occasion. For Matt Busby, five years of patient rebuilding was bearing fruit. A second golden age at Old Trafford was about to unfold.

1963

PRESTON PROUD TO BE HAMMERED

1964

WEST HAM
Standen, Bond, Burkett, Bovington, Brown, Moore ©, Brabrook, **Boyce (1)**, Byrne, **Hurst (1)**, **Sissons (1)**

PRESTON NORTH END
Kelly, Ross, Lawton ©, Smith, Singleton, Kendall, Wilson, Ashworth, **Dawson (1)**, Spavin, **Holden (1)**

After sleeping peacefully for the last couple of seasons, the first round burst into life with a netful of goals. Crystal Palace hit eight against Harwich, whilst Netherfield, Torquay and Coventry all managed six. For those in search of embarrassment for the league sides, Yeovil was usually the first port of call. The Somerset team obliged again when Southend lost at Huish for the second time in five years.

Millwall were another red-faced league club. The Lions had already endured defeat by Worcester and Bath in recent seasons. Kettering provided this year's embarrassment, winning 3-2 at the Den in a first round replay. Two-goal George Armour was the Poppies' hero, but Kettering were denied a shot at the third round by Oxford, who beat them 2-1 at the Manor Ground.

Yeovil stormed to the Third Round for the seventh time with a fine 3-1 win over free-scoring Crystal Palace. Dave Taylor with two and Ken Pound did the damage but Second Division Bury negotiated the Huish slope to win 2-0. Another Somerset team had made the third round, as Bath City saw off Maidenhead and Wimbledon (still a Southern League side) to take their place alongside the big boys. Bolton weren't the most glamorous side around, but they were still in the First Division (but only just, they were relegated). Bath emerged with honour, forcing a replay before going down 3-0.

Pride of the part-timers was Bedford Town, who reached the fourth round for the first and only time in their history. Newcastle, still struggling unsuccessfully to get out of Division Two, were the obliging patsies. Bedford took a 2-0 lead through Jack Fahy and a sloppy deflection off Newcastle's Bill McKinney. With the game held up by over-excitable fans throwing straw on the pitch, there was enough injury time for Newcastle to pull one back and give Bedford a jittery few moments. The Southern League team held on; Newcastle's worst cup moment was still to come, but this was a shocking performance. For Bedford, hopes soared when the fourth round draw gave them a home tie with Fourth Division Carlisle, but the lure of the last sixteen proved too great a distraction. The Cumbrian side ran out easy victors, winning 3-0.

The third round provided joy for some lower league teams too. Fourth Division Aldershot's 2-1 victory in a replay against top flight Aston Villa was a result of two goalkeeping errors. In the previous five seasons Villa's conquerors had won the Cup. Aldershot, somewhat predictably, ended that sequence when they lost to Swindon in the next round.

Bedford Town keeper Jock Wallace featured In an even more remarkable cup upset three years later. He was in goal when Berwick Rangers put out their Glasgow namesakes 1-0

1963-1964

Sheffield Wednesday were a pretty potent side in the sixties, so a trip over the Welsh border to Newport shouldn't have proved too much of an obstacle. Twice Wednesday took the lead and looked to have the game under control, but twice Newport skipper Joe Bonsor brought his side level. Ralph Hunt got Newport's third with twenty minutes to go and a superb save from Len Weare saw them home. Another great draw saw Newport travel to Burnley in the next round; a brave fight saw them eventually fall 2-1 to a John Connelly winner.

Less earth-shattering was Second Division Preston's victory over Nottingham Forest. Seventeen-year-old Howard Kendall scored an extra-time winner at Deepdale. Preston put out another First Division side in the fourth round when Bolton fell 3-2 in a replay. After a stiff examination Preston found that the questions got progressively easier. The draw opened up with two matches against Fourth Division opponents. Carlisle and Oxford were despatched with caution rather than style, but Preston were in the last four all the same.

Doug Holden, scorer of Preston's opening goal, had received his first loser's medal eleven years before, playing for Bolton against Blackpool. Happily, he was also in the Wanderers side which won in 1958.

1963-1964

Oxford had done particularly well to win through to the sixth round. They had joined the Football League after Accrington Stanley's financial melt-down, and were only in their second season. They avoided top notch opposition until round five, when they faced Blackburn at the Manor Ground. The former Headington United gave a splendid account of themselves, winning 3-1 without a trace of luck. Two goals from Tony Jones swung the day; United's inspiration was a sturdy, destructive half-back called Ron Atkinson, affectionately known as 'the Tank'.

Preston's other scorer, Alex Dawson, also played in the 1958 final, but for Bolton's opponents, Manchester United. Dawson was one of many reserves drafted into the first team after the Munich air-crash, and his hat-trick had won the semi-final for United. His experience was key to Preston's appearance in the final; his goal at Wembley was his sixth.

1963-1964

Preston were appearing in the semi-finals for the first time in a decade. They were joined there by another Second Division side – Swansea, who had knocked out three top flight clubs en route to their first appearance in the last four since 1926. The Swans finished the season in a relegation battle, ending in nineteenth place, which made their performance all the more remarkable. Swansea had already seen off Sheffield United and Stoke the hard way, earning draws away from home and winning the replays. United were thrashed 4-0 at the Vetch, Stoke 2-0. The sixth round draw made them travel to Anfield, where champions-elect Liverpool entertained hopes of the Double. Amazingly, Swansea won 2-1, goals from McLaughlin and Thomas securing the most famous

Cup victory in the Welsh club's history. The semi-final draw guaranteed that a Second Division club would again reach Wembley and it was Preston who edged home. Although McLaughlin scored for Swansea, goals from Alex Dawson and centre-half Tony Singleton saw North End through.

Joining them in the final were West Ham, whose wait had been even longer. Forty-one years had passed since they went down to Bolton, but Ron Greenwood was fashioning a side that would open a new chapter at Upton Park. Marshalled by Bobby Moore and spearheaded by Geoff Hurst, the Hammers began their journey by settling local difficulties against Charlton and Leyton Orient. Hurst scored twice against the Os, and then hit two more as Swindon were beaten at the County Ground. The quarter-finals pitted West Ham against top division opponents for the first time. Burnley's star was waning from their title-winning season four years earlier but they remained a top-half side. Two goals from Johnny Byrne helped the Hammers home 3-2.

In the semi-final at Hillsborough, West Ham took on favourites and holders Manchester United. United had scored twenty-one goals in their six matches, nine of them from Denis Law. The Lawman had finished off Sunderland with a top class hat-trick in the second replay of a classic tie. The Hammers were granted a much-needed leveller when torrential rain fell in the hours before the match, reducing the pitch to an ankle-deep mud pudding.

United dominated possession and pressed consistently, but the game was scoreless until the fifty-sixth minute. Ronnie Boyce conjured a goal out of nothing against the run of play, crashing a shot into the top corner from twenty-five yards. Seven minutes later, the Hammers' fans' thoughts turned to Wembley when Boyce headed home Jackie Burkett's cross. But back came United, who finally broke through after seventy-eight minutes when Denis Law converted a pass from George Best. As West Ham braced themselves for a nerve-wracking onslaught, Bobby Moore demonstrated his calmness under fire by bringing the ball coolly out of defence. Geoff Hurst completed the move, firing home past Dave Gaskell. West Ham had appeared in Wembley's first final, and they were finally back.

The Hammers may have started as favourites, but their Second Division opponents started more purposefully. West Ham's nerves were confirmed in the ninth minute when goalkeeper Jim Standen fumbled a shot from Alex Dawson. Doug Holden was on hand to poke in the rebound. The goal stirred West Ham into action and they levelled four minutes later when John Sissons carried the ball deep into the Preston half. The eighteen-year-old winger cut inside before hitting a low shot across Alan Kelly into the far corner.

West Ham, as the First Division side, may have expected to take charge from them on, but Preston were having none of it. They controlled possession for the rest of the half and deservedly regained the lead five minutes before the break through Alex Dawson.

The Hammers started the second half on the front foot, and their greater fluency paid dividends after fifty-two minutes. Kelly kept out Brown's header but Geoff Hurst headed the rebound towards goal. Again Kelly parried but could only divert the ball on to the bar. It bounced down on to the prostrate keeper before trickling agonisingly over the line. It may have been scrappy, but it threw West Ham the lifeline they needed.

With nothing to choose between the sides, the game looked destined for extra-time. In the ninetieth minute, however, Peter Brabrook received the ball near the touchline. With his socks around his ankles, the West Ham winger looked barely able to put one foot in front of the other, but he summoned enough energy to clip over one final cross. Arriving to meet it was Ronnie Boyce, whose tireless running had earned him the nickname 'Ticker'. He picked the perfect moment to demonstrate his fitness, heading across Alan Kelly into the far corner. Preston were left cursing their luck having been the better side for long periods. West Ham, after sixty-six years of trying, had won the Cup.

LIVERPOOL BREAK THEIR DUCK

LIVERPOOL:
Lawrence, Lawler, Byrne, Strong, Yeats ©,
Stevenson, Callaghan, **Hunt (1)**, **St John (1)**,
Smith, Thompson

LEEDS UNITED:
Sprake, Reaney, Bell, **Bremner (1)**, Charlton,
Hunter, Giles, Storrie, Peacock, Collins ©,
Johanneson

L iverpool v Leeds has a solid ring to it. That they met at Wembley in 1965 suggests the continuation of a long and illustrious Cup tradition. In fact both clubs were attempting to win the trophy for the first time and Leeds, flexing newly-honed muscles under the stewardship of Don Revie, were appearing in their first final.

This season's competition took several rounds to warm up. Crook and Scarborough beat league opposition in Carlisle and Bradford, but the highlight of the first two rounds was the north London derby between Enfield and Barnet. After a 4-4 cliffhanger, Barnet's 3-0 victory at Underhill was emphatic. Theirs was the only non-league presence in round three, and a 3-2 home defeat by Preston curtailed further progress. In a muted third round, Torquay nearly pulled off what would have been the day's only surprise. At Plainmoor they trailed Spurs 3-1 at half-time, but two second-half goals from Robin Stubbs completed his hat-trick and earned the Gulls an unlikely replay. They fell away 5-1 at White Hart Lane but a 55,000 crowd guaranteed the Fourth Division side a handsome pay day.

The Cup finally found its form in the fourth round. Third Division Peterborough attracted a record 30,056 to London Road for the visit of Arsenal. The sixties was a lean decade for the Gunners. While silky Spurs tasted Double and European glory, Arsenal made do and mended in mid-table. Their prospects looked bright when John Radford gave them an early lead but goals from Derek Dougan and Peter McNamee made this a famous day for 'the Posh'. Peterborough fancied their chances in the Fifth Round after the draw matched them with Second Division Swansea. The ground record at London Road was broken for the second time in three weeks as forty more squeezed on to the terraces. After forcing a goalless draw, the Swans looked to have wrested the advantage, but two goals from Peter Deakin ensured Peterborough took their place in the quarter-finals. A plum draw at Chelsea promised to swell the coffers and over 63,000 packed Stamford Bridge. It was the only bright spot for 'the Posh', who were reduced to ten men early on after Crowe was stretchered off. He eventually returned to cut a reduced, hobbling figure on the left wing but by then Peterborough were 4-0 down, and eventually lost 5-1.

Another team to hit a hurdle in round four were Liverpool. Unlike Arsenal, they stumbled but regained their balance. A draw at home to Fourth Division

Stockport appeared so comfortable that Bill Shankly preferred a spying mission on European Cup opponents Cologne rather than witness what would surely be a routine victory. At half-time, the Reds trailed 1-0 and headline writers were sharpening their pencils. It took a fifty-first minute equaliser from Gordon Milne to spare Liverpool, who were in no mood for such complacency in the replay. Two goals from Roger Hunt saw them through. They remained in Lancashire for the fifth round, travelling to Bolton. Nearly 60,000 jammed Burnden Park but home fans were disappointed by Ian Callaghan's late strike.

Liverpool's quarter-final tie at Leicester looked a tricky one. The Foxes had been their bogey side in recent seasons, but a solid performance from the Reds earned them a second bite after a 0-0 draw. As a tight replay at Anfield unfolded, it seemed ever more likely to be settled by a single moment of brilliance. So it proved, as Roger Hunt's spectacular volley flew past Gordon Banks for the only goal of the game.

By the semi-final, Liverpool, as with any team still competing in three trophies, were suffering a fixture pile-up. Their clash with Chelsea at Villa Park arrived three days after they had returned from a European Cup quarter-final against Cologne. The Blues looked to have grabbed the lead when centre-half John Mortimore headed home, but the referee decided that goalkeeper Tommy Lawrence had been impeded. It was the break Liverpool needed. Just after the hour Peter Thompson cut inside to lash the ball home and Willie Stephenson's penalty secured the win eleven minutes from time. The Reds were back at Wembley for the first time in fifteen years, but the team barring their way to a first FA Cup were formidable.

Three seasons earlier, Leeds had finished nineteenth in Division Two and only a late-season rally had saved them from the drop. Their change in fortune was due entirely to their new manager, Don Revie, who had transformed the team, bringing in top players like Bobby Collins and Johnny Giles. After running away with the Second Division, they took the top division by storm, failing only on goal average to pip Manchester United for the championship. The two had clashed in a tetchy semi-final at Hillsborough, which finished in scoreless stalemate. Four days later at the City Ground, a single goal from Bremner was enough to put Leeds through.

At Wembley, Leeds's reputation for professionalism bordering on the cynical looked well-founded. After ten minutes, captain Bobby Collins, a man whom football cards would euphemistically describe as 'tough-tackling', dropped his shoulder into Gerry Byrne's collar-bone. The resulting fracture left the full-back's arm dangling uselessly, but he continued, seemingly impervious to the pain. The remaining eighty minutes passed in similarly bruising fashion, but nothing could divide the teams. Three minutes into extra-time, Byrne looked to have gained his revenge. Overlapping down the left, he crossed for Roger Hunt to stoop and head home. In such a tight game it seemed certain that a single goal would settle it, so it was a surprise when Leeds replied eight minutes later. By now they were effectively down to ten men, with Jim Storrie a limping passenger on the wing. Jack Charlton had been thrown forward as an extra attacker, and it was his knock-down that fell for Bremner to volley past Lawrence in the Liverpool goal.

After 111 minutes, and with a first Wembley draw beckoning, Callaghan's cross eluded Sprake, and Ian St John dived to head into an empty net. If Liverpool prided themselves on superior fitness one doubts that it had ever been put to such effective use. The FA Cup was theirs at last.

1965

T(W)O ABSENT FRIENDS

1966

N on-leaguers started far more brightly than in recent years. Flying the flag were Bath City, 2-0 victors over Newport County, South Shields, who put out York 3-1, and pride of place went to Bedford Town, who reached the fourth round for the second time in three seasons. They announced their intentions with a 2-1 win at Third Division Exeter, then put out Brighton 2-1 in a second round replay. The Seagulls had been lulled into a false sense of security after thrashing Wisbech Town 10-1 in the first round.

The third round draw found the FA Cup in unromantic mood. Five non-league clubs had made it into the hat, but four got a rough deal, with Bedford Town and Hereford getting the shortest straws, at least financially. The two were drawn together, with Bedford taking the spoils 2-1. Folkestone went out with a whimper, 5-1 at home to Crewe, and there was a similar sense of anticlimax at Home Park, where Plymouth spanked Corby Town 6-0. Corby would have to live with the fond memories of an excellent away win at Luton in a second round replay.

The only non-league side without a grievance were Altrincham, whose reward for a fine 3-1 win at Rochdale was a trip to Molineux. Wolves had grown mouldy since the fifties and had lost their First Division status a year earlier. They were still too strong for Altrincham, running out convincing 5-0 winners.

Bedford at last gained their just desserts, drawing Everton at home in the fourth round. Two goals from Derek Temple and one from Fred Pickering gave Everton a comfortable afternoon, but the Southern League side had put the town on the map once again.

Holders Liverpool failed in their first defence of the trophy. Their home game against Chelsea looked the tie of the third round, and a high-quality encounter duly ensued. Roger Hunt was again on target, but goals from Bobby Tambling and Peter Osgood sent the Blues into round four. Having beaten the holders Chelsea next put out last season's beaten finalists. This was the first of three epic ties in five seasons involving Chelsea and Leeds, which started an enmity that lasts until this day. After Tambling put the Blues in front after only eight minutes, there followed a home rearguard that lasted for the rest of the game. Leeds threw everything at the home defence, but the team with a reputation for a soft underbelly held firm.

If Chelsea proved surprisingly steady, Manchester United were rocking. After winning convincingly at

Derby in the third round, Law and Best scoring twice in a 5-2 romp, they hosted Third Division Rotherham. The Yorkshiremen departed Old Trafford with a creditable 0-0 draw and a guarantee of a packed Millmoor for the replay. Once again, the combined talents of Best, Law and Charlton could find no way through, and it took an extra-time goal from John Connelly to settle the tie.

United hit their stride in the fifth round, winning 4-2 in another minor classic at Wolves with a brace from Denis Law. Chelsea, after two high-quality victories, found it was their turn to struggle. They made heavy weather of beating Shrewsbury at Stamford Bridge, two from Barry Bridges and a winner from George Graham seeing them home 3-2. In the quarter-finals, they looked to have the softest task after being drawn at home to Third Division Hull, but the Tigers were no pushover. Hull were leading their division and had already gained confidence from a 2-0 win over Nottingham Forest in the fourth round where Terry Heath had scored both goals. Hull showed their pedigree again at Stamford Bridge, holding their hosts to a 2-2 draw, courtesy of two goals from Ken Wagstaff, but Tambling was again Chelsea's saviour at Boothferry Park. The striker, who remains the Blues' record scorer, notched another two, and a third from George Graham earned a 3-1 win.

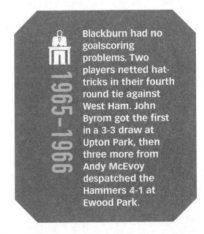

The sixth round saw the re-emergence into the limelight of two clubs whose previous Cup glories were a fading memory. Everton had been league champions three seasons earlier but their last Wembley appearance had been back in 1933, when Dixie Dean and company had earned them victory over Manchester City. These two were to meet this season at Goodison Park. Everton had started this season's Cup campaign in fine style, winning their first three ties 3-0. City were far less convincing, requiring replays to see off Blackpool and Leicester. The form guide gave little indication of the stalemate to follow, as they slogged out two matches and 210 minutes without a single goal. In the second replay at Molineux, Fred Pickering finally found a way through for Everton before Derek Temple's second bolted on victory.

In the semi-final at Burnden Park, their opponents were attempting to banish the bitter memories of last season. Manchester United had been put out in last four by the narrowest of margins, losing to Leeds in a replay. Lightning struck twice, Colin Harvey's goal being good enough to win the day.

1965-1966

Chelsea had finally emerged as a force in the game and had a League title to their name from 1955. But it was 1915 since they last appeared in a final. A two-leg win over Leicester in the previous season's League Cup was scant compensation.

The other club in the 'sleeping giant' category were Sheffield Wednesday. The Owls, like Everton, had not visited Wembley since the war and had been sustained for three decades by their thrilling 1935 victory over West Brom. Wembley apart, Hillsborough is arguably the most famous FA Cup venue, but in 1966 it didn't stage a single tie. Wednesday's far-flung route saw them visit Reading, Newcastle, Huddersfield and Blackburn, emerging victorious each time. Johnny Fantham, David Ford and Jim McCalliog provided the goals, but they lined up at Villa Park as underdogs in their semi-final against Chelsea. Tommy Docherty's side were keen to avenge their defeat at the same stage a year earlier but failed to cope with a heavy pitch. Graham Pugh and Jim McCalliog saw Wednesday home and Chelsea left Villa Park with that sinking semi-final feeling again.

Wednesday fans still wake up sweating over this final, and it all started so promisingly for them. After only four minutes, David Ford's cross was met by Jim McCalliog, whose shot was deflected by Ray Wilson past Gordon West. It was the first FA Cup goal that Everton had conceded this season, and it appeared to upset their disciplined game plan. They laboured for the rest of the half, but could make little headway.

Everton's Ray Wilson tasted even greater Wembley glory just two months later. He played as England's left-back in the World Cup final defeat of West Germany.

1965-1966

Everton's game looked well and truly up after fifty-seven minutes. Although Gordon West parried John Fantham's shot, David Ford turned from provider to goalscorer as he tapped home the rebound.

Many Everton fans were now looking accusingly at the bench. Manager Harry Catterick had sprung a major, and unpopular, surprise by dropping centre-forward Fred Pickering, a fan's favourite, and replacing him with the young and largely untried Mike Trebilcock. The young striker had been signed over the New Year from Plymouth but had made only seven league appearances. His status as a fringe player seemed unarguable when his details weren't even included in the match programme, but with Everton staring down both barrels, he responded in the best possible fashion.

Wednesday's Jim McCalliog was to return to Wembley in triumph a year later. He scored Scotland's winner in a memorable 3-2 triumph, as the auld enemy inflicted England's first defeat since their World Cup victory.

1965-1966

If Wednesday had held Everton for another ten minutes, the Cup would surely have been theirs. Having gained a two-goal lead they just needed to keep their shape and discipline. Within two minutes, though, Everton had scored, and the tide of the match had turned.

Wednesday's England international keeper Ron Springett looked to have kept Everton at bay as he blocked Derek Temple's header. The ball fell to Trebilcock, who drove home. Suddenly, Wednesday were a bag of nerves. Everton poured forward and five minutes later they were level. Alex Scott's free-kick was met by a feeble defensive header from centre-half Sam Ellis. Trebilcock was on hand to lash in his second.

Everything was now running Everton's way. With ten minutes left, they won the Cup with a goal out of nothing. A hopeful punt out of defence should have been meat and drink for Owls' centre-half Gerry Young, but he inexplicably took his eye off the ball at the crucial moment. It squirmed under his foot and Derek Temple hared after it from the centre circle. Springett's charge from his line was as panic-stricken as Temple's finish was unruffled. The ball nestled in the net and Wednesday's heartbreak was complete. The Cup stayed on Merseyside.

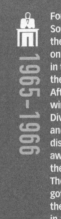

CAPITAL, SIR, CAPITAL!

CHELSEA:
Bonetti, Allan Harris, McCreadie, Hollins, Hinton, Ron Harris ©, Cooke, Baldwin, Hateley, **Tambling (1)**, Boyle, *sub: Kirkup*

TOTTENHAM:
Jennings, Kinnear, Knowles, Mullery, England, Mackay ©, **Robertson (1)**, Greaves, Gilzean, Venables, **Saul (1)** *sub: Jones*

London's FA Cup successes had been few and far between. Although the capital had staged the lion's share of finals, few of its teams had lined up at Kennington Oval, Crystal Palace, Stamford Bridge, Wembley or elsewhere. In 1967 the city finally provided both finalists for the first time.

Spurs were given a vigorous workout early on by Millwall. Emerging battered but still intact from the Den with a 0-0 draw, a goal from Alan Gilzean nudged Tottenham into round four. The Scottish forward was on target again against Portsmouth, scoring twice in a 3-1 win. The other Spurs goal came from Jimmy Greaves, who netted both against Bristol City in the fifth round. Tottenham's Cup run was at full tilt.

Chelsea were bidding to reach their third consecutive semi-final. They started well, negotiating a tricky tie at Huddersfield 2-1 with goals from Peter Houseman and Bobby Tambling. Tambling was on target again with the only goal at Brighton, and then scored for the third tie running as Sheffield United were beaten 2-0 at Stamford Bridge. In the sixth round, Chelsea had the chance for revenge. Sheffield Wednesday had surprisingly denied the Blues a Wembley appearance with victory in the previous season's semi-final, but Tommy Baldwin halted their progress with the only goal.

Chelsea must have approached Villa Park with some trepidation. Firstly, the opposition was Don Revie's Leeds. More importantly, this was the venue of both their semi-final defeats in 1965 and 1966, but this season they possessed a striker for whom the ground was a second home. In the close season, Tony Hateley had become the Blues' first six-figure signing, having arrived from Aston Villa. Back on his home turf, the striker (father of future England forward Mark) headed Charlie Cooke's centre past Sprake to put Chelsea one-up. With a minute left and the Blues hanging on by their fingertips, Leeds won a free-kick on the edge of the Chelsea area. Giles tapped it short to Lorimer, who thundered the ball past Bonetti. London hearts sank, as the Villa Park jinx appeared to have struck again, but Chelsea were reprieved by fussy officialdom. Referee Ken Burns ruled that the free-kick had been taken before he was ready. The goal was disallowed and Chelsea were through to their first major Wembley final.

Spurs route to the final was less fraught. After holding Arsenal's conquerors Birmingham to a goalless draw at St. Andrews, they overwhelmed them at White Hart

Rogers was on target again in the next round, as Swindon saw off Bury, and it took three attempts for Nottingham Forest to shake them off in the fifth round.

1966-1967

Lane. Jimmy Greaves and Terry Venables scored twice apiece in a 6-0 rout. At Hillsborough they faced Nottingham Forest, who had knocked out holders Everton in a 3-2 thriller at the City Ground, all the goals coming in the last half-hour. Their young striker Ian Storey-Moore had caught the eye with a hat-trick, but Spurs' know-how kept him in check at Hillsborough. Goals from Greaves and Frank Saul put them through to a third final in seven years, Terry Hennessey's effort proving mere consolation for Forest.

The two finalists appeared evenly matched. Chelsea had finished sixth in the league, one place ahead of their opponents, but Spurs had Wembley experience on their side. The final was only Chelsea's second; the first in 1915 was a distant memory. In Jimmy Greaves and Terry Venables, Tottenham had two ex-Chelsea players in their camp. The precocious Venables had fallen out with Chelsea boss Tommy Docherty, but this match proved sweet revenge.

Tottenham's continental tactics slowed the game and their possession starved Chelsea's ball-players, Cooke and Baldwin, of the opportunity to mount attacks. With half-time approaching, Alan Mullery's shot span off Ron Harris into the path of Jimmy Robertson, who shot Spurs ahead. The winger turned provider midway through the second half, his pass finding Frank Saul whose quick turn and shot outfoxed Bonetti.

With Swindon's exit, the romance was over for the year; seven First Division sides plus Birmingham made up the last eight.

1966-1967

The game was effectively over, although Chelsea kept interest going to the final whistle with Tambling's consolation four minutes from time. The narrow scoreline flattered the Blues, who had been beaten by technically superior and more experienced opponents. Tottenham and Wembley were now inextricably linked. This was their third win under the twin towers, and their fourth Cup maintained a 100% record in finals.

Once again the non-league stars were Bedford Town. The Southern League side reached round three for the third time in four seasons, and would have remained in splendid isolation but for the efforts of Nuneaton Borough, who knocked out Swansea 2-0. Borough were going well in the Southern League, and a goal from Crawley plus a goalkeeping howler were too much for Swansea.

To Nuneaton went the satisfaction of becoming the only non-league club in the fourth round draw. While Bedford were losing 6-2 at home to Peterborough, Nuneaton were battling to a 1-1 draw at home to Rotherham and proved no pushovers in the replay, going out by a single goal. North London fortunes were in sharp contrast. As Spurs started another victorious campaign, Arsenal's trough deepened. At St Andrews in the fifth round, they fell to Second

Swindon had an even finer moment two years later. With the Robins still in the Third Division, Coventry, Blackburn, Derby and Burnley were seen off en route to a League Cup final against Arsenal. Swindon had somehow hung on to their prize asset, and looked to Don Rogers for their inspiration. Swindon scored early and then spent the next eighty minutes defending their penalty area. Rogers couldn't get a look in. A late Arsenal equaliser took the game into extra-time where Rogers made his mark at last. A header for 2-1 and then a fine solo goal as he skipped over the muddy surface from the halfway line clinched Swindon's only major trophy. As a bonus, they also won promotion the same year.

Division Birmingham, Geoff Vowden scoring the only goal. The Gunners' embarrassment was shared by Manchester United, who also tripped up to opponents from the same tier. Norwich must have travelled to Old Trafford more in hope than in expectation despite a good cup record. United were en route to another league title, but Don Heath and Gordon Bolland wrote themselves into East Anglian folklore by scoring in a famous 2-1 win.

The competition's biggest patsies in 1967 were West Ham, three World Cup winning players and all. Swindon Town were a good Third Division side, and boasted a player of ability way beyond that level in Don Rogers, but they should still have been out of their depth. The first match at Upton Park was a real ding-dong affair, with a Geoff Hurst hat-trick earning the Hammers a draw despite a splendid twosome from Rogers, the mousta-chioed maverick.

In the return, Rogers and his colleagues really turned up the heat. West Ham were never given a moment's peace; even Bobby Moore looked panicky in the second half.

The Third Division team took the lead in the first half, and West Ham missed a succession of chances before equalising with just over ten minutes left. Rather than dig in, though, Swindon came straight back; full-back John Trollope floated a deep cross to the far post where Rogers lurked. Rogers' finish was an ancestor of Marco Van Basten at Euro '88. There was even time for Swindon to add a third on the break to rub it in.

BAGGIES BAG CUP

THE LAST 16

Portsmouth **1** West Brom **2**	
Tottenham (1) **1** Liverpool (1) **2**	
Arsenal (1) **1** Birmingham (1) **2**	
Sheffield Wed (2) **0** Chelsea (2) **2**	
Leeds **2** Bristol City **0**	
West Ham **1** Sheffield Utd **2**	
Rotherham (1) **0** Leicester (1) **2**	
Everton **2** Tranmere **0**	

QUARTER FINALS

West Brom (0)(1) **2** Liverpool (0)(1) **1**
Birmingham **1** Chelsea **0**
Leeds **1** Sheffield Utd **0**
Leicester **1** Everton **3**

SEMI FINALS

West Brom **2** Birmingham **0**
at Villa Park

Leeds **0** Everton **1**
at Old Trafford

FINAL, 18 MAY 1968, WEMBLEY

Everton **0** West Bromwich Albion **1**
after extra time

EVERTON:
West, Wright, Wilson, Kendall, Labone ©,
Harvey, Husband, Ball, Royle, Hurst, Morrissey
sub: Kenyon

WEST BROM:
Osborne, Fraser, Williams ©, Brown, Talbut,
Kaye *(Clarke, 91)*, Lovett, Collard, **Astle (1)**,
Hope, Clark

The competition came in like a lion. The first round was littered with shocks, with five league teams falling to less illustrious opposition. Sadly, though, Ryhope Colliery Welfare were not one of the victors but the Wearside club had crossed broken new ground simply by reaching round one. Formed in 1898 as Ryhope Villa, they had first entered the FA Cup in 1912, but this was their crowning achievement. Faced with the relative might of Fourth Division Workington, they lost 1-0 at home and have never troubled the first round since.

Among the major casualties was the Football League's oldest club. Notts County were trading on former glory. Their 1894 victory had never seemed more remote. These days they were languishing in the lower reaches of Division Four, and a 1-0 defeat at Runcorn hardly lifted the gloom at Meadow Lane. Elsewhere, Macclesfield beat Stockport, Brentford were knocked out by Guildford City and Oxford United succumbed to Chelmsford City. Mansfield pipped Notts County for the reddest-faces-in-Nottinghamshire award by crashing out 5-1 at Tow Law Town. The first attempt to play the tie four days earlier had been abandoned at half-time with the ground enveloped by a blizzard. Mansfield were clearly still suffering, with their defence still particularly prone to exposure. Tow Law scored two more in a replay at Shrewsbury in round four; unfortunately Shrewsbury scored six.

Disappointingly, after such a bonanza of nose-tweaking, only Macclesfield made it to the third round, where they were sent to Craven Cottage. Fulham were in the midst of a dismal League campaign, which ended with them five points adrift at the foot of Division One. Such parlous form made no opponents a formality, but the Cottagers prevailed 4-2 after an erratic performance.

Tie of the round was Manchester United v Tottenham, which pitted the champions against the holders. United were hoping Tottenham's goalkeeper Pat Jennings would be unable to repeat his feat from that season's FA Charity Shield, when his long punt upfield bounced over Alex Stepney's head and into the net!

Martin Chivers, Spurs' new signing from Southampton, repaid a slice of his fee with two goals to earn his side a replay. At White Hart Lane, the match was goalless until extra time, when Jimmy Robertson shot Tottenham into the fourth round. Newcastle and Wolves failed to join them. The Magpies lost 1-0 at home to Second Division Carlisle to continue a dire cup record in the sixties. Rotherham belied league form so dismal that it saw them relegated to Division Three. The Millers rallied to beat Wolves with a single goal from Jim Storrie.

West Brom nearly joined the list of high-profile casualties when they travelled to Layer Road in round three. Tony Brown's goal earned them a draw against Third Division strugglers Colchester. Without it, the prodigious campaign of Jeff Astle would have been strangled at birth. The Baggies' centre-forward opened his account with two in the replay as Albion cruised home 4-0, setting the ball rolling on a run that would bring him nine of his side's sixteen Cup goals. By the tournament's end, he had scored in every round, a feat that only Chelsea's Peter Osgood has managed since.

The strangest performance of the third round came from Manchester City. The team that would end the season as league champions played like relegation candidates when stuttering to a scoreless draw against Reading at Maine Road. In the replay they overwhelmed the Third Division side 7-0, including a hat-trick from Mike Summerbee. The City winger was again on target in the fourth, but Leicester edged through in a seven-goal thriller. Jeff Astle and Tony Brown were on target as West Brom won 3-2 at Southampton, but the round's scoring honours went to Mark Hateley. Now at Liverpool, his third club in as many seasons, Anfield's new centre-forward bagged four in the 5-2 defeat of Walsall.

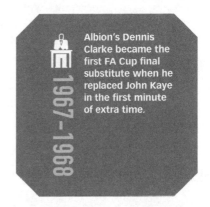

Liverpool's fifth round opponents would be a trickier proposition. Tottenham, having been drawn at Old Trafford in the third round, were being forced to defend their trophy the hard way. Goals from Greaves and Hateley cancelled each other out, but Liverpool won a hard-fought replay 2-1 thanks to Roger Hunt and a penalty from Tommy Smith.

Liverpool's neighbours from across the park were also in the sixth round draw, but Everton's passage had been a decidedly cushy one. Ties against Southport, Carlisle and Tranmere were hardly the stuff of legend but a trip to Filbert Street would be a step-up in class. Everton upped their game sufficiently to run out 3-1 winners, Jimmy Husband scoring twice.

Leeds booked a second successive semi-final place, a rare goal from Paul Madeley proving enough to beat Sheffield United 1-0. West Brom overcame Liverpool in a sixth round replay, after Astle and Hateley had embarked on their own private duel. Both had scored at Anfield in a 1-1 draw and the two strikers repeated the feat at the Hawthorns. Outside-left Clive Clark ended the stalemate with Albion's winner. The surprise package in the last four was second division Birmingham. Freddie Pickering secured their semi-final place with the only goal against Chelsea.

The sense that this might be West Brom's year strengthened as the semi-final draw sent them to Villa Park to play Birmingham. The reliable double act of Astle and Brown were right on cue, and Albion were back at Wembley for the second successive season. Last year's performance could scarcely have inspired confidence. They had started as red-hot favourites for the League Cup but were turned over by Third Division QPR.

This year they faced Everton, who under Harry Catterick were being moulded into a team that would win the title within another two years. The Toffees had ensured that Leeds again left the semi-finals empty-handed, Johnny Morrissey's goal winning the day at Old Trafford. The final was a tedious affair, with both teams labouring on a surface rendered unusually heavy after recent downpours. After ninety uneventful minutes, extra-time was not an inviting prospect for the neutral. Fortunately, the man of the tournament was to enliven proceedings within three minutes. Jeff Astle's winner was not without its good fortune, as his first attempt rebounded off Colin Harvey straight back into the Albion striker's path. For a man in such rich goalscoring form, a second chance proved lethal. The ball flew across Gordon West into the far corner, and Albion had their hands on the trophy for a fifth time. At the time, only Aston Villa, Blackburn and Newcastle had won more.

NEIL YOUNG'S HARVEST

MAN CITY:
Dowd, Book ©, Pardoe, Doyle, Booth, Oakes, Summerbee, Bell, Lee, **Young (1)**, Coleman
sub: Connor

LEICESTER:
Shilton, Rodrigues, Nish ©, Roberts, Woollett, Cross, Fern, Gibson, Lochhead, Clarke, Glover
(Manley 70)

The partnership of the experienced wiseacre Joe Mercer, and the brash tactician, Malcolm Allison, proved a dream ticket for Manchester City. In 1968, with their rivals United covering themselves in European glory, City made sure the town wasn't all painted red by winning the league. Adding the FA Cup the following year, and the League Cup and European Cup Winners' Cup in 1970, brought an unprecedented run of success to the blue side of Manchester.

It proved a false dawn. City have had almost three trophy-free decades while United have had to buy a bigger cabinet.

In the early stages, the Cup was in stern mood. No non-league sides triumphed over teams from the bottom two divisions. Some levity was provided by prodigious scoring from Southend United. The Shrimpers potted nine past King's Lynn, then went one better against Brentwood, who at least managed one in reply. Twin strikers Billy Best and Gary Moore gorged themselves. Best hit eight in the two ties, including five against Brentwood, while Moore managed seven. Best was to score twice more in the campaign to finish with ten, remarkable for a player whose team were knocked out by the fourth round.

Only one non-league side limped into the Third Round. Kettering gave a fair account, earning a 1-1 draw at Bristol Rovers before going out 2-1 in the replay. The rest of the round provided mild surprises rather than shocks. First Division Sunderland were particularly feeble, losing 4-1 at home to a Fulham side that finished bottom of Division Two. Second Division beat First again as Preston saw off Forest 3-0, while Third Division Mansfield started a run that was to see them through to the sixth round for the first time.

After disposing of Tow Law Town for the second season running (what odds that draw?), then Rotherham, Sheffield United were the Stags' first victims in the tougher rounds of the competition, beaten 2-1 with both goals from Mansfield icon Dudley Roberts. Next, free-scoring Southend were brought down to earth, a narrow 2-1 win with Roberts again firing the winner. West Ham had made a habit of providing headlines for the wrong reasons, so a trip to Field Mill in February had bounty hunters scenting blood. They were proved right, as the Hammers surrendered 3-0 with a pathetic performance. The end finally arrived at home to Leicester, when a solitary effort from Rodney Fern spoilt the party.

Leicester provided the final's youngest-ever goalkeeper, although at nineteen years and 220 days the best days of Peter Shilton's career stretched way ahead. Having begun in the sixties, he was still playing in 1990 at the World Cup in Italy. Remarkably, this remained his only FA Cup final.

The most bizarre tie was played at Stamford Bridge. Chelsea looked to be taking a fourth round replay with Preston in their stride. With seventeen minutes left they led 2-0, only for the match to be abandoned after sudden floodlight failure. Ian Hutchinson and Alan Birchenall, in particular, were left cursing their luck as their 'goals' now counted for nothing. The surreal air surrounding the tie continued as the rearranged fixture took place on a weekday afternoon. This didn't stop nearly 40,000 throwing one of West London's largest collective sickies, but the only genuine malaise looked to be in the home team's performance. With ninety minutes on the clock, the Blues trailed 1-0 to a Gerry Ingram goal, but then won an improbable victory with two extra-time goals from David Webb and Charlie Cooke. Inconsistent? Chelsea?

In Manchester both United and City reached the quarter-finals, but it was United's form that was the more eye-catching. They had swept aside Birmingham 6-2 in a fifth round replay, with an imperious Denis Law claiming a hat-trick. This brought the flying Scot's tally in this season's competition to seven, and continued a love affair with the competition.

Law and United drew a blank in the sixth round, going out to a goal from Joe Royle at Old Trafford. Everton faced City in the semi-finals, but Tommy Booth prevented the Toffees claiming a Manchester double by claiming the only goal at Villa Park.

The Foxes also provided the last professional cricketer to play in an FA Cup final. Graham Cross was a regular for Leicestershire.

In the other semi-final at Hillsborough, holders West Brom faced relegation-threatened Leicester. Albion had been the scourge of London, knocking out Fulham, Arsenal and Chelsea en route. That man Astle had nicked the winner against Chelsea in a close sixth round tie. The Foxes, despite fragile league form, had won at Anfield in the fifth round before seeing off Mansfield. Albion started favourites, but were beaten by the only goal of the game scored by Allan Clarke.

There is another unwanted statistic for Leicester. They became the most frequent finalists never to win the trophy, having also lost in 1949, 1961 and 1963.

The final was drab but at least provided consolation for City, whose defence of their league title had been pitiful. They had finished in thirteenth place, which was at least eight higher than Leicester who became only the second relegated finalists and the first since City themselves in 1926. Leicester had their chances, and Harry Dowd made one stupendous save from Clarke. The scorer of the only goal was Neil Young, the only Canadian singer-songwriter to score in an FA Cup final, or not, as the case may be.

1969

ALMOST BLUE

1970

This was a great FA cup year. There was lower division interest until the latter stages, moments of sensational individual brilliance, and a classic, albeit brutal, final.

Right from the first round, the shocks arrived. Even before the flawed genius of an ageing and alcoholic Jimmy Greaves arrived, Brentwood showed that they carried a threat. Their win over Reading was a major surprise, as Reading had half an eye on promotion to Division Two.

The West Midlands Regional League doesn't sound terribly glamorous. The reality reflected that feeling; it was an outpost of non-league football, and one of its teams, Tamworth, had done well to even reach the first round. Their opponents, Torquay United, were in the Third Division but possessed no Cup pedigree, having only once ventured beyond the third round, and that had been in 1955. Despite taking the lead, Torquay remained true to form, losing 2-1 to goals from Tamworth's prolific forwards Graham Jessop, a clay-worker, and Ray Holmes, a car plant man. Gillingham showed how to take care of lesser teams in the next round, beating Tamworth 6-0 at a canter. Tamworth have never since made the draw for the Second Round.

Pride of place in the third round went to Sheffield United, who hosted eventual Champions Everton. The Toffees boasted the midfield 'holy trinity' of Kendall, Harvey and Ball, who were sent cursing back to Goodison after a 2-1 defeat.

The Blades' 'reward' was a tough trip to Derby, where the Rams gave Everton a lesson in professionalism. John O'Hare grabbed a couple in a 3-0 win.

A Blackpool side good enough to win promotion (for one year) were also too good for Arsenal. After a creditable 1-1 draw at Highbury, the Gunners were spiked 3-2. Having cleared Becher's Brook, Blackpool then fell at the water-jump, surrendering 2-0 at home to Mansfield to prolong a dismal modern cup record.

Non-league Sutton United made it into the hat by winning their third match in the competition proper — all against other non-league teams. At last a prize draw — the mighty Leeds at home. Unfortunately for Sutton, Revie's machine was in good working order, Allan Clarke helping himself to four and Peter Lorimer to two in a 6-0 caning. As far as top flight opponents were concerned, Sutton were sent to Coventry for nearly twenty years until . . . read on.

Torquay United remain one of the league's dismal Cup teams. They have never gone beyond round four and never beaten a top division team. In the early 90s they were eliminated by non-league opposition for six consecutive seasons. Whether Farnborough, Yeovil, Slough, Sutton, Kidderminster or Enfield bother chalking those up as a giant-killing act, who knows?

Second Division teams were having a good time. By the time the Cup was down to the last sixteen, Division Two had as many representatives as Division One. While all the lower division teams fell, four Second Division sides won through, but none of them drew each other.

Swindon, after their League Cup heroics the previous year, were scoring for fun until they too were steamrollered by Leeds with two more for 'Sniffer' Clarke; Leeds were giving no quarter. Middlesbrough had seen off a poor West Ham in round three, and met Manchester United in the last eight. They fought tooth and nail, only going down 2-1 in a replay. This was a creditable effort considering the merciless way United had crushed the aspirations of Fourth Division Northampton in the previous round. You would have put your shirt on George Best's mind being elsewhere at the prospect of the County Ground in February. Maybe there was a desperately attractive blonde in the crowd who tempted George to turn on the style. Whatever the reason, Best showed his full repertoire in an amazing performance, scoring six in an 8-2 rout. It was Willie Morgan, one of the many shaggily-coiffured forwards to labour under the sobriquet of 'the new George Best', who saw United through with the winner against Middlesbrough.

Best's six goals in a match remains a record for Manchester United; Denis Law must have been fuming!

Chelsea, in the main, had made light of some heavy opposition. Wins against Birmingham and Burnley – in a replay, after a faltering performance in a 2-2 draw at home – were despatched before a convincing 4-1 away win at Crystal Palace saw them into the last eight. More London opposition in near neighbours QPR stood in their way. Another four goals away from home was a convincing response from the Kings Road dandies, Peter Osgood continuing his score-in-every-round streak with a classy hat-trick.

Only Watford of the Second Division sides prevailed. Bill Shankly ungraciously described them as the worst team ever to have beaten Liverpool. Beat them they did, all the same, with a Barry Endean header from a cross by the man of the match, the inspirational man with the film-star name, Ray Lugg. It wasn't a fluke, Liverpool were very poor.

Chelsea got the luck of the draw. Watford's course was run. They were hammered out of sight at White Hart Lane; the 5-1 scoreline reflects the game.

Shell-shocked Cobblers' keeper was Kim Book, whose brother Tony had lifted the Cup nine months previously as captain of Manchester City.

The other semi-final was a clash of the titans. There was no love lost between Manchester United and Leeds – actually, everyone hated Leeds – and they slugged it out for three matches totalling 300 minutes. A solitary Billy Bremner goal settled it. In a season truncated to accommodate the World Cup in the summer, the last thing Leeds needed was three semi-finals in twelve days. They may have reached the Cup final, but Everton had overhauled them in the league, and they still had to face Celtic in a European Cup semi-final second leg four days after the final.

The Cup final promised another rousing clash. Pragmatic Leeds against the Cavalier flair of Chelsea offered a fascinating contrast of styles. The uncompromising nature of both defences promised some fireworks. We got both.

Cup final protocol demands many rituals. Two polite, overawed teams produce a sporting yet sterile contest that is usually settled by a single goal. Barely a tackle is attempted in anger and the manicured sward that is the Wembley pitch remains billiard-table green throughout.

This year was different. A bizarre decision to allow the Horse of the Year show a few days before the final produced a pitch bearing an uncanny resemblance to the Baseball Ground in mid-January. After witnessing 120 minutes of furrows ploughed by 'Chopper' Harris, the groundsman would probably have preferred another round from Harvey Smith.

A mutual enmity laid low any prospect of a cagey opening. These were two teams that wanted blood and it was Leeds who drew it first. Charlton's header from a corner was barely worthy of the name but plopped agonisingly over the line after Harris and McCreadie's wild lunges only connected with each other.

The equaliser was equally comedic. Houseman's speculative twenty-five-yarder trundled towards Sprake, whose dive over the ball resulted in another addition to his thickening album of howlers. Jones looked to have spared his blushes six minutes from time, but his effort was cancelled out inside two minutes courtesy of Hutchinson's header.

The FA's plans to shorten the season were in tatters; the teams would have to wait eighteen days for the replay at Old Trafford. In the meantime Leeds were knocked out of Europe by Celtic and conceded the title to Everton.

After such a battle, it seemed unfair to expect the replay to maintain such high-octane excitement. Instead, it was just a battle. The tone was set within minutes, after Harris had lived up to his nickname by reducing Eddie Gray to the role of limping passenger. The tactic was cynical and deliberate, as Gray had tormented David Webb at Wembley. Chelsea responded by moving Webb to centre-half and transferring their hit-man to right back.

An incensed Leeds traded fire with fire, so that large parts of the game became reminiscent of the True Blues v the Dirty Yellows in *Bedknobs and Broomsticks*. Hutchinson and Charlton traded punches and the studs of an airborne McCreadie hurtled into Bremner's face; just two of the more 'memorable' incidents in this combustible contest.

Occasionally, a game of football would break out. Jones again looked to have won it for Leeds, before Osgood's magnificent diving header levelled proceedings with twelve minutes left.

After fourteen minutes of extra-time, with both teams having slugged each other to a virtual standstill, Chelsea poked their noses in front. Hutchinson summoned up enough energy for a final, prodigious long throw, which deflected to Webb at the back post, who squeezed it into the net via his left ear.

It was the knockout punch. In 210 minutes of football, Chelsea were only ahead for six of them. Leeds had given everything but had nothing left. For an exhausted but delighted Chelsea, there was the euphoria of their first Cup.

1970

CHARLIE GETS UP LIVERPOOL'S NOSE

1971

ARSENAL:
Wilson, Rice, McNab, Storey *(Kelly (1))*,
McLintock ©, Simpson, Armstrong, Graham,
Radford, Kennedy, **George (1)**

LIVERPOOL:
Clemence, Lawler, Lindsay, Smith ©, Lloyd,
Hughes, Callaghan, Evans *(Peter Thompson
70)*, **Heighway (1)**, Toshack, Hall

ootball in the seventies wasn't the wonderland of riches that wearing our rose-tinted glasses would have us remember. It was, however, a rich decade for the FA Cup. High profile shocks, even in the finals, and some tremendous individual stories made sure the Cup remained a blue riband event.

1970 had seen a monumental battle for the trophy. 1971 would see monumental achievements of a different sort. The trend started early; Barnet, Grantham Town, Rhyl and Boston United were the non-league headline-grabbers in the opening round. Newport, Stockport, Hartlepool and Southport were the guilty parties. Newport, especially, had a shocker. That a decent Southern League side should host a god-awful Fourth Division outfit and send them packing is, in itself, unworthy of featuring here. What is remarkable, though, is Barnet's 6-1 win, which equalled the worst post-war defeat by a league side to non-league opposition. North London's other George scored a hat-trick.

Yeovil went one better in the second round, winning away at a Bournemouth side promoted to Division Three by the season's end. Yeovil's principal task was achieved by keeping a clean sheet – Cherries' striker Ted MacDougall had scored six in the previous round as Oxford City were thrashed 8-1 in a replay.

They were still trumped by Rhyl, who could only draw at home to Barnsley, but won through against the Third Division team when they won a second replay 2-0 in the palatial surroundings of Old Trafford.

Wigan's defeat of Peterborough, some seven years before they won admission to the league, completed the rout. Not a result that would raise eyebrows nowadays. They were joined in round three by Barnet, the winners of an all non-league tie.

The third round draw was fickle. Rhyl travelled the length of Wales only to get thrashed 6-1 by Swansea. Yeovil were handed the plum of Arsenal at home and heads were held high throughout, despite the 3-0 reverse.

Non-league pride was well and truly maintained at Maine Rd. Wigan were expected to turn up and be grateful to collect their handsome share of the gate money. Instead, they held City for more than seventy minutes until Colin Bell finally found a way through. Barnet, too, fell at this stage, beaten 1-0 by Colchester United.

Rochdale provided the round's surprise, beating Coventry City 2-1 at Spotland. The Sky Blues have good reason to thank Ray Crawford, as events later in the

1970-1971

This was not Ray Crawford's first taste of glory. The veteran striker had won a league championship medal with Ipswich nine years earlier, and won a couple of England caps the same season.

season means that this result has been largely forgotten. Not in Rochdale, though, where Messrs. Cross and Butler ensured the club's first appearance in the fourth round for sixty-three years. Fifty league places separated these clubs at the season's end. Coventry may thank Crawford, but Rochdale won't. He scored twice in a 3-3 draw at Spotland in the next round, and scored again in the replay, a 5-0 blitz. Maybe Colchester were eliminating the other Davids to ensure there own niche in football history was preserved, because what happened next is one of the biggest Cup shocks of all time, rivalling Walsall-Arsenal in 1933 as the shock of shocks.

Lest we forget, Don Revie's Leeds were *the* team to beat. True, they blew more trophies than they won, but their failings had tended to be at the final hurdle. In general, they were pipped by their peer group:

Liverpool, Arsenal, Celtic (Sunderland was a nightmare not yet visited), but Colchester?

Layer Road was jammed with 16,000 fans, but all gathered out of a sense of occasion rather than to witness a genuine contest. The spectators in the first hour were joined by the Leeds defence.

After eighteen minutes, Ray Crawford rose unchallenged after Gary Sprake had flapped at a cross. Ten minutes later the crowd's elation turned to disbelief as Crawford grabbed an unlikely second. There seemed little danger as he and Paul Reaney fell on top of a loose ball, but striker reacted quicker. Swinging a trailing left leg, he directed the ball just inside the post.

1970-1971

Colchester manager Dick Graham may have regretted his pre-match promises. As a win bonus, he had pledged a fortnight's holiday to the players and their wives. He had also vowed to scale the ancient walls of Colchester castle. He was as good as his word on both counts.

Surely Leeds would regroup at half-time, courtesy of Revie's harsh words and tactical nous? Whatever was said, the effect was only to send Leeds into a tailspin.

Ten minutes after the break, a speculative punt forward saw the ball bounce comfortably between Sprake and Reaney. With a politeness not normally associated with Leeds's defence, they left it for each other, allowing an initially hopeful Simmons to head into a gaping goal.

1970-1971

Arsenal's win was a reward for their stamina. The Cup final was their sixty-fourth game of the season. The first Double of all was achieved by Preston in just twenty-seven.

Finally, Leeds woke up. A desperate Revie dropped Clarke into the hole and pushed Giles into attack. The tactic took effect within five minutes, as a distracted Colchester allowed Hunter to head home Lorimer's corner. With fifteen minutes left, Giles himself poached a second, and Leeds were within touching distance.

There were high jinks at Blackpool. Unfortunately for West Ham, most of them took place the night before the game, as players broke a pre-match curfew. Four were fined by manager Ron Greenwood after a 4-0 defeat, including Bobby Moore. The Hammers' captain was dropped to the bench for the next league game.

1970-1971

The last fifteen minutes were an agony of desperate Colchester clearances, local watches being checked incessantly and a cacophony of whistling which started fully five minutes before the referee's blast sent the ground into rapture. The Fourth Division side had won it. FA Cup ties don't come any better than this.

Colchester's bounty continued in round six with a trip to Goodison Park. Although the dream ended harshly with a 5-0 defeat, as Kendall and co ran riot, the 53,028 crowd generated £26,000. For a Fourth Division side, their one-third share was something of a bounty.

The semi-final draw threw up a Merseyside derby for the ninth time. Liverpool were by far the stronger side on paper, but were forced to battle back with second-half goals from unlikely sources. Alun Evans and Brian Hall sent the Reds to Wembley after Alan Ball had put Everton in front.

The other semi-final matched Arsenal with Stoke. City, labouring at the wrong end of the First Division, had taken seven matches to get through four rounds, including three against Huddersfield. They did, however, have the memory of a 5-0 thrashing of Arsenal in September to feed on. At Hillsborough, the Potters looked the form horses by racing into a 2-0 lead within half-an-hour. Their second seemed to sum up Arsenal's afternoon. Charlie George's back pass was woefully under-hit, allowing John Ritchie to intercept and draw Bob Wilson before slotting home into an empty net.

Huddersfield's win at Birmingham in a third round replay was a triumph over adversity. Keeper Terry Poole was carried off with a broken leg. His replacement, winger Steve Smith, broke his thumb. The Terriers still kept a clean sheet, winning 2-0.

1970-1971

In the second-half Stoke continued to press, but Arsenal finally managed to break swiftly, Storey shooting home from twenty yards. The Gunners remained unconvincing and, as ninety minutes elapsed, the game looked to have drifted away. Deep into injury-time, Arsenal won a final corner. McLintock's goal-bound header was palmed away by Stoke midfielder Mahoney and referee Partridge pointed to the spot, despite Gordon Banks's protestations that he was fouled as the corner came over. Storey shot coolly past Banks to level.

Stoke had shot their bolt. In the replay, Arsenal took a firm grip early on and never looked back after Graham's bullet header gave them a thirteenth-minute lead. Stoke, forty seconds from their first final, were out.

Just over a month later Arsenal played Stoke in a crucial league match at Highbury, squeezing through 1-0 to leave themselves two points behind Leeds. The amateur-

Eddie Kelly became the first substitute to score in an FA Cup final.

1970-1971

The exit of holders Chelsea ruined a potentially great day for Peter Bonetti, who was playing his 500th match for the Blues. The opposition were Manchester City, the same club against whom he made his debut.

Chelsea failed to hold their trophy, but did win the European Cup Winners' Cup, beating Real Madrid 2-1 in a final replay. Peter Osgood scored in both matches, and John Dempsey atoned for a horrible error in the first match with the opener in the second.

ish scheduling still prevalent meant they knew exactly what they needed to do in their last league game two days later – beat Tottenham at White Hart Lane to win the league. Spurs' ground was packed to the rafters with prayerful Gunners and Lilywhites hoping to pull the rug from under their rivals. Young Ray Kennedy's header, three minutes from the end, put an end to a tense match and a nail-biting championship race.

Despite Arsenal's domestic dominance, Liverpool must have fancied their chances. The Gunners had an exhausting run-in, making up a seven point deficit from the end of February. Arsenal sides are usually resilient and this one was no different. Bertie Mee had built a team without prima-donnas; their virtues were work-rate and discipline, with George 'Stroller' Graham adding a touch of guile, and Charlie George a dash of flair and glamour.

After ninety minutes light on action, the pendulum swung towards Anfield. An exhausted Arsenal had already reshuffled after midfield henchman Peter Storey had been forced off with an ankle injury. In the first minute of extra time, they fell behind. Bob Wilson met Heighway's advance too mindful of a prospective centre. The winger surprised him with a low shot that beat him at the near post.

Lesser sides than Arsenal would have wilted. With Radford a tireless threat, they forced their way back ten minutes later. An innocuous centre found Kelly, whose inadvertent shot-cum-deflection dribbled embarrassingly under Graham's foot and into the net, with the entire Liverpool defence rooted to the spot. A fluke certainly, but Arsenal had earned it.

By contrast, their winner was unequivocal. With nine minutes left, and with most players running on empty, Charlie George summoned one last burst of energy. Taking Radford's pass thirty yards out, he sidestepped Smith and advanced before planting an unstoppable shot past Clemence. George's cele-bration, a mixture of elation and exhaustion as he lay prostrate on the floor with his long hair billowing out, remains etched in the memory. A shattered Liverpool barely had strength to restart the game, let alone mount a comeback. The Gunners had matched the Double of their North London rivals.

LEEDS AT LAST

LEEDS:
Harvey, Reaney, Madeley, Bremner ©,
Charlton, Hunter, Lorimer, **Clarke (1)**, Jones,
Giles, Gray *sub: Bates*

ARSENAL:
Barnett, Rice, McNab, Storey, McLintock ©,
Simpson, Armstrong, Ball, George, Radford
(Kennedy 80), Graham

B efore Ted MacDougall became another in a long line of white elephants at Old Trafford, he was rattling them in for the Cherries at a remarkable rate. True, a first round home tie against Margate was akin to shooting fish in a barrel, but how often have players scored nine goals in one match in the competition proper? Just this once. For the record, Bournemouth won 11-0. One of the other scorers was Cave, probably the same one into which Margate's defence disappeared after the game.

In the early rounds, the glory-hunting spotlight fell on the north east. South Shields won at Scunthorpe, Blyth Spartans knocked out Crewe and Stockport before running out of steam at Reading.

The third round was thin on shocks, with one exception. Notts County had run away with division four the previous year, and ran away with their cup tie at Watford, winning 4-1 against a team that made the semi-finals two years before. Alan Durban scored a hat-trick as Derby taught County the real meaning of a gulf in class in the next round.

Now to that one exception. When the Newcastle v Hereford tie at St James's Park was delayed because of the weather, it seemed only to delay the inevitable. Hereford were still in the Southern League, and Newcastle had assembled their best team for over a decade, spearheaded by the bandy-legged but explosive goalscorer, Malcolm Macdonald. A goal from player-manager, Colin Addison, and a second from Brian Owen earned Hereford another go. MacDonald boasted that Newcastle would score double figures in the replay. Not for the only time in his career, Supermac's words turned into his post-match dinner. Further delays due to weather meant the replay took place on fourth round day. Several previous pitch inspections had found a frozen, rutted and wholly unfit surface. Now the sublime had become the ridiculous, as the thaw had reduced the pitch to the consistency of chocolate blancmange.

The unusual Saturday replay gave Match of the Day cameras an excuse to visit unknown territory. There were bigger TV fish to fry that day, so junior commentator John Motson was given the job. If this was a day that changed players' lives, Motty's career was propelled into the limelight, as his familiar ecstatic braying entered the living rooms of the nation.

Despite this match's notoriety, it could all have been so different. The spectacle of twenty-two men wading through mud was an unedifying one for eighty minutes,

1971–1972

Forty-eight-hours after Wembley, with Liverpool labouring to break down a disappointed but resilient Arsenal, Leeds had the chance to win the Double by avoiding defeat against Wolves. They failed, blaming two rejected penalty appeals; Derby were champions.

before MacDonald's far-post header looked to have resumed normal service. With two minutes left, Colin Addison charged from defence but stumbled over a loose ball. It ran to Ronnie Radford, who advanced a couple of paces before unleashing a thirty-five-yarder that McFaul wouldn't have stopped with a stepladder and Kenny Everett's 'Brother-Lee-Love' gloves. Radford was no Ray Crawford; he was a journeyman footballer, and it was only his third goal in his first season for Hereford after an undistinguished time at Newport.

Mayhem ensued. A pre-pubescent tide of parkas and flares swarmed over the pitch, doubtless ensuring a maternal ticking off for getting their shoes muddy. Newcastle had bigger problems in store. Slumbering peacefully and waiting for the final whistle, they had to rouse themselves for extra time.

The initiative was now with Hereford. Twelve minutes after the restart, the virtue of a fresh pair of legs was vividly illustrated. Ricky George, an eightieth-minute substitute, ghosted round a statuesque Newcastle defence to send a cross-shot beyond McFaul. Newcastle were out, and they have never been allowed to forget it.

Hereford were drawn at home to West Ham in the fourth round, a tie that was played only four days later. A heroic 0-0 draw produced the unusual prob-

1971–1972

Allan Clarke, after loser's medals with Leicester in 1969 and Leeds the following year, was a winner at last. Alan Ball was still waiting, having also lost with Everton in 1968. He waited in vain for his entire career.

lem at Edgar Street of forged tickets. Such was the interest in the replay at Upton Park that the 42,211 crowd was within 111 of the ground record. Hereford lost the battle 3-1, but won the war at the end of the season when their exploits earned them election to the Football League.

By the time the fifth round took shape, most of the big clubs were still in the competition. Of the four in contention for the title, Manchester City and Liverpool had fallen; City at Second Division Middlesbrough and Liverpool in a replay to title favourites, Leeds. Allan Clarke had again done the damage, scoring both goals in a 2-0 win at Elland Road after a goalless struggle at Anfield. A strong London contingent, plus Everton and a smattering of Division Two sides, joined Leeds and Derby in the fifth round draw.

Only Orient upset the natural order. The Chelsea team of Osgood, Hudson and co. breezed into a two-goal lead, but their performance thereafter brought knowing glances from those who had dubbed them champagne Charlies. Hoadley and Bullock made the match all square,

1971–1972

Derby banned the TV cameras from their fourth round tie with Notts County after a dispute over the fee. The Rams' claim of a derisory offer seemed justified, as they were offered the less than princely sum of £87.50!

and the O's pinched it through Barry Fairbrother's eighty-ninth-minute winner. Chelsea fans, realising their players had given up the ghost, invaded the pitch in a forlorn attempt to get the match abandoned. The hooligans were beginning to make their mark; their best-forgotten exploits would attract the attentions of irresponsible tabloid editors for years to come.

Orient fell at home to Arsenal in the next round, and only Birmingham of the Second Division cadre survived, winning comfortably at home to Huddersfield; no great surprise, they would take Huddersfield's place in the top division the following season. Birmingham boasted formidable strike-power, with seventeen year-old wonderkid, Trevor Francis, as well as the two Bobs, Latchford, later of Everton and England, and Hatton. They were no match for the wiles of Leeds, and fell at the semi-final stage again.

Arsenal were approaching their second successive final the hard way. Two replays were needed to overcome Derby, then Stoke City were offered a chance for revenge for their narrow defeat twelve months earlier, as the semi-final draw repeated itself. This time Arsenal appeared to be in no mood for nonsense. Armstrong put them ahead and they were coasting but the game turned on an injury to Bob Wilson. Unwisely, the hobbling keeper was deemed fit to continue, and Stoke seized their chance. With fifteen minutes left, a speculative cross was intercepted by Peter Simpson. Mindful of Wilson's predicament, he attempted a cushioned header to his keeper but succeeded only in deflecting it past him. Radford immediately took over in goal, but the horse had already bolted. It was off to Goodison Park for the replay.

Stoke looked to have slain their ghosts with Jimmy Greenhoff's penalty, but redemption turned into Groundhog Day with two pieces of cruel luck. A penalty looked harsh punishment for Peter Dobing's challenge on Armstrong, but Charlie George accepted the opportunity. With fifteen minutes left, a clearly offside Radford broke free to shoot past Banks. The linesman had mistaken a programme seller for a Stoke defender. Lucky Arsenal had committed robbery. They would travel to Wembley determine to hold on to at least one part of their Double; their chance in the league had gone weeks before.

Despite Leeds' success under Revie, their glory years threw up more bogeymen than trophies. The previous season's nightmares, namely the championship surrender to Arsenal and the Cup fiasco at Colchester, were still open wounds. The Cup was a competition to be approached with trepidation. This was their third final in eight years, the first two had both slipped away from promising positions.

The days preceding had been tense; a four-way fight for the title had taken shape. With one game to go for Leeds and Liverpool, both lay adrift of Derby, with their final matches to be played only forty-eight hours after the FA Cup final. (Yes, the Football League really were that stupid).

Precisely 100 years after the first final, the centenary match has lived in the memory for this statistic only. Both teams were old hands at the big game and knew each other inside out. Both were pragmatic teams, even to the point of cynicism, and a free-flowing classic was never on the cards.

Eight minutes into the second half, Lorimer fed Mick Jones on the right-wing, who eluded McNab on the by-line and crossed for Clarke to score with a diving header. Although lacking power, Arsenal's stand-in keeper Geoff Barnett was late in reacting, the ball finding his left-hand corner in virtual slow-motion.

The remaining moment of drama occurred in the game's final attack. Jones, attempting to repeat his assist, dislocated his shoulder after falling awkwardly. His heavily-strapped ascent up the thirty-nine steps to receive his medal was painful to watch. After two near-misses, it completed the first victorious collection by a Leeds team.

MONTY'S DOUBLE

LEEDS:
Harvey, Reaney, Cherry, Bremner ©, Madeley,
Hunter, Lorimer, Clarke, Jones, Giles, Gray
(Yorath 75)

SUNDERLAND:
Montgomery, Malone, Guthrie, Horswill,
Watson, Pitt, Kerr ©, Hughes, Halom,
Porterfield (1), Tueart *sub: Young*

The shocks just kept on coming. Only this year we had to wait until the final for the biggest shock of all. Sunderland not only provided Wembley with one of its most memorable finals, they also grabbed most of the headlines in a truly phenomenal run. Many Second Division teams who reached the final did so via the luck of the draw; but for Sunderland it was a hard slog. Notts County and Reading were despatched only after replays and by the fifth round, Sunderland's odds lengthened as they contemplated a trip to Maine Road. Micky Horswill and Billy Hughes earned them a replay where, in a memorable night at Roker Park, they overran City 3-1 with two more from the diminutive Hughes.

The semi-final draw looked a classic case of 'lucky Arsenal'. While a high-flying Wolves were paired with Leeds, Arsenal travelled to Hillsborough more in expectation than in hope. Arsenal had seen off Chelsea in a sixth round replay despite an exquisite volley from Peter Osgood that was voted Match of the Day's Goal of the Season. The replay was no less action packed. After Houseman put Chelsea ahead, George Armstrong was toppled on the edge of the box. The referee awarded a free-kick, which he altered to a penalty after consulting a linesman. Alan Ball converted, and Ray Kennedy sealed the win.

In the semi-final, urged on by a Kop filled to bursting with Rokerites, Sunderland shocked Arsenal by taking a 2-0 lead through Vic Halom and, inevitably, Billy Hughes. Charlie George's reply with five minutes remaining was mere consolation. The muted celebration from the normally flamboyant Arsenal striker suggested that even the Gunners knew their hopes of a third successive final were done for.

The rest of the competition had been a trifle mundane, despite a rash of league clubs falling to disrespectful interlopers from the regions. The roll of honour reads Hayes, Margate, Bangor City, Yeovil and Scarborough. Their respective victims were Bristol Rovers, Swansea, Rochdale, Brentford and Oldham. Only Margate made it to the third round, where Tottenham added six to Bournemouth's eleven from the previous season.

The fourth round did see the Second Division having fun at the expense of their supposed betters. Carlisle, only two seasons from their nirvana, saw off Sheffield United before losing narrowly to Arsenal. Hull City, with their veteran forward line of Ken Wagstaff and

Ken Houghton, beat West Ham 1-0 with Houghton the scorer. Sheffield Wednesday, a mediocre side, took two replays to get past an equally mediocre Crystal Palace, a Brian Joicey hat-trick settling the third game 3-2. Pride of place goes to Luton Town and Millwall. Luton won 2-0 at Newcastle with both goals scored by winger John Aston, surplus to requirements at Man United. Luton weren't Hereford, but this was still a stinker of a result for the Geordies. Millwall won by the same score at Everton, and an off-season for the Toffees had just got worse. Another veteran, full-back Harry Cripps, scored Millwall's opener. Sunderland's only moment of good fortune was the quarter-final draw, which paired them at home to Luton, the only other team from outside Division One to survive the cull of the fifth round.

Leeds' passage to a third final in four years was not always a smooth run. They took three games to see off Norwich, their emphatic 5-0 win serving only to make the two previous ties all the more puzzling. An Allan Clarke hat-trick continued the striker's fine record in the competition. A quarter-final at Derby proved their highest hurdle, Lorimer's strike proving the difference in a tight encounter. The customary semi-final appearance on the scoresheet from Bremner was good enough to see off Wolves.

That, apparently, was the hard work over. Sunderland's previous efforts cut little mustard with the bookies, as Leeds arrived at Wembley the hottest final favourites in years.

Any post-mortem on Don Revie may well have found a single word impressed on his heart – Montgomery. This was not as embarrassing as Colchester, nor as important as the European Cup defeats by Celtic or Bayern Munich. But for anyone searching for an epitome of Leeds' propensity to snatch defeat from the jaws of victory, it came twenty minutes from the end of this pulsating match.

Against the odds, Leeds were still a goal down but such was their dominance of the second-half that the breaching of Sunderland's defence seemed only a matter of time. Paul Reaney's cross picked out Trevor Cherry, stealing behind the right-flank, whose downward header brought a full-stretch save from Jim Montgomery. His efforts looked in vain, as his parry fell into the path of an advancing Lorimer. The man with the thunderbolt right foot, instead of burying the chance with a

trademark bullet, chose to take the ball on his instep. A back-pedalling Montgomery spotted a sliver of salvation, and twisted in mid-air to parry against the bar. Commentators, crowd and players seemed momentarily frozen, unable to fathom what had taken place. It took a slow-motion replay to highlight the extent of Montgomery's heroics.

At that moment, the game changed. Leeds sensed their chance had gone, and the remaining twenty minutes ebbed away in a mixture of disjointed attack, frenzied clearances and unbearable tension.

Sunderland's lead was earned after a spirited performance in the first half-hour. In the first minute, rookie defender Richie Pitt left Allan Clarke a crumpled heap after an ill-timed lunge. Had it occurred today, Pitt may well have been sent off. His tackle served to distract the Leeds striker, who spent the rest of the game seeking revenge rather than the ball. His only contribution was a booking after flooring Sunderland captain Bobby Kerr. On thirty-two minutes the first major turning point in the game arrived. A corner from Kerr eluded Watson's head but rebounded from Halom's chest to Ian Porterfield. The former Raith Rovers man smashed the ball home from ten yards. The rest was all about Montgomery.

Such was the cacophony of Wearsiders whistling at the death that Ken Burns's final blast was barely heard. It sparked a frenzy of disbelieving celebration, capped by Bob Stokoe's dash across the pitch to embrace his keeper. The manager's Midas touch had taken Sunderland from relegation candidates to a creditable sixth place in Division Two. It is for this day, though, that his name became forged in Sunderland folklore.

SHANKS FOR THE MEMORY

LIVERPOOL:
Clemence,Smith, Lindsay, Phil Thompson,
Cormack, Hughes ©, **Keegan (2)**, Hall,
Heighway (1), Toshack, Callaghan *sub: Lawler*

NEWCASTLE:
McFaul, Clark, Kennedy, McDermott, Howard,
Moncur ©, Smith *(Gibb 70)*, Cassidy,
Macdonald, Tudor, Hibbitt

T hird Division strugglers Brighton, managed by an ill-at-ease Brian Clough, faced a potential first round banana skin with a trip to an Isthmian League side. Brighton were in a mess; an 8-2 defeat by Bristol Rovers had shown that much. They played the first match in near-copybook fashion, keeping it tight and defusing spirited opponents. The replay on their home turf would be a different story. It was. They fell apart. To be beaten 4-0 at home is unfortunate. To be beaten by a hat-trick in ten minutes from a man called Foskett from the stockbroker belt looks like carelessness of the highest order. To be fair to Walton & Hersham, they were holders of a cup won at Wembley. Their victory over Slough Town seven months earlier had won them the FA Amateur Cup. This must have been where Walton's midfield battler Dave Bassett learned to put one over on the big boys.

A hundred miles and more along the south coast at Exeter, Midland Combination team Alvechurch were playing only their second match in the competition proper. To the amazement of all, including themselves, they won it. A late goal by Graham Allner saw them home, and paved the way for a 6-1 thrashing of King's Lynn and the chance of a plum in the third round. Fourth Division Bradford City were more of a damson, and a pretty sour one, emerging 4-2 winners. Alvechurch have never made the first round since.

The plums went to Boston United and Hendon, drawn away at Derby and Newcastle respectively. Both earned fantastic draws away from home, and their opponents looked ripe for a fall. Newcastle still had the memories of Hereford and Luton preying on their minds, and Derby were still rebuilding after Brian Clough's departure the previous year. The ghouls were disappointed; Newcastle won 4-0, Derby 6-1 with the rarity of a hat trick from Archic Gemmill.

Hereford themselves were paired against West Ham for the second time in three years. Again they forced a draw in the first match, but this time their replay chance came at Edgar Street. Successive promotions had leapfrogged Hereford into the Third Division, and proof of their improving pedigree was underlined with a 2-1 win.

It was left to Bolton, 3-2 winners over a talented Stoke team, to provide the round's other surprise. Another hat-trick, from the prolific ex-Blackburn striker John Byrom did the job for the Wanderers.

1973-1974

Third qualifying round: Falmouth Town v Bideford lased for five matches and nine hours before Bideford go through 2-1.

The fourth round followed a similar pattern; nothing seismic, although Second Division Nottingham Forest weren't expected to beat Manchester City, and certainly not 4-1. The honours went to Wrexham, who beat run-away Division Two leaders, Middlesbrough 1-0. Wrexham's finest hour against Arsenal was still eighteen years away, but their largely forgotten effort this season is worth noting. The Middlesbrough triumph was followed by a 1-0 win at First Division Southampton. David Smallman's winner started work on the Saints' coffin; relegation at the end of the season hammered in the final nail.

Liverpool, like many eventual winners, nearly fell at the first. Doncaster, despite two goals from old boy Kevin Keegan, forced a 2-2 draw at Anfield. These rarefied heights eventually proved beyond the Fourth Division side as they lost the replay 2-0. Fortune smiled on Liverpool in the fourth round draw, which paired them at home to Second Division strugglers Carlisle. Again the task nearly proved beyond them, as the red machine choked on a 0-0 draw. Boersma and Toshack used the Reds' get-out-of-jail-free card at Brunton Park. When confronted with Ipswich in round five, opponents of genuine quality, Liverpool raised their game and saw them off comfortably.

1973-1974

On 6 January 1974, four Cup ties kicked off on a Sunday, the first time that any FA Cup match had been played on the Sabbath. The upward curve of attendances was dramatic. Bolton's 3-2 win over Stoke was watched by 40,000, twice the season's average at Burnden Park. Cambridge attracted a season's best 8,479 to the Abbey Stadium for the visit of Oldham.

1973-1974

Alan Mullery's fourth-minute volley at Craven Cottage stunned opponents Leicester and earned the veteran midfielder the BBC's Goal of the Season award. He was almost matched at Luton in the sixth round, when Keith Weller waltzed round the entire Hatters' defence before finishing off Leicester's 4-0 victory in style.

Newcastle were given yet another headache in the fourth round, needing a replay to see off Scunthorpe after drawing at home again. They too responded better to a tougher task, winning 3-0 at Second Division West Brom.

Defeat by Sunderland appeared to have steeled Leeds's resolve. They looked to be walking away with the championship, playing thirty league games before tasting defeat. That Bristol City, lounging around in the lower half of the Second Division, held Leeds to a 1-1 draw was a surprise. That they held them for seventy-three minutes of the replay at Elland Road was even more of a shock. To pinch the game with a Don Gillies' goal was the stuff of screaming headlines. Liverpool succeeded where Leeds failed in round six.

The sixth round saw one of competition's most controversial ties. No, it isn't a misprint. Newcastle were going well in the top half of Division One, and, in

Malcolm MacDonald, boasted (frequently and loudly) one of the most potent strikers in the country. Forest were languishing in the lower reaches of the Second Division, with Brian Clough and salvation two years in the future.

A packed and expectant St James's Park turned up expecting a Newcastle procession. What they witnessed was a skilful and motivated performance from the visitors, who established a 2-1 lead with goals from Ian Bowyer and Liam O'Kane. Midway through the second half, events turned from bad to worse for Newcastle. Firstly, Forest were awarded a penalty. Pat Howard's protests tested the patience of referee Gordon Kew to breaking point and earned him an early bath. After Lyall had converted the spot-kick to put Forest 3-1 up, the Geordie crowd decided that if their team couldn't settle the issue, they would do the job themselves.

A deliberate mass-invasion covered virtually every blade of grass, forcing referee Kew to lead the players from the pitch. After eight minutes they returned, but spectators still ringed the pitch. Forest, having had their concentration broken, were clearly rattled.

A resurgent Newcastle seized their chance. Bobby Moncur pulled one back, McDermott levelled with a contentious penalty given by an understandably nervous referee, and David Craig scored a late winner.

That appeared to be the end of the matter and Newcastle's name entered the velvet bag for the semi-final draw. A furious Forest were not prepared to let it drop. Two days later, they lodged a protest with the FA, who upheld their appeal on 14 March. The judgment argued that the crowd had unfairly influenced the outcome and declared the game null and void. A rematch was ordered on neutral ground.

What would have resulted at St. James' Park, pitch invasion notwithstanding, has been the subject of bitter bar-room reflection in Nottingham. The whole affair was rough justice on Forest, but hooliganism blighted the game in the seventies like no other era before.

Nine days after the original game, the teams lined up at Goodison Park. The last thing this episode needed was the publicity of a replay, which naturally ensured the resulting 0-0 draw. Three days later, they did it all again. Malcolm MacDonald proved the difference, scoring the game's only goal.

After the saga of their sixth round tie with Forest, two goals from Malcolm Macdonald thwarted Burnley's attempt to reach Wembley for the first time in twelve years. For the Magpies, the wait had been even longer. Nineteen years had elapsed since the last of their golden years, when winning the Cup had seemed a regular finale to their season. They would meet Liverpool in the final. Bill Shankly's side had seen off Leicester in a semi-final replay and would start favourites, with the proviso that they could stifle Macdonald and his canny partner, John Tudor. The league matches between the two had been close, a 0-0 draw and a tight 2-1 win for Liverpool at Anfield.

In the event, once Liverpool hit their straps in the second-half, Newcastle were simply overwhelmed. It took nearly an hour for the Reds to break through. Tommy Smith's cross looked to carry no danger, but in an instant Keegan had chested it down and volleyed from twenty yards. Caught off guard, McFaul could only help the ball into the goal. From then on it was one-way traffic. Heighway threaded his way through the inside-right channel, his precise finish eluding the unimpressive McFaul at the far post. With two minutes remaining Heighway's dribble set up Keegan for a tap-in.

For Bill Shankly, it was the perfect parting gift as he announced his retirement from the incessant pressures of management shortly afterwards. His satisfaction at conducting the Kop choir during the lap of honour was evident. Little did he realise the scale of the success that would be built on his foundations. For now, Liverpool's second FA Cup was reward enough.

TAYLOR MADE

THE LAST 16

Ipswich **3** Aston Villa **2**

Derby **0** Leeds **1**

Arsenal (0)(1) **1** Leicester (0)(1) **0**

West Ham **2** QPR **1**

Mansfield **0** Carlisle **1**

Everton **1** Fulham **2**

Birmingham **2** Walsall **1**

Peterborough (1) **0** Middlesbrough (1) **2**

QUARTER FINALS

Ipswich (0)(1)(0) **3** Leeds (0)(1)(0) **2**

Arsenal **0** West Ham **2**

Carlisle **0** Fulham **1**

Birmingham **1** Middlesbrough **0**

SEMI FINALS

Ipswich **1** West Ham **2**
at Stamford Bridge after 0-0 at Villa Park

Fulham **1** Birmingham **0**
at Maine Road after 1-1 at Hillsborough

FINAL, 3 MAY 1975, WEMBLEY

Fulham **0** West Ham United **2**

FULHAM:
Mellor, Cutbush, Lacy, Moore, Fraser. Mullery
©, Conway, Slough, Mitchell, Busby, Barrett
sub: Lloyd

WEST HAM:
Day, McDowell, Tommy Taylor, Lock, Lampard,
Bonds ©, Paddon, Brooking, Jennings, **Alan
Taylor (2)**, Holland *sub: Gould*

his was a great year for the non-leaguers. No less than five entered the fourth round draw: Leatherhead; Wimbledon; Altrincham; Stafford Rangers and Wycombe Wanderers. Although Altricham and Wycombe fell in replays, all emerged with glory.

Wycombe lost at First Division Middlesbrough but conceded the only goal a minute from time in the replay. Altrincham rocked Everton at Goodison Park when John Hughes gave them the lead. The home side were eventually reduced to nine men, after Gary Jones was dismissed and John Connolly was stretchered off with a broken leg. It took a penalty from Dave Clements to rescue them and the rebellion was quelled in the replay courtesy of a 2-0 win. Altrincham became regular participants in the competition proper, and their physical style discomfited more than one league club.

Stafford Rangers won their replay against Rotherham, who became their third league scalp of the season following Stockport and Halifax. A disappointing draw at home to Peterborough proved doubly so when the Posh won through 2-1.

The other non-leaguers didn't need replays. Wimbledon had Mickey Mahon in their ranks, a man who had played for Colchester in their remarkable win against Leeds. It was Mahon who came up with winner at First Division Burnley, but the key to the win was the tactical shackling of Burnley's star, winger Leighton James. The uncompromising Dave Bassett played almost as second full-back and gave James some of his own special brand of t.l.c.. Wimbledon produced even greater heroics in the next round, a tie they eventually lost. To be drawn at champions Leeds was a prospect at which most First Division teams would have baulked. The Dons, in a style that was to serve them well in the years ahead, simply gave it a go. They held Leeds for eighty-two minutes, and then looked destined for the 'plucky' headlines as the home side won a penalty. Lorimer's spot kicks normally carried goalkeeper and ball into the net but on this occasion Dons' keeper Dickie Guy, who was inspired throughout the Cup run, pushed a tame effort around his right-hand post to hand Wimbledon a memorable draw.

Nearly 46,000 packed Selhurst Park for the replay, where rough justice was meted out. Wimbledon went out to a shot from Johnny Giles that took a cruel deflection off Bassett. 'Harry', and Wimbledon, would be back.

Leatherhead had already knocked out another Third

At the end of the season, Bremner's entire club were banned for four years by UEFA after rioting fans wrecked the Parc des Princes stadium during Leeds's defeat in the European Cup final by Bayern Munich.

1974-1975

Division side, Colchester, so went to Brighton with high hopes. The public were introduced to the 'Leatherhead Lip', a cocky centre forward called Chris Kelly. The rent-a-quote striker proved a tabloids' dream and filled the back pages with his winner at Brighton. Leatherhead's victory earned them a trip to Leicester, where a stunned Filbert Street witnessed the visitors leave the pitch at half-time with a two-goal lead. A buoyant Kelly had notched the second, but that was as good as it got. Leicester powered back to take the tie 3-2 but they had received the fright of their lives. Kelly's non-league obscurity didn't last for long – he signed for Millwall four days later.

The non-league upstarts' feats diverted attention from really big teams who sauntered through that third round. Both Manchester teams went out; City to Newcastle, United, embarrassingly, to Walsall. These weren't great sides, though; City were on the slide and United were suffering their only season in Division Two since 1938. Walsall added Newcastle's scalp in the next round before succumbing in a local derby against Birmingham. These were odd times for Newcastle; this was their third embarrassment in four years with a final sandwiched in between.

An equally poor Tottenham side also came a cropper. Nottingham Forest were having a horrible season near the bottom of the second division. At the start of the campaign Brian Clough had an eventful forty-four days as manager of Leeds. Clough took over at Forest just in time for a third round replay at Tottenham and had an instant effect; Forest's 1-0 win was one of the results of the year. Forest played four games in the next round before losing a third replay to Fulham. 'Old Big 'Ead' was clearly disgruntled

In a curious break with tradition, 'Abide with Me' was not sung before the final. After much protest, it was reinstated the following year.

1974-1975

after the third stalemate. 'If nobody wins this on Monday, we ought to line up the players and shoot them,' was his typically unceremonious verdict.

The eventual winners, West Ham, progressed by winning two London derbies in rounds five and six. They saw off a talented QPR side before facing Arsenal at Highbury. They chose this stage to unveil their secret weapon, Alan Taylor. The 'Rochdale whippet' had joined the Hammers from his local club three months earlier. At Highbury, he helped himself to two goals against one of the poorest Arsenal sides anyone could remember.

Their semi-final opponents were Ipswich. Bobby Robson's team were a growing force in the game, and they would push hard for the title before being edged into third by Derby, the winners, and Liverpool. Ipswich were doing all the hard work in the competition. Wolves, Liverpool, Aston Villa (promoted from the Second Division along with Man United at the end of the season) and Leeds was hardly a cakewalk to the semis. A goal from full-back Mick Mills did for Liverpool and after three draws yielded only two goals, a 3-2 win at Filbert

The season began and ended badly. The showpiece opener, the FA Charity Shield between Leeds and Liverpool, was shown on live TV for the first time. So thousands of people saw Kevin Keegan and Billy Bremner sent off for fighting and then compound their offence by throwing away their shirts as they left the pitch. Football was coming under pressure for its bad image, so the FA responded with an eleven-game ban for both the culprits. Bremner's crime was slightly the more heinous; younger viewers should never have been exposed to his deathly pale and rather weedy torso.

Street saw them deny Leeds another crack at the trophy. Whymark, Woods and Hamilton were the scorers, all integral parts of Ipswich's finest era. The semi-final against West Ham produced another replay, but at Stamford Bridge Ipswich, like Arsenal, were undone by the tyro Taylor, who scored two more in a narrow 2-1 win.

Their Wembley opponents, Second Division Fulham, had reached their first final by quietly taking out good opposition. After a win over Hull, and the marathon against Forest, Fulham were given a tougher assignment at Goodison Park. Viv Busby was the two-goal hero at Everton and young striker John Mitchell rose to the occasion in the semi-final against Birmingham. He fired the opener at Hillsborough with a sumptuous volley, and bagged the winner in a tense 1-0 win at Maine Road in the replay. There were just seconds remaining when Mitchell's winner squeezed Fulham into the final.

The Wembley build-up centred on Fulham veterans Alan Mullery and Bobby Moore, an unexpected swansong for two illustrious pros playing out the added time of their careers. The fairy story that would have been their winners' medals was rewritten by Alan Taylor. Showing a natural striker's instinct, Taylor pounced twice when Peter Mellor couldn't hold onto stinging shots, and London pride was confined to the East End.

1975

SAINTS IN HEAVEN

1976

MAN UTD:
Stepney, Forsyth, Houston, Daly, Brian Greenhoff, Buchan ©, Coppell, McIlroy, Pearson, Macari, Hill *(McCreery 66)*

SOUTHAMPTON:
Turner, Rodrigues ©, Peach, Holmes, Blyth, Steele, Gilchrist, Channon, Osgood, McCalliog, **Stokes** (1) *sub:* Fisher

'The other semi-final is a bit of a joke, really,' said Manchester United manager Tommy Docherty, as his team braced themselves for a tie with Derby, leaving Second Division Southampton and Crystal Palace to contest the other place at Wembley. To the undiluted joy of anyone who enjoyed seeing an obnoxious big-head made to eat his words, they turned to ashes in the final. The First Division was put to the sword. Only four of its members survived until the quarter-finals and the top flight failed to provide the trophy's winners for only the second time since the war.

The fun started before the big boys even took their place in the draw. Here's the first round roll-call of honour:

Seventies Cup heroes Colchester took their turn at a sheepish exit, becoming the first and only league scalp for Dover Athletic, thumped 4-1 in a replay. Southport joined them; perennial strugglers, they would cede their league place to Wigan a couple of years later. A 4-1 defeat at Spennymoor United of the Northern League probably hastened their departure. Former league club Gateshead restored some pride with a 3-1 win at Third Division Grimsby. Reading, near the top of the fourth, lost to the only goal at Isthmian League Hendon. Compared to these shocks, Leatherhead beating Cambridge barely got on the radar. Cambridge's manager, former Oxford cup hero Ron Atkinson, would have to wait until the following year to get his mojo working, when Cambridge stormed two divisions in successive seasons.

One of the finest goals of this campaign was scored by a non-league player. Marine's Bill Morrey dribbled down the wing from the half-way line. Just when he appeared to have run the ball out of play, he curled the ball into the net from near the corner flag. It helped Marine knock out Fourth Division Barnsley 3-1.

The *Palme d'Or* of the round went to the conquerors of Tranmere. Like Reading, Tranmere were nestling at the top end of the fourth, but couldn't cope with Coventry at Highfield Road. So what? It was Coventry Sporting of the West Midlands Regional League, borrowing their more illustrious neighbours ground for the day. It was the only time the amateur side ever made it into the fourth round draw. They must have had such fun.

In the circumstances, maybe the biggest shock of the round was Yeovil failing to beat Millwall! Not that the Lions had it easy; they finally wrapped up the tie in a second replay at Aldershot.

Sadly, none of these teams lasted beyond the next

round, although Gateshead took Rochdale to a replay. It was left to Scarborough to carry the baton into the Third Round. Having seen off Morecambe in a seaside Roses match, they saw off another Lancastrian team, the once-mighty Preston, in round two.

They were joined in the third round by Tooting & Mitcham. Having scrapped past Romford and local rivals Leatherhead, they found themselves 2-0 down at Swindon within five minutes of the start but forced a replay with two in the last four. At Sandy Lane Alan Ives covered them in glory with the winner in a 2-1 victory. T&M's manager was Roy Dwight, who scored for Forest, won a winner's medal and broke his leg in the 1959 Final. (Remember? Elton's uncle?)

Baton passing often happens in the Cup; a team beats a giant-killer, and then seizes the initiative to achieve glory themselves. Scarborough's conquerors were Crystal Palace, managed by former Manchester City boss, Malcolm Allison.

The lasting image of this season's competition was Big Mal's fedora. The ex-Manchester City boss may have been reduced to managing a Third Division club, but you couldn't keep him away from the limelight for long. Victories against Walton and Hersham, Millwall and Scarborough were hardly the stuff of headlines, but success at Elland Road in the fourth round changed all that. The sight of Big Mal parading before away fans, gesturing his forecast of the impending victory, would today have ensured his conviction on incitement to riot charges. In the gauche days of the seventies, it was all part of the entertainment. The first indication that a post-Revie Leeds were yesterday's men came with this mugging at the hands of Allison's side. Dave Swindlehurst's header continued a famous run.

Chelsea were next. Another team in decline, they were enduring a treading-water season in Division Two. In the Cup, they drowned in front of over 50,000 at Stamford Bridge, flying winger Peter Taylor scoring twice in a 3-2 Palace win. Sunderland must have been dreaming of the heroics of three seasons earlier when they drew a Third Division side in the sixth round but their glory hunting was snuffed out by a single goal from Alan Whittle.

By the semi-finals South London hopes were high that the Eagles could become the first Third Division side to reach the FA Cup final, as they avoided the big guns. Back at Stamford Bridge,

1975-1976

two Southampton goals from Paul Gilchrist and David Peach ensured that Palace would not repeat their success of two rounds earlier.

Southampton had already pooped one party in the round before. Bradford City were only a Fourth Division side, but a previously kind draw saw them up against Norwich in the fifth round. The Canaries had won promotion to the top flight in 1975, and were already through to the League Cup final. Bradford were flat broke and not very good. The tie was twice postponed, as the Bantams were laid low by a flu virus. Never slow with an ill-advised quote, Norwich boss John Bond sneered that Bradford's inability to raise a team should jeopardise their league status. Goals from Bradford's Don Hutchins and Billy McGinlay made him eat his words; Villa scuppered his chances of silverware a week later by winning the League Cup.

While Southampton sneaked through against modest opposition, the big sides were carving each other up. Holders West Ham fell to Liverpool at the first hurdle. Derby beat Everton at the same stage and made it a Merseyside double in round four. With Charlie George added to a championship-winning side, Derby were a tough prospect. A sixth round demolition of Newcastle proved the point. 4-2 flattered Newcastle; Derby scored four outstanding goals, one of them a trademark rocket of a free-kick from Scotland international Bruce Rioch.

Manchester United faced them after seeing off Leicester and Wolves, but it took extra-time in a replay for them to pull through at Molineux, Stuart Pearson's winner settling affairs. United's 2-0 win in the semi-final was a bit of an anti-climax to an eagerly awaited match, a double from Gordon Hill seeing the reds home. United had won the 'real cup final' as Docherty put it.

United were amongst the hottest of Wembley favourites. The Red Devils finished only four points off the pace in their first season back in the big time. That their failure was not greeted with the open-mouthed astonishment that received Leeds's defeat to Sunderland was down to the nous of their opponents.

Despite their inferior league status, Southampton were an experienced team and in Channon, Osgood and McCalliog had canniness to spare. United were hugely talented but were a younger side with limited experience of big matches. Saints endured only sporadic pressure from a younger and more nervous United, and then stole the game eight minutes from time when Bobby Stokes's precise angled shot eluded Alex Stepney and sneaked into the far corner.

Still, why should Docherty care? United had already won the 'real' cup final.

For the Saints, whose last final in 1900 had ended in 4-0 ignominy at the hands of Bury, it had been worth the wait.

Wembley, 5th May 1956. Play is delayed whilst Manchester City keeper Bert Trautmann receives treatment. He soldiered on as City beat Birmingham 3–1, only to be later diagnosed with a broken neck. (Getty Images)

Wembley, 3th May 1958. Bolton manager Bill Ridding (left) serves a celebratory tipple to centre-forward Nat Lofthouse after Wanderers' 2–0 victory over Manchester United. Lofthouse had earned it, scoring both goals. (Empics/PA)

7th May 1960. The Wembley 'hoodoo' strikes again, as Blackburn's Dave Whelan is stretchered off after breaking his leg in a challenge with Wolves' winger Norman Deeley. Whelan never played again, but realised a handsome profit on his compensation. He now boasts a multi-million-pound business empire and owns Wigan Athletic. (Colorsport)

Wembley, 6th May 1961. Tottenham's players celebrate the century's first Double after beating Leicester 2–0.

(Colorsport)

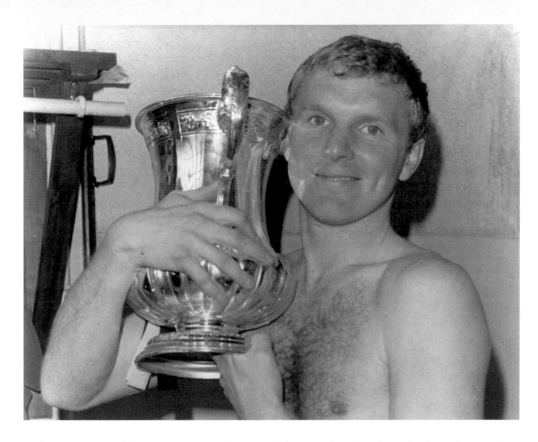

2nd May 1964. Bobby Moore covets West Ham's first trophy after they edged out Preston 3–2 in a thrilling final. The FA Cup was the first of three trophies Moore collected at Wembley in consecutive years. Twelve months later he lifted the Cup Winners' Cup, then led England to World Cup glory the following season. (Colorsport)

Wembley, 11th April 1970. A rare moment of bonhomie in the 1970 final, as Leeds' Eddie Gray (left) bonds with Chelsea's Charlie Cooke at the end of a pulsating 2–2 draw. The replay at Old Trafford eighteen days later is widely regarded as the dirtiest final ever. Chelsea won it 2–1 in extra time.
(Getty Images)

Wembley, 8th May 1971. Charlie George lies prostrate after firing Arsenal's winner against Liverpool. Arsenal had come from behind in extra time to snatch the trophy. (Getty Images)

Wembley, 5th May 1973. Sunderland's skipper Bobby Kerr is hugged by manager Bob Stokoe after his team had provided one of the FA Cup's biggest shocks. Sunderland, then a second-division club, had beaten the mighty Leeds 1–0 to win their first trophy in forty-six years. (Getty Images)

Wembley, 18th May 1985. A disbelieving Kevin Moran (centre) is sent off by referee Peter Willis and becomes the first player to be dismissed in an FA Cup Final. Bryan Robson (left) rushes to his defence, whilst John Gidman (no.2) and Gordon Strachan (no.8) look on helplessly. (Coloursport)

Wembley, 20th May 1989. Ian Rush celebrates yet another goal against Everton, as Neil McDonald (no.2) experiences a familiar sinking feeling. Rush's double helped Liverpool defeat their rivals 3–2 after extra time, repeating the dose he served up three years earlier against the same club. For good measure, he bagged another against Sunderland in the 1992 final. (Colorsport)

Layer Road, Colchester, 13th February 1971. A despondent Gary Sprake (far left), Paul Reaney (kneeling) and Eddie Gray (no.11) watch aghast as fourth-division Colchester score again. The home side's 3–2 victory in their fifth-round tie was one of the biggest upsets for years. (Empics)

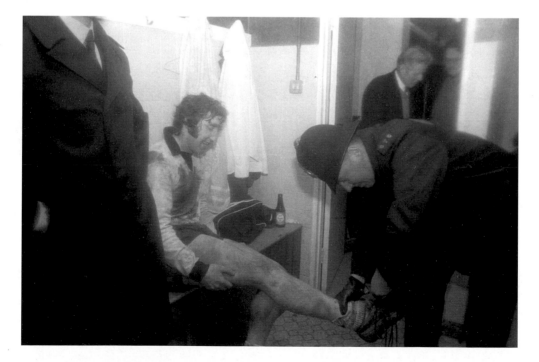

Below: Edgar Street, Hereford, 5th February 1972. Even the constabulary paid homage after non-League Hereford dumped out first-division Newcastle in a third-round replay. Billy Meadows feels the long arm of the law. (Empics/PA)

The Racecourse Ground, Wrexham, 4th January 1992. Mickey Thomas smashes home a late free kick as lowly Wrexham humble league champions Arsenal in a third-round encounter. (Empics/PA)

St James' Park, Exeter, 19th January 2005. Exeter City players huddle before their third-round replay with Manchester United. The Grecians had already created this century's biggest Cup headline by holding United 0–0 at Old Trafford. Although they lost the replay 2–0, the extra revenue threw a lifeline to this cash-strapped club. The FA Cup has often provided financial salvation for smaller teams. (Empics)

The Millennium Stadium, Cardiff, 12th May 2001. Michael Owen (left) watches his 88th-minute strike elude the diving David Seaman (right) and win the Cup for Liverpool. Arsenal had led but were undone by two late goals. (Colorsport)

The Millennium Stadium, Cardiff, 21st May 2005. Arsenal's players and fans celebrate Patrick Vieira's winning penalty. In the first final to be decided by a shoot-out, the Gunners sneaked home 5–4 against Manchester United after being outplayed during 120 scoreless minutes of open play. For Vieira, it was his last kick in an Arsenal shirt. (Getty Images)

REMEDY FOR THE DOC

LIVERPOOL:
Clemence, Neal, Jones, Smith, Kennedy, Hughes ©, Keegan, **Case (1)**, Heighway, Johnson *(Callaghan 64)*, McDerrmott

MAN UTD:
Stepney, Nicholl, Albiston, McIlroy, Brian Greenhoff, Buchan ©, Coppell, Jimmy **Greenhoff (1)**, **Pearson (1)**, Macari, Hill *(McCreery 81)*

outhampton were in determined mood. The holders, despite their continued Second Division status, proved that they were in no mood to give up their trophy without a fight. Promotion-chasing Chelsea were sent packing 3-0 at Stamford Bridge, then fellow hopefuls Forest were beaten 2-1 in a replay at the Dell. The first match at the City Ground had been a classic ebb-and-flow Cup tie which finished 3-3. Saints' scorers were an advert for experience over youth – Alan Ball, Mick Channon and Peter Osgood. Forest's scorers reflected the future; two from John Robertson and one from Tony Woodcock. Clough's team were taking shape; they would scrape promotion at the end of the season.

Now came the Saints' greatest test, the visit of Manchester United in a replay of the final from the year before. The first match was a blood-and-thunder affair with nothing to choose between the teams. The holders eventually succumbed to the eventual winners with two goals from Jimmy Greenhoff. The United striker's goals would prove crucial, as he was to score the winner in both semi-final and final.

For the most part, the top sides avoided slipping up against modest opposition. Only Sunderland, newly pro-moted, came a cropper. They discovered their own Achilles heel in Wrexham, two divisions below them. A goal from Billy Ashcroft dumped them out.

The latter round belonged exclusively to the big boys. Of the last eight, only Wolves were from outside the top division, and they won division two. Liverpool were scenting a treble. Bob Paisley was building on Shankly's legacy to create a side whose dominance would be unprecedented in the English game. Four home draws had provided their springboard to the semis. At Maine Road they faced an Everton side desperate to maintain local pride. They would have won it, but for the customary, publicity-seeking meddling by referee Clive Thomas.

The match had been a thriller, making it doubly irk-some that it was spoiled at the death. Bryan Hamilton timed his forward dart to perfection, deflecting a curl-ing, near-post cross to apparently win it 3-2. With the linesman motionless, Thomas blew up. His post-match blustering claimed that Hamilton must have handled, but admitted that he hadn't seen the 'infringement.' Everton had been robbed. Liverpool were in no mood to hand them a second chance in the replay. Manchester United would meet them; they reached their second successive final after the customary battle against Leeds at

Hillsborough. Goals from Steve Coppell and Jimmy Greenhoff gave Docherty's maturing side the win.

After this huge slice of luck, Liverpool's name looked on the Cup, but it deserted them in the final. After a limp first half, the game burst to life with three goals in five minutes at the start of the second. Case's splendid shot on the turn had cancelled out Pearson's opener, but when Macari fluffed a close-range shot three minutes later, United's chance to strike back immediately looked to have gone. Instead of spinning harmlessly wide, the Scot's shot hit an unsuspecting Jimmy Greenhoff on the chest, before arcing gently past Clemence into the net.

For Tommy Docherty, who had managed Chelsea to the final ten years earlier, this was his first and only Wembley triumph. His joy at landing United's first Cup in fourteen years was to be very short-lived.

The non-league teams gave a good account of themselves again, six of them seeing off league teams in the first round. The introduction of automatic promotion from the Conference curtailed this activity, as the persistent 'giant-killers' were able to take the place of the poorer Division Four sides without the self-serving protectionism of the re-election procedure.

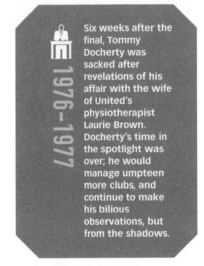

A good example of this was the defeat of Workington, an abysmal side, by Southern League Wimbledon. The only surprise was Workington keeping it to 1-0. Wimbledon were clearly the better team, and justice was done when they took Workington's league place the following year. The assault on Olympus had begun.

Leatherhead did their usual trick and took out a league side, but that hardly constituted a shock; Northampton were struggling at the foot of the Third Division having been promoted the year before. Leatherhead were a persistent thorn in the seventies. They would meet Wimbledon in round two, with the Dons easing to a comfortable 3-1 away win. Next up, just as Wycombe had done two years earlier, Wimbledon forced a goalless draw with Middlesbrough before losing 1-0.

Their Southern League colleagues Hillingdon Borough and Minehead both pulled off excellent away wins, at Swansea and Torquay respectively. Neither got past the next round. Portsmouth and Watford, temporarily slumming it in the lower divisons, saw to that.

Kettering Town's player-manager was former Northern Ireland international, Derek Dougan, who had appeared in the final as long ago as 1960 with Blackburn Rovers. His side looked to have given their all in the first

1976-1977

match, a 1-1 draw. Dougan clearly decided that if you want a job done, it's best to do it yourself. He duly scored the winner in the replay.

Matlock Town avenged a first round thrashing by Wigan the previous season, beating their Northern Premier League rivals 2-0. The goals were scored by two of the three Fenoughty brothers playing for the club. There was player-manager Tom, Mick, and Nick, a lively forward. It was Nick Fenoughty who put Mansfield Town to the sword in round two, scoring twice in a 5-2 win, a remarkable scoreline given that Mansfield hadn't been beaten at home for over a year. A draw against Carlisle was a miserable result in the next round; a 5-1 thrashing was even more difficult to bear.

The season's great non-league survivors were Northwich Victoria. They started off with Rochdale, winning a second replay 2-1 at Maine Road. No great surprise, as Rochdale were perennial whipping-boys for non-league sides. Peterborough were significantly better than Rochdale and were leading 1-0 when the first attempt at playing the match was abandoned due to fog. Northwich had obviously learnt a lot about their opponents in a mere twenty minutes – they won the rescheduled game 4-0. A disappointing draw saw them at home to Watford, but they had another sniff of payola when they beat the Hornets 3-2. The Cheshire side scooped their well-deserved pay-day by again switching their fourth round tie against Second Division Oldham to Maine Road. They were rewarded by a 29,000 attendance.

OSBORNE TAKES THE BISCUIT

Recent giant-killers found themselves on the receiving end this year. Wimbledon and Hereford had both earned their league status due to recent Cup exploits. Now they were dumped out in the first round by their former peers. Enfield stuffed the Dons 3-0 and Hereford lost 3-2 at home to Wealdstone. The rich vein of non-league wins was drying up – even Leatherhead lost their first round replay at Swansea.

There was always Rochdale to offer succour to the needy, and Scarborough accepted it gleefully by winning 4-2 and then seeing off Crewe in a replay. A rapidly improving Brighton team, approaching their heyday, were too strong in the third round, winning 3-0. Wigan's Cup followed a similar pattern. Their last season as a non-league team saw them enhance their claims for election by beating York and Sheffield Wednesday, a team in sorry decline. Southport's defeat to non-league Runcorn did Wigan a favour, and they duly took the place of the Fourth Division's perennial strugglers the following year.

Oxford, like Rochdale, exited red-faced for the second year running. Nuneaton Borough took only their second ever league scalp, but then crashed disappointingly against Tilbury, giving the docks' team their only foray into the 'big' draw. It worked out well for them with a good crowd guaranteed at Second Division Stoke. The result worked out less well; Stoke won 4-0.

One team remained to carry the flag for the non-leaguers. Blyth Spartans' journey began in earnest in the second round, when they accounted for Third Division Chesterfield 1-0. The excitement of the third round draw was snuffed out, as they were paired with Enfield from the Isthmian League. With only two other non-league sides in a draw containing sixty-four clubs, it was cruel luck on both. Alan Shoulder scored the only goal to leave the North London side cursing their misfortune. The fourth round draw sent Spartans to the Victoria Ground, where Stoke were waiting to dish out the same treatment they had handed to Tilbury.

If Spartans were over-awed, then it didn't show. Terry Johnson looked to the manor born as he fired them in front after ten minutes. Viv Busby and Garth Crooks appeared to have resumed normal service for Stoke but Spartans equalised deep into the second half through Steve Carney. With two minutes remaining, Terry Johnson grabbed his second of the game to send them into the last 16.

By rights, this was the game that should have seen

Spartans into the last eight. Terry Johnson scored what had become a customary early goal after seizing on an appalling back pass. Roared on by an enormous travelling support, they held on until the eighty-ninth minute when Wrexham were wrongly awarded a corner. The kick was easily dealt with but referee Alf Grey ordered a re-take on the grounds that the corner flag had fallen over! Astonishingly, the re-take produced the exact same sequence. With the flag now upright, the third corner was headed in at the back post by 'Dixie' McNeill. We'll never know Mr Grey's motivations, but it was an inexplicable and disreputable decision, and deprived Blyth of a place in football history as the first non-league team to reach the sixth round.

Spartans won a victory of sorts before a ball was kicked. The game had been switched to St. James's Park, and such was the Geordie public's enthusiasm that 42,000 had swarmed in half-an-hour before the kick-off, leaving an estimated 15,000 fans locked out. For once the occasion overwhelmed the apparently nerveless non-leaguers. A Whittle penalty and a second from McNeil put the game out of reach, despite the redoubtable Johnson's strike seven minutes from time. At the final whistle, Spartans' received a richly deserved standing ovation from the Newcastle fans.

Part of the reason for the passionate support for Blyth was love of the underdog. The other part was that Wrexham had already visited St James's Park once that season. Two goals from McNeil, a prolific centre forward for a short period, earned the Welsh side a draw and two more in the replay helped them to a 4-1 win over the Geordies. No wonder the Toon were shouting for Blyth! Newcastle had been Wrexham's second top flight victims. Bristol City had been easily beaten at the Racecourse as well after an extraordinary 4-4 draw at Ashton Gate.

Crystal Palace had been London's underdogs two years ago. Now the mantle passed to Orient. The Second Division side punched above their weight by knocking out First Division Norwich and Chelsea, both after being held at Brisbane Road. This was a particularly galling result for Chelsea. They had beaten champions Liverpool in the third round with a scintillating performance, especially from winger Clive Walker, who scored twice and made a fool of England full-back Phil Neal. A 6-2 demolition of Burnley followed and it looked as if the Blues were in business.

They reckoned without Orient's secret weapon, Peter Kitchen. He finished the campaign with seven of his side's nine goals, including both in the 2-1 win at Stamford Bridge. After putting paid to another top-flight team,

Two divisions may have separated Newcastle and Wrexham that year, but the following season they met in the league. Newcastle were relegated and Wrexham won Division Three. Their stars were McNeil and a tricky young winger called Mickey Thomas, later of Manchester United and Chelsea. Thomas, a cocky, but likeable, character would later serve time for dealing in forged currency. Now, about those corner flags, Mickey . . .

Middlesbrough in the sixth round, the O's first semi-final saw Arsenal barring their path to the dreamland of Wembley.

This was threatening to be a season of 'lucky' Arsenal. Walsall, Wrexham and Orient was hardly the most testing run to the final, yet even against Orient they needed slices of fortune. Despite the 3-0 scoreline, outrageous deflections played a part in two of the goals. Their finest moment was 1-0 away win in the fifth round against eventual champions Nottingham Forest.

Facing the Gunners at Wembley were Ipswich, making their first final appearance. Bobby Robson's side had been one of the teams of the decade, but this league season had been an odd glitch, and eighteenth place in the league ensured the Suffolk side started as underdogs. The pre-match odds ignored the fact that Ipswich's Cup run had been of a far higher standard than their opponents. They had avoided a potential banana skin at Cardiff, and had brushed aside the hostile atmosphere at the Den to crush Millwall 6-1 in the quarter-finals with a hat-trick from England centre forward, Paul Mariner. Their finest performance, in another portent of doom for Arsenal, came at Highbury in the semis. In a crunching encounter, they battled toe-to-toe with an excellent West Brom side before prevailing 3-1. Brian Talbot scored Ipswich's opener with a diving header but knew precious little about it. He was concussed while scoring in a clash of heads with John Wile. The Albion skipper fared even worse, playing the rest of the game with blood seeping from a heavily-bandaged skull. Further goals from captain Mick Mills and the young Scots midfielder John Wark saw Ipswich making their Cup Final debut.

The final started brightly and, for a while, the first-half threatened to buck the trend of cagey openings. It proved a false dawn as the game lapsed into scrap and stalemate. Arsenal, despite a resurgence of league form, looked off colour. With thirteen minutes left, their position became terminal. Clive Woods jinked down the right and fed David Geddis. The blond striker eluded Sammy Nelson and centred a low cross which squirted off the outstretched boot of Willie Young. Roger Osborne, twelve yards out, sent a low drive past Jennings. Osborne had to be substituted after scoring. The official reason was 'nervous exhaustion.' Osbourne had been so overwhelmed by the euphoria of the moment that he was close to collapse. Bless!

For Bobby Robson this was an overdue first trophy after years of near misses, although the league continued to elude him, the English one at any rate.

THE FIVE MINUTE FINAL

ARSENAL:
Jennings, Rice ©, Nelson, **Talbot (1)**, Young,
O'Leary, Brady, **Sunderland (1)**, **Stapleton
(1)**, Price, Rix *(Walford 83)*

MAN UTD:
Bailey, Nicholl, Albiston, **McIlroy (1)**,
McQueen (1), Buchan ©, Coppell, Jimmy
Greenhoff, Jordan, Macari, Thomas *sub: Brian
Greenhoff*

Arsenal were to finish the decade as they started it, with an efficient if unspectacular team bringing home the silverware. Typically, it proved a slog.

When the Gunners hosted Notts County in the fourth round, it was their sixth game of the competition. All the previous five had been against Third Division Sheffield Wednesday, a team they faced five times in seventeen days. The last three replays saw both teams carving up neutral Filbert Street before goals from Steve Gatting (brother of future England cricket captain Mike) and Frank Stapleton produced a collective sigh of relief. The marathon contrived increasingly entertaining matches. After a pair of 1-1 draws, the next two finished 2-2 and 3-3. It was tough on Brian Hornsby, who scored three goals in the tie and finished a loser. In all Wednesday played nine FA Cup ties this season; winning two, drawing six and losing one.

Smaller fish than Wednesday also proved difficult to land. Non-league Maidstone hopped up the A2 to frighten Charlton at the Valley before falling 2-1 in front of a record five-figure home attendance in the replay. Altrincham nearly caused a sensation at White Hart Lane, forcing a 1-1 draw only for Colin Lee's hat-trick to burst their bubble. Altrincham's robust, highly physical game was at odds with the affluent, leafy Manchester suburb that housed them. Their goal at Spurs was scored by Jeff Johnson. A club legend and long-time servant, he was no mean player, winning eighteen semi-pro England caps.

West Ham were having a breather in the Second Division, but that was no excuse for a shocking performance at Newport, where they lost 2-1.

Shrewsbury Town were on a roll, pushing for promotion from Division Three, and altogether up for the Cup. City viewed the bone-hard, frostbitten pitch and tightly-packed Gay Meadow as though it were a Channel swim in November. Their humiliation was recorded by the cameras, Maguire and Chapman's goals becoming an oft-repeated sequence on Football Focus.

In the fifth round Shrewsbury met Aldershot, who broke new ground by venturing that far. The Shots had seen off Sheffield United in a replay then Third Division Swindon. They matched Shrewsbury in the first game, a tense 2-2, but a pair from Wayne Biggins put paid to their hopes in the replay.

By the quarter-finals, the First Division has asserted its authority. Only Shrewsbury flew the underdogs' flag. They forced a brave draw at Molineux and had the thrill of rubbing shoulders with Manchester United, Arsenal and Spurs in the semi-final draw. The task of winning rather than simply defending proved beyond them in the replay. Despite feverish excitement at Gay Meadow, Wanderers picked them off 3-1.

The semi-final line-ups produced four sides steeped in Cup tradition. At Villa Park, Stapleton and Sunderland tamed Wolves without undue alarm.

By contrast, blood and thunder were the order of the day at Maine Road. In a magnificent game, goals from Kenny Dalglish and a rare strike from Alan Hansen were cancelled out by efforts from Joe Jordan and Brian Greenhoff. In the replay at Goodison Park, tension replaced action. A single goal from Jimmy Greenhoff, Liverpool's Cup scourge for the second time in three years, sent United to their third final in four attempts.

If this final had lasted for eighty-five minutes, it would have been recorded merely as a statistic. As with most finals the burden of the occasion made free-flowing football a rarity and no individual player would decorate their CV with a memorable performance. By half-time the game looked a non-event. Although a two-goal margin flattered Arsenal, they had at least exploited the meagre scoring opportunities that had come their way. United were fielding a rookie keeper in Gary Bailey, but it was the naivety of his defence that allowed Stapleton to thread a pass to the unmarked David Price after twelve minutes. The advancing midfielder drew the keeper before squaring to the onrushing Alan Sunderland and Brian Talbot. Such was their eagerness to unwrap the gift that they virtually tackled each other. Talbot got the touch.

Maidstone's Third Round exploits at Charlton threw another spotlight on goalkeeper Dickie Guy. Wimbledon's hero of '75 took another burst of the limelight in customary phlegmatic fashion.

1978-1979

As half-time approached, it was unwise of United to gift Liam Brady space on the right. To allow the game's deadliest crosser to find the unguarded head of one of the aerial game's finest exponents was downright negligent. Frank Stapleton duly made it 2-0. United's game looked well and truly up.

The second-half was largely a matter of Arsenal running down the clock. With seven minutes left Graham Rix was swapped for the extra ballast of Steve Walford. This apparently innocuous move served only to trip the Gunners up. It nearly overturned them completely.

When centre-half Gordon McQueen, still loitering in the opposing penalty area after a free-kick, turned in Joe Jordan's centre with four minutes remaining, Arsenal's

Liverpool even had a hiccough in the third round. Southend, in a rearguard action worthy of Rorke's Drift, held them 0-0 at Roots Hall before falling valiantly at Anfield to goals from Case, Dalglish and Ray Kennedy.

1978-1979

Arsenal and Sheffield Wednesday have met each other in twelve FA Cup ties. Half have been played on neutral ground, including three of their five games this season.

1978-1979

1978-1979

Comment from the losing finalists:
'It was like picking eight draws and finding the pools coupon still in your pocket.' Sammy McIlroy, having hauled United back into the game with the equaliser, sums up that sinking feeling.'

panic button was pressed. Two minutes later they were mesmerised by a dribble from Sammy McIlroy, who left David O'Leary and Walford as mere spectators before toe-ending the ball under a charging and unusually rattled Pat Jennings. The ball trickled like a flat-green wood approaching the jack before settling inside his right-hand post.

United celebrated as though they had won the Cup. Within a minute, Arsenal had. Brady summoned up one last turn of pace down the left wing. His beautifully arced cross fell beyond the fingertips of Bailey, landing perfectly on to Sunderland's right boot. A sliding touch and the net billowed. Millions lip-read the scorer's Anglo-Saxon expression of relief and glee. Wembley hadn't seen a final like it since Matthews and Morty in 1953.

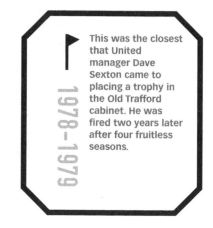

1978-1979

This was the closest that United manager Dave Sexton came to placing a trophy in the Old Trafford cabinet. He was fired two years later after four fruitless seasons.

1979

ON YER 'EAD, TREV!

1980

THE LAST 16

Wolves **0**	Watford **3**
Bolton (1) **0**	Arsenal (1) **3**
Tottenham **3**	Birmingham **1**
Liverpool **2**	Bury **0**
Everton **5**	Wrexham **2**
Ipswich **2**	Chester **1**
West Ham **2**	Swansea **0**
Blackburn (1) **0**	Aston Villa (1) **1**

QUARTER FINALS

Watford **1**	Arsenal **2**
Tottenham **0**	Liverpool **1**
Everton **2**	Ipswich **1**
West Ham **1**	Aston Villa **0**

SEMI FINALS

Arsenal **1**	Liverpool **0**

*at Highfield Road after 0-0 at Hillsborough,
then 1-1 and 1-1 again at Villa Park*

Everton **1**	West Ham **2**

at Elland Road after 1-1 at Villa Park

FINAL, 10 MAY, WEMBLEY

Arsenal **0**	West Ham United **1**

ARSENAL:
Jennings, Rice ©, Devine *(Nelson 61)*, Talbot,
Young, O'Leary, Brady, Sunderland, Stapleton,
Price, Rix

WEST HAM:
Parkes, Stewart, Lampard, Bonds ©, Martin,
Devonshire, Paul Allen, Pearson, Cross,
Brooking (1), Pike *sub: Brush*

The rash of non-league victories in the seventies dried up as the competition moved into a new decade. Yeovil, inevitably, made the third round draw, but only by beating other non-league teams, and they were easily knocked out by Norwich.

Altrincham's muscular football saw them beat Crewe 3-0 and grab an excellent away win at Third Division Rotherham. It took Second Division Orient two games to make them lie down. At the end of the season Altrincham were a whisper away from joining the league; Rochdale clung on by just one vote at re-election.

Harlow Town of the Isthmian League were in the competition proper for the first time. The second round, after a win over Leytonstone & Ilford from their own league, saw them draw Southend United, no great shakes near the bottom of the Third Division. A 1-1 draw at Roots Hall, and finish the job at Harlow was the order of the day. They applied the same clinical process to a much tougher assignation with Leicester City, a team who would win Division Two that season. The names of Neil Prosser and John MacKenzie passed into Essex folklore after these displays. Prosser silenced Filbert Street with an eighty-ninth minute goal to earn a replay. MacKenzie finished the job to send Harlow into new pastures. The bookies responded by cutting their odds . . . to 5,000-1. A 4-3 defeat at Vicarage Road wasn't a shameful way to exit the competition. The same two players were on the mark, MacKenzie scoring twice as Harlow gave the Hornets a run for their money.

Leicester's shame was masked by the humiliation of Manchester City. In the previous season they had countered United's third final in four years with inglorious defeat at Shrewsbury. This season, if such a thing were possible, the ignominy was even greater.

City were the 'cheque-book Charlies' of the day. Malcolm Allison had recently, and inexplicably, shelled out nearly £1.5m for Steve Daley, a price tag that would look expensive for the same player even today. Halifax were stony broke and had the league's most ramshackle ground. This particular mid-season found them locked in their habitual battle for re-election.

On the eve of the game, the Yorkshire side's much-needed pay-day was in the balance. The pitch was a pond but an enthusiastic if primitive mopping-up operation, involving the liberal of use of . . . er . . . towels, persuaded the referee against his better judgment that the ground was fit for play.

Over 12,500 were shoehorned into the Shay. Once

the game started City's distaste for the proceedings was clear. They tiptoed through the swamp for most of the game, clearly dreaming of the lush sward that awaited them in the replay at Maine Road.

It was not to be. With fifteen minutes left, even the most partisan home supporter would have settled for a replay and another fat cheque. Then, Halifax won a throw-in near the half-way line. Down the line it went towards Andy Stafford, who eluded a half-hearted challenge before swinging over a cross. Sprinting through the mud to collect was Paul Hendrie, bought from Bristol Rovers for a princely £5,000. Hendrie scooped the ball on his instep and smashed it past the onrushing Joe Corrigan. Finally City were aroused from slumber, and the kitchen sink was thrown. Halifax keeper John Kilner stood firm under the bombardment. For the second successive season City were in disgrace, but this time their ineptitude cost Allison dearly and he was out before the end of the season.

Three third division sides made the last sixteen. Blackburn, in a fallow period, beat Coventry before falling in a replay at Villa. Bury crept through but were dismissed by Liverpool. Chester had fun; they beat Newcastle 2-0 away in the third round and Millwall by the same score. The scorer of the second goal on both occasions was a young Welshman making a bit of a name for himself – Ian Rush. Ipswich were too strong for Chester in the fifth round.

The semi-finals threw together the two strongest remaining teams. For once Liverpool and Everton avoided each other. Everton, having a poor season, were handed the easier task, against Second Division West Ham. The Hammers were in their second season in that league and though they had bags of talent and experience, they couldn't get the consistency to mount a promotion challenge.

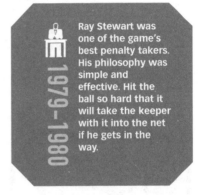

They had saved this season's best form for the Cup. Their run to Wembley left three First Division clubs in their wake and some indelible memories. Trevor Brooking, still picked for England despite the club's lowly predicament, got the winner in a replay against West Brom. Full back Ray Stewart scored twice from the spot as Orient were seen off 3-2. The same man's nerveless late penalty saw off Villa in the sixth round. Their winner against Everton in the semi came from the most unlikely of players. Veteran Frank Lampard's goal celebration, a mad dash to the corner flag before cavorting round it like a demented maypole dancer, was born as much out of surprise as elation.

The Gunners' disappointment was compounded when, after a seventy-game season, they lost the European Cup Winners' Cup on penalties to Valencia.

1979–1980

Arsenal skipper Pat Rice made his fifth final appearance for the Gunners, becoming the first player to reach that milestone with a single club.'

1979–1980

Arsenal's progress to yet another final looked inexorable. The draw had been kind giving them four ties against unremarkable opposition with only struggling Bolton from the same division. The Gunners were doing just enough to win, but knew that the performance bar would need to be raised to cope with semi-final opponents Liverpool.

Although the Reds were sweeping everything before them, the FA Cup proved perennially elusive for Bob Paisley's team. Their second successive semi-final was again to end in disappointment. That it took four games to finish them off only piled on the agony. Like all marathon ties, it was a relief when it finished. In contrast to Arsenal's epic the previous year against Wednesday, the longer this contest lasted, the greater the stalemate. Alan Sunderland had kept the Gunners in the hunt by scoring in the first and second replays. Brian Talbot finally put everyone out of their misery at Highfield Road (staging its one and only semi-final).

West Ham's winner in a poor final sprang from another unlikely source. Trevor Brooking had been the creative force of West Ham and England's midfield for years. His gifts were evident but scoring headers was not amongst them. Imagine his glee on thirteen minutes as Stuart Pearson's cross-shot was diverted into the net by his usually unused noggin. It was the third goal Brooking had scored with his head in a long career.

They should have had a second. At seventeen years 256 days, Paul Allen became the youngest player in an FA Cup final at Wembley. A mature performance should have been capped with a goal, had he not been cynically up-ended by Willie Young when clean through. He only revealed his tender years after receiving his medal, when he burst into tears.

Maybe Arsenal had nothing left in the tank, but they offered precious little threat. Brooking's goal was enough to win West Ham their third FA Cup.

1980

OSSIE'S GOING TO WEMBLEY

1981

Nottm Forest 2 Bristol C 1

Ipswich 2 Charlton 0

Southampton (0) 0 Everton (0) 1

Peterborough 0 Manchester C 1

Tottenham 3 Coventry C 1

Newcastle (1) 0 Exeter C (1) 4

Middlesbrough 2 Barnsley 1

Wolves 3 Wrexham 1

QUARTER FINALS

Nottm Forest (3) 0 Ipswich (3) 1

Everton (2) 1 Manchester C (2) 3

Tottenham 2 Exeter C 0

Middlesbrough (1) 1 Wolves (1) 3

SEMI FINALS

Ipswich **0** Manchester C **1**

at Villa Park

Tottenham **3** Wolves **0**

at Highbury after 2-2 at Hillsborough

FINAL, 9 MAY 1981, WEMBLEY

Manchester City **1**
Tottenham Hotspur **1**

MAN CITY:
Corrigan, Ranson, McDonald, Reid, Power ©,
Caton, Bennett, Gow, MacKenzie, **Hutchison (1)**
(*Henry 82*), Reeves

SPURS:
Aleksic, Miller, Hughton, Roberts, Perryman ©,
Villa (*Brooke 68*), Ardiles, Archibald, Galvin,
Hoddle, Crooks **OG: Hutchison**

FINAL REPLAY, 14 MAY 1981, WEMBLEY

Manchester City **2**
Tottenham Hotspur **3**

MAN CITY:
Corrigan, Ranson, McDonald (*Tueart 79*), Reid,
Power ©, Caton, Bennett, Gow, **MacKenzie (1)**,
Hutchison, **Reeves** (1p)

SPURS:
Aleksic, Miller, Hughton, Roberts, Perryman, **Villa
(2)**, Ardiles, Archibald, Galvin, Hoddle, **Crooks
(1)** sub: Brooke

T his was the only season that the club who would have enjoyed the shortest-ever trip to the twin towers reached the first round. Sadly for Wembley, their sniff of the big time ended with a 3-0 defeat at Enfield, which was not that much further away. Enfield went on to enjoy their most successful Cup season. Their name was still in the hat for the fifth round draw, having forced a 1-1 draw at Barnsley. They lost 3-0 at home in the replay. Good for Barnsley, but Hereford and Port Vale fans still shudder a little at the name of Enfield.

Altrincham reached the third round yet again, removing Scunthorpe along the way. A 4-1 defeat at Liverpool was no disgrace. Scorer Graham Heathcote later became the club's manager.

The romantic tale of the year was the team from St James's Park. Not Newcastle, who made themselves a laughing stock, but Exeter City. A 5-0 thrashing of Leatherhead put the perennial upstarts in their place, and a 1-0 away win at Millwall saw Exeter make one of their infrequent sorties into round three. Hoping for a big draw, they got Maidstone United away. They coped better than Gillingham in the previous round, and won through 4-2 at the first time of asking. Leicester City, promoted at the end of last season (and down again at the end of this one) was a better draw. First Division, decent crowd, yes, but beatable. A 1-1 draw at Filbert Street saw the sides reconvene in Devon. Exeter's spearhead was their long-serving centre forward Tony Kellow. The dog had his day; a Kellow hat-trick saw Exeter into uncharted territory, and another tie at St James's Park, only this time it *was* the one in Newcastle.

Again the Grecians forced a draw, so back to the other . . . you've got the picture by now. If Newcastle fans thought their team had reached a nadir in recent years, they were wrong. The club with one of the proudest cup records of all were roundly thrashed. By Exeter City, and 4-0 to rub the salt in. Exeter fans, if requested, will repeat, mantra-like, the names Hatch, Pearson, Roberts (P), Rogers (M) . . .

Tottenham spoilt the party in the last eight, but what fun they had!

After watching Arsenal parade at Wembley in five FA Cup finals since their last appearance in 1967, the cockerel chose this year to crow again. Spurs' first meaningful run since the days of Dave Mackay began with an undistinguished goal-less draw at Loftus Road. Tottenham won the replay 3-1 and never looked back.

Spurs had brought in the Argentinians Osvaldo

The third and fourth rounds saw a lot of the top sides take each other out. Aston Villa would win the league, pipping Ipswich to the title, but the Suffolk side won their cup encounter 1-0. Everton beat Arsenal in the third round and won a Merseyside derby in the fourth. Peter Eastoe and Imre Varadi were the scorers, not the most feted names in an Everton roll of honour. Everton saw off another fancied side, Southampton in the fifth, before falling to City.

1980-1981

Ardiles and Ricardo Villa after the 1978 World Cup had showcased their talents. Just as the Dutch pair of Muhren and Thijssen had added to Ipswich Town, the South American pair, Ardiles especially, added strength and guile to a team built around the languid talents of Glenn Hoddle. With a natural finisher in Scots international Steve Archibald, only a creaky back four let them down. But fortune smiled on them. QPR, Hull, Coventry and Exeter were all despatched at White Hart Lane. Only Wolves barred their way.

After an entertaining 2-2 draw, Tottenham enjoyed the distinct and unfair advantage of a replay at Highbury. Urged on by local support packing three sides of the ground, two from Garth Crooks and a rocket from Ricky Villa sent Spurs' fans streaming from N5 with an unaccustomed warm glow.

Manchester City was another club to be found filed under the misnomer 'sleeping giant'. Their recent Cup forays had ended in humiliation but John Bond had added some resolve and this season found them in no mood for charity. Crystal Palace and Norwich, both top flight clubs, were hit for four and six respectively and a tie at Peterborough that in recent seasons would have brought about their downfall was negotiated without mishap. The sixth round brought a battle with Everton, City winning through after a replay at Maine Road, thanks to two goals from full-back, Bobby McDonald. This left the little matter of Bobby Robson's Ipswich at Villa Park. These were heady days for the Suffolk side. Riding high in the League, they were to win the Uefa Cup the following month and started this semi-final as favourites. Normal time produced little in the way of action or goals, and a replay looked on the cards until Paul Power popped up with an extra-time winner.

Two of the Cup's most celebrated names had endured a decade of watching deadly rivals hog the limelight. Now their bridesmaid years were over, and Wembley was in for a treat.

No-one remembers the first game, save for Tommy Hutchison's peculiar achievement in scoring for both teams. His shoulder had deflected a Hoddle free-kick past the unlucky Joe Corrigan only ten minutes from the end.

By contrast, the replay was a classic. For Ricky Villa it was a renaissance. Out of sorts on Saturday, he was substituted midway through the second half and cut the most mournful of figures as he wandered round the perimeter towards the dressing room. He could hardly have been quicker out of his blocks on the Thursday night, smashing home the opener after only eight minutes.

Coventry beat Leeds, Forest took out Man United and Middlesbrough cut down Ron Atkinson's strong West Brom side.

1980-1981

Within three minutes City had replied with a goal that under normal circumstances would have been replayed ad infinitum as one of Wembley's greatest. Such was the control of the teenage McKenzie's waist-high, falling volley that the ball arrowed into the top corner from the edge of the box.

That it was eclipsed is some measure of Villa's effort. As the match ended its final quarter-hour, the game could not have been more finely balanced. Reeves's penalty early in the second half had been answered on the hour by the opportunism of Crooks, who had pounced on a loose ball in the box.

There looked no danger as Galvin fed the Argentinian on the left wing. City's right flank was policed heavily, but Villa embarked on a mazy dribble, appearing to pick up speed as he did so. He slalomed past Ranson and Caton, then cut back in a single movement to throw both off balance. As Corrigan advanced, he conjured enough room to stab the ball under his body and into the net. Having appeared to cover every blade of grass in creating the goal, his wild celebration threatened to mow a fresh pattern into the famous turf. It was a goal fit to win any game. For the 100th final, it seemed the most fitting of tributes.

RETURN OF THE COCKEREL

QPR:
Hucker, **Fenwick (1)**, Gillard, Waddock, Hazell, Roeder ©, Currie, Flanagan, Clive Allen *(Micklewhite 50)*, Stainrod, Gregory

SPURS:
Clemence, Hughton, Miller, Price, Hazard *(Brooke 105)*, Perryman ©, Roberts, Archibald, Galvin, **Hoddle (1)**, Crooks

QPR:
Hucker, Fenwick, Gillard, Waddock, Hazell, Neill, Currie ©, Flanagan, Micklewhite *(Burke 84)*, Stainrod, Gregory

SPURS:
Clemence, Hughton, Miller, Price, Hazard *(Brooke 67)*, Perryman ©, Roberts, Archibald, Galvin, **Hoddle (1p)**, Crooks

S even months before Glenn Hoddle was strutting his graceful stuff at Wembley, the first round tie between Sheffield United and Altrincham demonstrated that the beautiful game sometimes failed to wear its make-up.

That the Blades were playing in the first round was in itself a comeuppance. That they were outplayed and out-muscled at home by Altrincham was a double humiliation. The tone was set within a minute, as the visitors' John King was led from the field, blood streaming from a butt-induced head wound. He returned with twelve stitches, and a roused Altrincham grew from his inspiration to force a 2-2 draw. A timid United, mindful of the treatment that may have been meted out in the replay, failed to compete. A 3-0 drubbing completed their disgrace. A contrite manager Ian Porterfield, nine years after he delivered one of the great shocks as a player, delivered his sheepish verdict: 'We go away humbly'. United were slumming it in Division Four for the first time in their history. They escaped at the first attempt, remaining unbeaten at home.

Altrincham picked off York City to reach the third round. Tiny Cumbrian side, Penrith, after a famous victory over Chester City, couldn't repeat the dose against Doncaster. Joining Altrincham were the pride of North London, Barnet and Enfield.

Barnet even took Brighton, by now a First Division team, to a replay, and Enfield gave Palace a run for their money before going down 3-2. Enfield had previously thrashed former non-league colleagues Wimbledon 4-1 – the biter bit. Altrincham suffered the indignity of a 6-1 thrashing at Turf Moor, Burnley's Northern Ireland international Billy Hamilton grabbing a hat-trick.

The third round provided North London with another little matter, holders Tottenham against Arsenal. Pat Jennings, so often a hero at White Hart Lane, renewed his love affair with the home crowd. Now an Arsenal man, he fluffed an easy shot from Garth Crooks to hand victory to his old club with the only goal. That 1-0 final score, normally associated with their North London rivals, became the order of the day for Spurs as they beat Leeds and Villa by the same margin. A clean sheet against Villa was impressive – the Villains had beaten First Division Notts County 6-1 away from home in round three, helped by a David Geddis hat-trick.

Despite Spurs' purposeful progress, all eyes as usual were fixed on Liverpool. The Reds had started the season

In Europe Spurs got sucked into a kicking match with Barcelona, and went out 1-0 in Camp Nou after a 1-1 draw at home. Even bruisers like Roberts found the Spaniards hard to handle. The best Spurs side since the double-winners nearly came away with nothing.

1981-1982

indifferently, but by New Year the machine was purring. Closing in on another league title, they were taking the Cup in their stride. Swansea and Sunderland were brushed aside with an aggregate of seven goals to nil. The fifth round draw sent them to Stamford Bridge. Ten years previously, this would have been the tie of the round. But the Blues' vintage years had long since turned sour, with the 1982 crop barely good enough to hold its own in Division Two. Their 2-0 victory in front of their biggest crowd in over four years was jaw-dropping. Their hero was a young winger bearing the burden of the distinctly un-football sounding name Peter Rhoades-Brown. Double-barrel ran from his own half to score, outpacing a crop of seasoned international defenders.

The lower orders had shot their bolt by the fifth round; the last Third Division side Oxford United were well beaten by Coventry. Oxford were an up-and-coming team about to enter their purple period. In round four they pulled off a terrific result against Brighton, winning 3-0 at the Goldstone. The Second Division, by contrast, was heavily represented, boasting more teams in the last sixteen than the top flight. The winners of three all-Second-Division-ties were joined by Chelsea and Shrewsbury. The Shropshire team had taken Ipswich to a replay the season before; they went one better this year, beating Bobby Robson's side 2-1 at Gay Meadow.

The sixth round draw smiled on the contingent from the second tier; two semi-finalists were guaranteed, and it was Leicester, emphatic 5-2 winners against Shrewsbury, and QPR, who edged out Crystal Palace with a Clive Allen goal, that made the last four. Young Allen, cousin of Paul Allen who played in the 1980 final for West Ham, was proving a natural goalscorer; he had scored four times in a 5-1 fourth round demolition of Blackpool, and another in the fifth round against Grimsby.

Chelsea's reward for reaching their first quarter-final in nine years was a London derby against the holders. Mike Fillery put the Blues 1-0 in front just before the break with a pinpoint free-kick, but the Blues had reckoned without Glenn Hoddle. The future Chelsea boss ran the show in a masterful second-half display, capped by a sumptuous twenty-yard drive that gave Tottenham a lead they never looked like relinquishing.

With struggling West Brom completing the semi-final line-up, Tottenham looked odds-on to return to Wembley. They did; Leicester City gave them few alarms at Villa Park, a Crooks strike and a spectacular own goal sealing their place in the final.

That man Clive Allen ensured they would be facing Second Division opponents in the fourth all-London final. He scored the only goal in a tight semi-final against the Baggies. It was Rangers' first FA Cup final appearance, but their second time at Wembley, having won the League Cup as a Third Division side in 1967.

This was Spurs' seventh final and their fifth at Wembley since 1961. They also became the first side to reach both domestic Wembley finals in the same season.

Rangers must have fancied their chances. Sunderland, Southampton and West Ham had all tied their ribbons on the trophy at the expense of top-tier opposition, and in Ian Gillard and Tony Currie they boasted experienced ex-England internationals. Spurs, on the other hand, were deprived of the services of both their Argentine imports. The Falklands War had just broken out, and the nation was whipped into a jingoistic frenzy by the tabloid media. Ossie Ardiles was loudly booed in the semi-final and left early to help his country prepare for the coming World Cup. Both manager Keith Burkinshaw and Ricky Villa reluctantly conceded that it would be unwise for last season's hero to play at Wembley.

Both the final and replay were tedious affairs. In the first game Tottenham looked to have negated the need for a replay when Hoddle's shot deflected off Currie to beat Peter Hucker ten minutes into extra-time. Rangers refused to lie down, and suckered Spurs five minutes later with a classic set piece. Simon Stainrod's long throw was helped to the back post via Bob Hazell's head where Terry Fenwick, later of Spurs, rose to plant the ball past Ray Clemence.

Spurs made no mistake in the replay. This time the lead was theirs on six minutes. In a peculiar role reversal, playmaker Tony Currie brought down Tottenham hatchet-man Graham Roberts in the box. Hoddle put away the penalty as though it were a practice match. Rangers huffed and puffed, but to little effect. Spurs, with an extra layer of class, deserved their second successive Cup.

The Cup final win prevented the season turning into a nightmare for Tottenham. At the beginning of March, everything looked hunky-dory for Burkinshaw's classy side. The recruitment of Ray Clemence, deemed surplus to requirements at Liverpool, had added solidity at the back, and Tony Galvin, the Republic of Ireland winger, gave much needed pace and width to a midfield rich in passing and creativity. A League Cup final against Liverpool loomed. In the Cup Winners' Cup Eintracht Frankfurt had been seen off to set up a semi-final encounter with Barcelona. Even the title was within striking distance if Spurs could pick up points from their games in hand.

But it all went tits-up. At Wembley in March, Tottenham were leading through Steve Archibald and running down the clock when Ronnie Whelan took the match into extra time. Another Whelan goal and a snaffle from Ian Rush kept the League Cup at Anfield. The win set Liverpool up for a characteristic surge towards the title; Spurs' fixture pile-up became insurmountable and the old adage that points in the bag are better than games in hand was proved true. Tottenham faded and finished fourth, still their best finish since 1971.

. . . BUT HE DIDN'T

BRIGHTON:
Moseley, Ramsey *(Ryan 56)*, **Gary A Stevens (1)**, Pearce, Gatting, Smillie, Case, Grealish ©, Howlett, Robinson, **Smith (1)**

MAN UTD:
Bailey, Duxbury, Moran, McQueen, Albiston, Davies, **Wilkins (1)**, Robson ©, Muhren, **Stapleton (1)**, Whiteside *sub: Grimes*

BRIGHTON:
Moseley, Gary A Stevens, Pearce, Foster ©, Gatting, Smillie, Case, Grealish ©, Howlett *(Ryan 74)*, Robinson, Smith

MAN UTD:
Bailey, Duxbury, Moran, McQueen, Albiston, Davies, Wilkins, **Robson © (2)**, **Muhren (1p)**, Stapleton, **Whiteside (1)** *sub: Grimes*

There was plenty to keep the big game hunters interested after a couple of lean years. That Crewe and Halifax went out to non-league opposition produced scarcely a flicker among the pundits. Nor did Altrincham beating Rochdale at home – a reversal of that result would have constituted more of an upset. Slough Town provided a genuine early headline by knocking out Millwall, while Northwich earned local bragging rights in the Cheshire footballers' wives belt by eliminating Chester.

A new scourge of the lower divisions took a bow here. Telford United would reach the first round every year for the next ten years, and only once would they fail to make the second. Their victims this year were Wigan Athletic, finding their first season in Division Three hard work. They would not have enjoyed a non-league team meting out the treatment they had, until recently, been proud of handing out themselves.

It was a wretched second round for Welsh teams. Cardiff were chasing promotion from Division Three (and achieved it), and a 2-0 half-time lead against Weymouth was about par. But complacency set in and Weymouth clawed a goal back, and then equalised twelve minutes from time. Panic took over and Weymouth completed a memorable comeback with Gerry Pearson's volleyed winner five minutes from the whistle.

Worcester City turned over Wrexham on the same day, and earned a visit to Coventry, where the Sky Blues were too much for them. An away tie against Cambridge, a no-nonsense Second Division team with lousy support, was less than Weymouth deserved. They coped as well as could be expected with Cambridge's physical game and lost to a solitary George Reilly goal.

Bishop's Stortford joined these two in the draw after they followed up an outstanding win at Reading with a 4-1 cruise down the road at Slough. Stortford, ninety-nine years after their formation, enjoyed their fifteen minutes of fame at Middlesbrough: 2-0 down at the break, they also took advantage of second-half complacency to force a draw. The replay saw their tiny ground at Rhodes Avenue brimming with over 6,000 fans, who witnessed a glorious 2-1 defeat.

The fifth round provided the season with a shock eclipsing anything that Slough or Worcester could muster. Technically it was no such thing as both teams were in the same division. That Brighton, bottom of the table, could travel to Anfield and beat a Liverpool side who would eventually take the title by eleven points was still a sensational effort. The Reds' frustration was compounded by a rare penalty miss from Phil Neal and a winner from Anfield old boy Jimmy Case.

The side that finished runners-up to Liverpool were Watford, but they too suffered a setback, getting pounded 4-1 at Villa Park. Merseyside neighbours, Everton, fared better, putting paid to Tottenham's chance of a third successive Cup triumph.

Norwich were beaten in the next round – the Canaries presumably still celebrating Keith Bertschin's fifth round winner over the old enemy Ipswich. The semi-final brought Brighton's reward for their Herculean performance at Anfield. Second Division Sheffield Wednesday looked a far better bet than either Arsenal or Manchester United, who were left to slug it out at Villa Park. Wednesday were an ordinary side who had had an easy draw, and Jimmy Case and Michael Robinson sent the Seagulls flying to Wembley for the first time.

The Final was a mismatch. Brighton's run masked a non-existent Cup pedigree and dire league form – they were relegated a couple of weeks before the big day. They had never even reached a quarter-final. Ron Atkinson was threatening to make United a league force again, (they finished third), and they boasted the country's best player in Bryan Robson. They beat every Cup opponent (including Everton and Arsenal) at the first attempt. They came up against an Albion whose relegation seemed to

lift the shackles. They led at half-time courtesy of Gordon Smith's header, but Frank Stapleton, a scorer against United in the 1979 final, brought them level ten minutes after the break.

Eighteen minutes from time, United looked to have won it in style. Ray Wilkins, in a rare foray forward, curled a delicious twenty-yarder beyond Moseley that drew comparisons with his goal-scoring youth at Chelsea. That looked enough, at least until Gary Stevens popped up to fire past Bailey with only three minutes remaining.

Extra-time was goalless, but Brighton fans still dwell on an incident in the last minute. Accepting Robinson's pass, only ten yards and Gary Bailey separated Brighton from the Cup. 'And Smith must score!' bellowed the BBC's Peter Jones. But he didn't, firing straight at the keeper instead and Albion's chance was gone. So symbolic was the moment that these words became the title of a Brighton fanzine.

Brighton appeared still to be dwelling on Smith's miss in the replay five days later. Their defence should have been strengthened by the return of captain Steve Foster, gypsy ringlets, silly headband and all. With Gatting switched to right-back, it only served to throw them off balance. By half-time they were 3-0 down, and Muhren's second-half penalty rubbed in the heaviest defeat in a Wembley final.

EVERTON DRAW HORNETS' STING

EVERTON:
Southall, Gary M Stevens, Bailey, Ratcliffe ©, Mountfield, Reid, Steven, Heath, **Sharp (1)**, **Gray (1)**, Richardson *sub: Harper*

WATFORD:
Sherwood, Bardsley, Price *(Atkinson 58)*, Taylor ©, Terry, Sinnott, Callaghan, Johnston, Reilly, Jackett, Barnes

The 1980s was a decade that gave opportunities to previously unsung clubs. Brighton, Swansea, Oxford, and Wimbledon flirted with the top division, Luton and Oldham returned after long-forgotten gaps. Two of these clubs, Oxford and Luton, won the League Cup, while Oldham got to the final of that competition. Brighton made their only Cup final appearance, and Wimbledon went one better.

Add a name to this list; Watford. Promoted from the Fourth Division in 1978, four years later they finished runners-up to Luton in Division Two and entered previously uncharted territory. The club's success was founded on the enthusiasm and cash of lifelong fan, pop-star Elton John, and the team-building and tactics of Graham Taylor. Taylor's philosophy was simple; play the ball long into the heart of the opposition's territory and then apply pressure to capitalise on any mistakes. Unlike Wimbledon a few years later, Watford didn't set out to physically intimidate their opponents, just discomfort them. The super-talented John Barnes on the wing gave them an extra dimension, and the aristocrats couldn't cope. Watford finished runners-up to an imperious Liverpool in their first season, even beating the champions in their last match to clinch second over Manchester United.

Watford's sojourn in the top flight lasted six years; their effectiveness dimmed as Elton's readiness to bankroll them waned, and Taylor eventually left for the England job via Aston Villa. He tried to apply the Watford virtues to England, work-rate and simplicity to the fore. In the end he only proved the folly of the FA in appointing a manager with so little experience of either European football or big egos. A shame because, like Bobby Robson the England manager before him, Graham Taylor is a genuinely nice man with a wealth of knowledge and deep passion for football. Taylor was reunited with Watford in the late 1990s; promotion through the play-offs in 1999 was for one year only – the club wisely refused to spend recklessly and the team was ill-equipped for the top flight. Taylor remains in the game as a sensible and honest pundit, and deserves better than to be remembered as a fatuous, though admittedly amusing, tabloid headline.

A refreshing wind of change blew through this season's competition. Arsenal, Manchester United and Nottingham Forest crashed out in the third round. By the last sixteen, the balls of Spurs and Liverpool had also been discarded from the velvet bag.

Just before Christmas, Manchester United had been

The first round welcomed back illustrious opponents for the first time in eighteen years. Corinthian Casuals provided a whiff of nostalgia, but not of romance. After a goalless draw, Bristol City finished the job 4-0 at Ashton Gate.

1983-1984

knocked out of the League Cup by Third Division leaders Oxford. A repeat against Bournemouth looked unlikely; the Cherries were struggling in Division Three, and even an injury-hit United would surely take the FA Cup a bit too seriously. Or perhaps not. United were dire, confirming Bournemouth manager Harry Redknapp's theory that they wouldn't like it up 'em. Milton Graham and Ian Thompson became the toasts of the South Coast, the latter robbing a dithering Bryan Robson to smash home the Cherries' second. As Harry himself put it: 'We don't get many days like this in Bournemouth.' A Middlesbrough side struggling to keep out of Division Three spiked the Gunners 3-2, avenging a fifth round defeat the year before. The two giant-killers met in round four, Middlesbrough coming out on top.

Forest exited with less eggy faces. A defeat by a Lawrie McMenemy's Southampton, replete with ex-England players, was no disgrace. It was a new Saints star, the small but nimble Steve Moran, who got both goals. Moran was the toast of the city when he scored the only goal in the next round – it eliminated hated rivals Portsmouth at Fratton Park.

For Liverpool, the fourth round was Groundhog Day. Brighton became the Reds' nemesis by knocking them out in successive years. Now a Second Division club, last season's finalists triumphed with goals from Gerry Ryan and Terry Connor.

Tottenham, for whom Wembley had

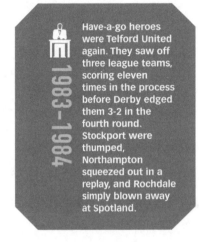

Have-a-go heroes were Telford United again. They saw off three league teams, scoring eleven times in the process before Derby edged them 3-2 in the fourth round. Stockport were thumped, Northampton squeezed out in a replay, and Rochdale simply blown away at Spotland.

1983-1984

almost become a suburb of E17 in recent seasons, went out to Norwich in a replay at Carrow Road. Canary-come-lately Mick Channon struck the winner.

By the sixth round, the tournament was wide open. Only one of the eight, Southampton, had reached the final in the last sixteen years. After an easy draw in the early rounds, Third Division Plymouth had pulled off a fine win at The Hawthorns in the fifth round. Tommy Tynan was the West Country's hero. Another 1-0 win, over Second Division Derby in a replay, saw Plymouth entertaining thoughts of Wembley. When the draw was made, the Cup was guaranteed a new finalist as Argyle were paired with Watford. The Hornets had scored plenty of goals on their way through; John Barnes, future Celtic and Rangers player Mo Johnston, and the towering George Reilly all carried a threat.

Villa Park was no place for the purist, but Watford's

Everton's Wembley line-up included midfielder Kevin Richardson, who was transferred to opponents Watford two years later.

1983-1984

1983-1984

Watford's run was nearly strangled at birth. In the third round, they found themselves two goals down to local rivals Luton. John Barnes and Maurice Johnston hauled them back into the tie. The replay at Vicarage Road was a thriller. The score was 3-3 after normal time when Super Mo applied the coup de grace. For some locals, the Cup run never got any better than this.

long-ball style paid immediate dividends when lofty centre-forward George Reilly headed them in front inside ten minutes. It was the Pilgrims who finished the stronger but Watford survived a late battering despite having their woodwork rattled in the last few minutes.

Everton were flying a lone flag for the traditionalists. Despite their pedigree, the trophy cabinet had been bare for fourteen years, as their neighbours from across Stanley Park dominated Europe. Manager Howard Kendall, one third of the revered 'holy trinity', was the sole link with the glory years and was rebuilding the team in his own image. Neville Southall, Kevin Ratcliffe, Peter Reid and Andy Gray formed a spine that promised Everton the first chance of Merseyside parity in years.

Early signs weren't promising. Two excruciating games with Gillingham failed to produce a goal, let alone a winner. A laboured win over Notts County set up a semi-final with Southampton, which most neutrals thought would provide the winner of the competition. It was in the semi-final that Everton finally showed their mettle. They started as underdogs against a Southampton team still in with a chance of the Double. Two parsimonious defences made a tight tie inevitable; a goalless ninety minutes stretched it into extra-time before Adrian Heath squeezed them home.

Wembley was a colourful mixture of blue and yellow, old and new. One sensed that Watford were glad just to be there and were rather overcome by the occasion. After Elton set the tone by blubbing through 'Abide with Me', Watford simply petered out. In Nigel

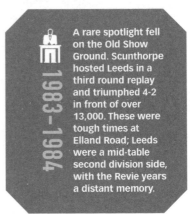

A rare spotlight fell on the Old Show Ground. Scunthorpe hosted Leeds in a third round replay and triumphed 4-2 in front of over 13,000. These were tough times at Elland Road; Leeds were a mid-table second division side, with the Revie years a distant memory.

Callaghan and John Barnes they had the skill and pace to unlock even a sound defence like Everton's, but their route one, bustling style failed to unsettle more accomplished opponents.

Ironically, Watford were undone by a piece of physical opportunism. Everton had already turned round a goal up, Sharp's strike eight minutes before the break having found the net via Sherwood's left-hand post. They sealed victory after fifty-two minutes, thanks to the aerial dominance of Andy Gray. The Scottish striker appeared to have nodded the ball from Sherwood's gloves as the keeper rose to gather a cross, but referee Hunting correctly signalled a goal. For Watford, their adventure was over. For Everton, this was the dawning of a new, golden age.

Goal of this season's tournament came from John Barnes. Against Birmingham in the quarter-finals, he picked up the ball wide on the left, advanced a few paces before arrowing a looping drive into the far corner.

STORMIN' NORMAN

THE LAST 16

Blackburn **0** Manchester Utd **2**

Wimbledon (1) **1** West Ham (1) **5**

Southampton **1** Barnsley **2**

York C (1) **0** Liverpool (1) **7**

Luton T (0)(2) **1** Watford (0)(2) **0**

Millwall **2** Leicester **0**

Everton **3** Telford **0**

Ipswich **3** Sheffield Wed **2**

QUARTER FINALS

Manchester Utd **4** West Ham **2**

Barnsley **0** Liverpool **4**

Luton T **1** Millwall **0**

Everton (2) **1** Ipswich (2) **0**

SEMI FINALS

Manchester Utd **2** Liverpool **1**
at Maine Road after 2-2 at Goodison Park

Luton T **1** Everton **2**
at Villa Park

FINAL, 18 MAY 1985, WEMBLEY

Everton **0** Manchester United **1**

EVERTON:
Southall, Gary M Stevens, Van Den Hauwe,
Ratcliffe ©, Mountfield, Reid, Steven, Sharp,
Gray, Bracewell, Sheedy *sub: Harper*

MAN UTD:
Bailey, Gidman, Albiston *(Duxbury 91)*,
Whiteside (1), McGrath, Moran, Robson ©,
Strachan, Hughes, Stapleton, Olsen

After last year's glorious run to the fourth round, expectations were high at non-league Telford. They were a team who believed, with justification, that they were a match for anyone in the lower divisions. After squeezing past Lincoln in a replay, they faced a declining Preston at Deepdale. A win was always a possibility, but a 4-1 slaughter was an undignified exit for a once proud club. Colin Williams followed up a pair against Lincoln with two more. Williams added more goals as Bradford and Darlington were seen off before Telford got the draw they deserved, a trip to league leaders Everton. There were to be no more fairytales, just cash; Everton were too good and won 3-0.

Manchester United's continuing failure to land a league title was a source of much Merseyside mirth (laughter that would be returned with interest in the following decade). It was the Cup where United grabbed their glory, and they were keen to avoid the pratfall of the previous season's defeat when they drew Bournemouth in the third round. They exorcised the demons of Dean Court by thumping Bournemouth 3-0. From then on it was plain sailing; Coventry, Blackburn and West Ham were dismissed at the first attempt, the precocious Norman Whiteside firing a terrific hat-trick against the Hammers. The little matter of Liverpool awaited them at Goodison Park in the semi-final.

Before such serious business, the comic relief had been provided by Arsenal. In the third round Hereford nearly provided a banana skin at Edgar Street, but thoughts of a slip-up looked to have been banished by a replay that finished 7-2 in Arsenal's favour. The next round saw a trip to Bootham Crescent, where a tie with Third Division York did not threaten serious danger. It was an awful game on a frozen pitch, and the Gunners looked to have slithered to a replay until Steve Williams gifted their hosts a penalty one minute from time. Keith Houchen, for whom greater FA Cup glory lay in store, remained as cool as the conditions to despatch the spot-kick and consign Arsenal's season to oblivion.

Arsenal weren't the only ones who were prey to Captain Cock-up. West Brom were embarrassed for the second year running at Orient, and Doncaster enjoyed a rare bright-spot in a truly abysmal Cup record by beating QPR 1-0. Chelsea had regained First Division status under John Neal, and would have gone into their tie at home to Millwall full of confidence after a 5-0 win at Wigan in the previous round. Four of the goals had been scored by their centre-forward Kerry Dixon. Never the most accommodating of opponents, Millwall muscled Chelsea out of the game, a 3-2 win clinched by a young bruiser of a striker called John Fashanu. He was on target again when Leicester found The Den traditionally inhospitable in round five.

Luton's tricky goalscorer, Brian Stein, stifled the Lions' roar. But the sixth round tie between Luton and Millwall was marked by one of the worst displays of hooliganism yet witnessed. Seats were ripped out and used as missiles and a mass pitch invasion delayed the game by twenty-five minutes, footage all recorded by BBC cameras. Prime Minister Margaret Thatcher, having watched the scenes on television news bulletins, entered the fray, demanding that the game's governing body and the courts tackle the issue once and for all but the FA, led by Ted Croker, responded by denying any responsibility for 'society's problem'. The Kenilworth Road riot was followed a few months later by the twin disasters at Bradford and Heysel. Both owed much to the dilapidated condition of the stadia.

The passage of holders Everton to a second successive final looked to be as direct as it was comfortable. After winning at Elland Road against a Leeds side still drifting in Division Two, home draws against Doncaster and Telford hardly tested them. Another tie at Goodison against an Ipswich side struggling without the magic touch of Bobby Robson, should have provided easy pickings. The visitors surprised Everton with a 2-2 draw, only for the champions elect to reassert themselves at Portman Road and take the tie with a Graeme Sharp strike.

Liverpool put Arsenal's performance into perspective, annihilating York with John Wark scoring three of their seven goals. It was Ian Rush's turn to score three in the next round against Barnsley, and Liverpool went into the semi-final draw half expecting to meet Everton at that stage for the fifth time.

As it transpired, the semi-final draw favoured Everton yet again that season. Luton would have been the choice of both Manchester United and Liverpool, but the two giants were pitched together, leaving the Toffees to face Luton at Villa Park. Not that this was a soft touch; the Hatters were enjoying their third successive season in the top flight and possessed genuine match-winners in Ricky Hill and Brian Stein. Everton found them a tough nut to crack and it took extra-time before Kevin Sheedy's fourth goal of the campaign saw them home.

The other semi was momentous. After seventy minutes, and with a goalless game poised on a knife-edge, Bryan Robson's shot was blocked and Mark Hughes forced the loose ball over the line. The game exploded, and Ronnie Whelan curled a breathtaking equaliser in the eighty-sixth minute. United looked to have won it when Frank Stapleton's deflected shot found the net eight minutes into extra time. With the clock showing 120 minutes, and Goodison Park drowned in Mancunian whistles, Paul Walsh levelled to spark furious United protests. George Courtney ignored the linesman's offside flag.

At Maine Road in the replay, the pendulum seemed to have had tilted towards Liverpool. It swung even further when Paul McGrath, in attempting to divert a cross over his own crossbar, succeeded only in planting it past Gary Bailey. United's get-out-of-jail card was played, not for the first time, by Bryan Robson. Almost directly from the second-half kick-off, he fired past Grobbelaar for the equaliser. On the hour, Mark Hughes latched on to Strachan's pass to shoot United's winner.

Waiting for them were the holders and league champions. Everton knew the Double would give them the one honour that had always eluded their neighbours. For nearly eighty minutes familiarity bred stalemate, until the moment arrived that would inspire United's victory. As Peter Reid broke from midfield, he was upended by a clumsy lunge from Kevin Moran. Reid was still fifty yards from goal, but referee Peter Willis pointed to the touchline, and a distraught and protesting Moran eventually accepted the awful truth. He had become the first player to be sent off in an FA Cup final.

Far from being weakened, United were inspired. Adrenalin coursed through tired limbs, putting Everton on the back foot. With the match deep into extra-time, one goal would be enough for victory. It was a strike worthy of winning any game. Mark Hughes sent Norman Whiteside marauding down the right wing and with an energy belying his efforts of the previous 110 minutes, the young Ulsterman cut inside and bent a shot from the edge of the area. It arced towards the far corner before finding the one square of netting left unguarded by Neville Southall. The red half of Wembley went berserk.

It was too late for Everton to reply. The Double dream was over, and United, still seething with righteous indignation, had won their sixth Cup.

MERSEY BEATS MERSEY

THE LAST 16

Luton (2)(0) **3**	Arsenal (2)(0) **0**
Tottenham **1**	Everton **2**
Derby (1) **0**	Sheffield Wed (1) **2**
West Ham (1) **2**	Manchester Utd (1) **0**
York C (1) **1**	Liverpool (1) **3**
Watford (1) **3**	Bury (1) **0**
Peterborough (2) **0**	Brighton (2) **1**
Southampton (0) **1**	Millwall (0) **0**

QUARTER FINALS

Luton (2) **0**	Everton (2) **1**
Sheffield Wed **2**	West Ham **1**
Liverpool (0) **2**	Watford (0) **1**
Brighton **0**	Southampton **2**

SEMI FINALS

Everton **2**	Sheffield Wed **1**

at Villa Park

Liverpool **2**	Southampton **0**

at White Hart Lane

FINAL, 10 MAY 1986, WEMBLEY

Everton **1**	Liverpool **3**

EVERTON:
Mimms, Gary M Stevens *(Heath 65)*, Van Den Hauwe, Ratcliffe ©, Mountfield, Reid, Steven, **Lineker (1)**, Sharp, Bracewell, Sheedy

LIVERPOOL:
Grobbelaar, Lawrenson, Beglin, Nicol, Whelan, Hansen ©, Dalglish, **Johnston (1)**, **Rush (2)**, Molby, MacDonald *sub: McMahon*

T he season started in sombre mood after Bradford and Heysel. The football authorities, beleaguered and, quite frankly, clueless, responded by introducing the Full Members' Cup. Nobody cared and nobody turned up to watch.

As if to catch the mood, the early rounds of the Cup failed to turn up the heart-warming stories normally associated with the entry of the league clubs to play the hopeful semi-pros. Telford beat Stockport for the second time in three years – nobody fell off their chair. Dagenham beat Cambridge; again, no surprise as Cambridge were rubbish. Up and coming non-leaguers Wycombe saw off Colchester, a minor shock, and Altrincham won away at Third Division Blackpool in round two. The second round also saw Frickley Athletic, formerly Frickley Colliery, claim their only league scalp with a win at Hartlepool.

Altrincham saved their stunner for round three. Birmingham City were having a ghastly season. Ron Saunders had got them promoted the year before, but they were heavily in debt and the squad couldn't cope with the top flight. Even home advantage didn't help them, nor did taking the lead early in the second half. Birmingham's goal was against the run of play and Altrincham stayed patient, forcing their way back into the match. Their winner was a bizarre own goal, Birmingham scorer Robert Hopkins and young David Seaman conspiring to let a tame back-pass trickle into the net. Seaman would have better Cup memories.

The early rounds were hardly classics. Lots of replays and second replays and most of the ties going with form. A tough winter made the draws a farce. The sixth round draw featured all sixteen teams still in the competition; all but one tie went to a replay. Only one team outside the top flight made the last eight, as Brighton capitalised on a dreadful Newcastle performance in the third round. Southampton quelled their rebellion with ease.

Sheffield Wednesday had come through impressively, Carl Shutt's goals seeing off Derby in a replay and West Ham in the last eight.

Everton and Liverpool, with the odd minor hitch, had made imperious progress through the competition. Everton had an awkward tie with Exeter, and Liverpool were taken to a replay by York City for the second successive year. A 3-1 defeat restored York's self respect after their 7-0 mauling in 1985.

The Merseyside pair, comfortably the best two

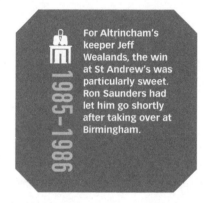
sides in the country, needed replays to book their places in the semis. Gary Lineker saw off Luton after a 2-2 draw, while Ian Rush finished off Watford in extra time after the Hornets forced a courageous draw at Anfield. For the second year running, both Everton and Liverpool were in the semi-final. They were kept apart again.

The goal against Watford was, surprisingly, Ian Rush's first of the campaign. Perhaps mindful of his meagre contribution, he bagged both in the semi-final to end Southampton's hopes in extra time. Extra time was needed at Villa Park, too, where Graeme Sharp's winner settled a tense match against an improving Sheffield Wednesday.

It had taken 114 years, but the twelfth pairing in FA Cup history of Merseyside's old rivals eventually took place in the final. It was a match that, had capacity proved no object, could have emptied Liverpool itself.

At Wembley, it was Everton who drew first blood, as Lineker outpaced Hansen to shoot past Grobbelaar at the second attempt. The Toffeemen seemed determined to avenge their surrender of the Championship to Liverpool seven days earlier and pressed forward in an attempt to double their advantage. Again, it was Rush who came to Liverpool's rescue.

With the second half twelve minutes old, he stole round the back of Everton's defence, drew Mimms and slotted the ball into an unguarded net. Six minutes later Craig Johnston fired Liverpool ahead. It was tough luck on Everton, but an object lesson from Liverpool in how to make the most of an opportunity. As the game entered the last six minutes, Everton's risk-taking became ever more desperate. The influential Molby turned defence into attack with a pass to Whelan. The Irishman broke down the left, checked, and picked out an unmarked Rush, who drilled in a clinical finish.

Everton, so close to a Double the previous season, were forced to watch Liverpool take their bow as Merseyside's first winners of the honour. Kenny Dalglish, in his first season in management, had achieved something that had evaded Bill Shankly and Bob Paisley in all their long years with the club.

SKY BLUE HEAVEN

COVENTRY:
Ogrizovic, Phillips, Downs, McGrath, Kilcline © *(Rodger 88),* Peake, **Bennett (1)**, Gynn, Regis, **Houchen(1)**, Pickering **OG Mabbutt** *sub: Sedgley*

SPURS:
Clemence, Hughton *(Claesen 97)*, Thomas, Hodge, Gough, **Mabbutt © (1)**, **Clive Allen (1)**, Paul Allen, Waddle, Hoddle, Ardiles *(Gary A Stevens 91)*

More than usual, the advent of the competition proper joined together a curious mixture of sleeping giants and local-league chancers. Middlesbrough v Blackpool made strange reading in the first round. Another club trading on past glories, Burnley, discovered that mere reputation counts for nothing. Every other Third and Fourth Division club breathed a collective sigh of relief as the Clarets were forced to make the journey that they all had hoped to avoid. Telford's derring-do of recent years had secured a financial position healthier than many league sides. The 3-0 home win felt more like a banker than an upset.

If Burnley were embarrassed at Telford, this was nothing compared to the humiliation felt by Wolves. Last season's first round baptism had been a 6-0 hammering at Rotherham. This year they laboured for two games against Chorley of the Northern Premier League before crashing out 3-0 in the second replay at Burnden Park. Two-goal Charlie Cooper had Wolves well and truly over a barrel. Wolves manager Graham Turner, their fifth in two years, had only been with the club a month and was distraught at the lack of heart and desire in the squad. His response was to sign a bumptious reserve striker from West Brom, Steve Bull. Wolves, although they didn't know it yet, had found their Moses. The second round draw brought Chorley a richly-deserved local derby at home against Preston. Once again, the match was switched, this time to Ewood Park, where over 15,000 witnessed a frenetic 0-0 draw. Chorley's undoing proved to be Deepdale's artificial pitch. They slithered to a 5-0 defeat in the replay, but could console themselves with a bumper payout from a 16,308 crowd.

Telford reached round three for the third time in four years. More eyebrows were raised at the similar journey of Caernarfon Town. The Welsh part-timers took their place at the prefects' table for the first time, this after making it beyond the qualifying competition for the first time in fifty-seven years. Stockport, habitual patsies in the eighties, and York, were their victims. They even denied Telford (who lost 2-1 at home to Leeds) the accolade of becoming the last non-league side standing after holding Barnsley 0-0. Oakwell may not be everyone's idea of the big time, but every Caernarfon player can bore his grandchildren with tales of a tie, lost by only a single goal in the replay.

The third round draw ensured heightened local rivalry in East London and Manchester. Orient achieved the best financial result by earning a replay at Upton

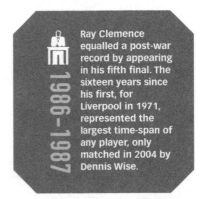

Welsh side Ton Pentre could not have wished for a better draw. Having reached the first round for what remains the only time in their history, Lady Luck paired them at home to Cardiff. A 4-1 defeat scarcely dented local pride.

1986-1987

Park, where West Ham sent them back up the road with a full wallet and a 4-1 defeat.

United and City were paired at Old Trafford and Norman Whiteside took up where he left off in last year's final with the match-winner.

There would be no return to Wembley for the Double winners. Luton showed just how far they had come by keeping a clean sheet three times against the Reds. Two goalless draws were followed by a comprehensive 3-0 win, the height and strength of Mick Harford giving Liverpool a torrid time. The tie was subject to much controversy; Luton's ban on away fans nearly saw them thrown out of the competition, and the first replay had to be rescheduled after Luton's flight to Liverpool was unable to leave. Cue whingeing from beaten manager of big club, Kenny Dalglish.

The first division sides claimed six of the last eight berths, but they all played each other. The Wigan – Leeds tie guaranteed the lower orders a presence in the semis. Wigan had claimed a good win over Norwich, enjoying a good league season in Division One, in the fourth round. Paul Jewell scored the only goal and was on target again when Wigan beat Hull 3-0 in the next round. Leeds were slowly dragging themselves out of a slough; after ending Telford's latest adventure they beat QPR at Elland Road to set up the Wigan game. Leeds proved too strong for the Third Division side and made a date with Coventry at Hillsborough.

Ray Clemence equalled a post-war record by appearing in his fifth final. The sixteen years since his first, for Liverpool in 1971, represented the largest time-span of any player, only matched in 2004 by Dennis Wise.

1986-1987

Coventry City, for once, were not distracted by their perennial struggle against the drop; a comfortable mid-table position allowed them a crack at a rare Cup run. Keith Houchen's goal to win a tricky fourth round tie at Old Trafford gave them the kick-start they needed. Wins at Stoke and Sheffield Wednesday, with two more from Houchen, put them in the semis for the first time.

It was back to Hillsborough for Coventry in their quest for that first trip to Wembley. Coventry went behind, but then took the lead with another Houchen goal after an equaliser from Mickey Gynn. A late Leeds goal took the game into extra time, but Dave Bennett's goal clinched it. Bennett, a loser with Manchester City in 1981, was returning to Wembley with his new colleagues. The opponents would be the same as on his last trip.

Tottenham stuttered to a 3-2 win over Scunthorpe at White Hart Lane in the third round. It took a winner from Chris Waddle to avoid a potentially parlous replay. Successive home wins against Crystal Palace and Newcastle sent them to a ground where few would volunteer to

In the opposite goal was Steve Ogrizovic. For years he waited patiently as Clemence's understudy at Anfield before moving to Highfield Road.

1986-1987

Spurs' Clive Allen had played in the 1982 Final for QPR against Tottenham. He was maintaining a family tradition, as father Les had been part of Spurs' Double-winning team in 1961. Cousin Paul was also appearing in his second Cup final for a London club. In 1980, he had lined up for West Ham against Arsenal.

travel. Plough Lane, with its promise of roughhouse treatment from Jones, Wise and co, appeared the ideal abbatoir for a fancy dan outfit like Spurs. The recording duo of Hoddle and Waddle put paid to any thoughts of such slaughter, leading to suggestions that they may have sung to their hosts in the tunnel before the game.

Arsenal had ambitions of following Spurs to the semis, but came unstuck in the sixth round at home to Watford. Graham Taylor's side were building a reputation as seasoned Cup campaigners and set up the Highbury tie after squeaking through against Walsall after two replays. They would need to defend better than they did in the 4-4 draw in the first replay at Vicarage Road. That they did and carved out an excellent and merited 3-1 win. Two of the goals came from Luther Blissett, back at Watford after an unhappy spell at Milan; the other came from John Barnes, who left for Liverpool at the end of the season.

David Pleat's side would have started as favourites at Villa Park in any circumstances, but their odds shortened considerably by a bizarre injury crisis at Watford. A few days before the game, not a single registered keeper remained outside the treatment room. In desperation, they turned to a director's son. West Country restaurateur Gary Plumley would have been more at home as Basil Fawlty's locum. He had played a few league games as keeper at Halifax, but was hardly equipped for an FA Cup semifinal. The contrast in fortunes was sharpened even further by the sight of

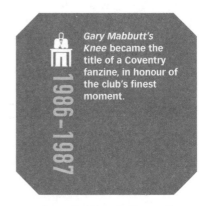

Gary Mabbutt's Knee became the title of a Coventry fanzine, in honour of the club's finest moment.

Ray Clemence warming up in the opposite goalmouth. The challenge facing Plumley was keeping out Clive Allen, who finished the season with forty-four goals.

Predictably, with such a rookie keeper, Watford's defence was a shambles. It took half-an-hour to resemble anything approaching a cohesive unit. By then, they were three goals down. The remaining hour passed as one of the least tense in semi-final history as Spurs cantered to a 4-1 win.

The two finalists approached Wembley with widely varying pedigrees. At the time, Spurs had won the trophy on a record seven occasions, with a 100% record in finals. They had lifted the Cup twice already in the eighties, and arrived at Wembley on the back of their best league season in years, finishing third behind Everton and Liverpool. They were clear favourites, but most neutrals were cheering for the opposition. The Sky Blues

For Glenn Hoddle, playing his last game for Tottenham, the match proved an unfitting finale. He left in the close season to join Monaco, where he would learn the art of management under a cerebral young French coach called Wenger.

were enjoying their twentieth consecutive season in the top flight, but not a glimmer of a trophy had come their way. Their FA Cup record was particularly bad; two appearances in the sixth round, one as a Third Division side.

The dye looked cast as early as the second minute, when PFA Footballer of the Year Clive Allen stole in front of Trevor Peake to head home Waddle's cross. It was the quickest Cup final goal since Nat Lofthouse had fired home for Bolton in 1953. Within seven minutes, the Sky Blues were level. Full-back Greg Downs crossed, Houchen's head flicked the ball on, and Dave Bennett eluded Ray Clemence before shooting past a desperately covering Hodge.

The goal inspired Coventry and as half-time approached they remained ahead on points. Spurs were creating little, but Coventry conspired to invent their own danger. A Glenn Hoddle free-kick looked aimless but Steve Ogrizovic checked his dash from the line. Brian Kilcline, under pressure from Gary Mabbutt, succeeded only in diverting the ball past his own keeper.

With luck like this, Coventry's name hardly looked destined for the trophy. They refused to lie down, but their harrying and chasing seemed in pursuit of a lost cause until one moment of inspiration turned the match on its head. Keith Houchen, picking up the ball in central midfield, laid the ball wide to Bennett and continued his run towards the box. The winger's cross looked to be too far ahead of him, but he threw himself full-length to send a header rocketing past Clemence's despairing right glove. Two years earlier, Houchen's penalty for York had sent Arsenal spinning out of the Cup. Now he had sent their North London neighbours reeling.

The remaining twenty seven minutes failed to produce a winner. Six minutes after the restart, Coventry were gifted a slice of luck as Spurs paid back the first-half own goal. Lloyd McGrath, overlapping down the left wing, looked to have sent over a harmless cross. Gary Mabbutt, in attempting to charge down the centre, succeeded only in looping it via his kneecap over a stranded Clemence into the far corner of the net.

For Coventry, this was the crowning glory of the managerial duo of John Sillett and George Curtis, who had played more than 500 games for the Sky Blues two decades earlier. Their workaday team was never to scale such heights again, but few outfits have appreciated their big day with such relish.

1987

DONS. MK 1

LIVERPOOL:
Grobbelaar, Gillespie, Ablett, Nicol, Spackman
(Molby 72), Hansen ©, Beardsley, Aldridge
(Johnston 63), Houghton, Barnes, McMahon

WIMBLEDON:
Beasant ©, Goodyear, Phelan, Jones, Young,
Thorn, Gibson *(Scales 63)*, Cork *(Cunningham
56)*, Fashanu, **Sanchez (1)**, Wise

T his was a campaign for neither the traditionalists nor the purists. A season that ended with the nouveau riche Wimbledon cavorting round the hallowed turf with their first trophy began with nine previous winners in the first round. Burnley v Bolton made strange reading at the same stage as VS Rugby v Atherstone United, but such is the arbitrary nature of the draw.

Sunderland were playing a first round tie for the first time since 1925, the last year that the big clubs were forced to slum it at that stage. Near-neighbours Darlington were the beneficiaries, as the two were drawn together at Roker Park. Although Sunderland won 2-0, a trip further down the North Sea coastline in round two proved their undoing, as Fourth Division Scunthorpe dumped them out 2-1. The days of Porterfield, Montgomery and Stokoe had never seemed more distant.

This season's non-leaguers to avoid were Macclesfield. The Conference side reached the Third Round for the first time in twenty years courtesy of two thumping wins against League opposition. Carlisle were despatched 4-2 at the Moss Rose Ground, which then became a graveyard for Third Division Rotherham. Steve Burr grabbed a hat-trick as the distinctly unmerry Millers were trounced 4-0.

After such derring-do, Macclesfield were entitled to feel under-whelmed at being sent to Port Vale in the third round, especially when they lost. Nothing like as under-whelmed as Spurs felt after their fourth round trip to the same venue. In an instant, Vale had turned from potential big-boy scalp to plucky underdog. Spurs were the most successful Cup team in history, and had started their campaign well with a tidy 4-2 win away at Second Division Oldham. But this was Vale Park, a mud-bath of a pitch in a ramshackle ground on a windswept hill. Ardiles was left out, and one or two others might as well have stayed at home with him. Ray Walker, Vale's ex-Villa playmaker, scored a wonderful free-kick, and Phil Sproson added a second before half-time. A Neil Ruddock header reduced the lead, but Ruddock was alone in his appetite for the battle. Vale's 2-1 victory delighted most *Match of the Day* viewers and revived memories of the glory days of 1954. But there was no semi-final this year; Watford saw Vale off in the fifth round, to set up a match direct from the Charles Hughes' coaching manual: Wimbledon v Watford.

In only their second season as a top division club, Wimbledon were doing more than consolidating their

league position. In last year's competition they had reached the last eight before losing to Tottenham. This season, they had seen off West Brom and Mansfield before facing a genuine test at Newcastle. They brushed the Geordies aside, 3-1. Goals from the towering centre half Eric Young, and the formidable John Fashanu saw them win the aerial battle against Watford to set up a semi-final against those other Johnny-Come-Latelys, Luton Town.

This was a tie that provoked a snobbish reaction from many commentators, who felt that two such humble clubs were unworthy of a semi-final appearance. The position of both in the top half of the First Division was conveniently ignored. Predictably, what the tie lacked was not tradition, but finesse. If you consider that the respective centre forwards were John Fashanu and Mick Harford, then the tactics aren't difficult to second guess. Both were on target, Fashanu from the penalty spot, but it was Dennis Wise, a player of very different build, who popped up with the winner.

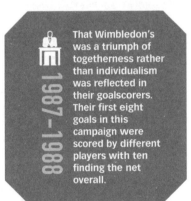

1987 - 1988

That Wimbledon's was a triumph of togetherness rather than individualism was reflected in their goalscorers. Their first eight goals in this campaign were scored by different players with ten finding the net overall.

While one side of the draw saw the arrivistes battling it out, the other side saw the established clubs going at each other. In the fifth round Liverpool drew Everton once again, the Reds knocking out their rivals with a Ray Houghton goal. Their other victims were Stoke, Villa and Manchester City. That looks impressive but they were all in Division Two that year. Manchester United, still to deliver for Alex Ferguson, had gone out to Arsenal, a Mike Duxbury own goal settling the issue. Arsenal fell in turn to Nottingham Forest but they, in turn, were no match for Liverpool at Hillsborough, two goals from the season's top scorer John Aldridge saw Liverpool through to a comfortable 3-1 win.

Like the previous year, the contrast in the pedigree of the finalists could hardly be greater. Wimbledon were a team with a reputation of backs-to-the-wall aggression. Their Cup exploits in the 1970s had propelled them from the Southern to the Football League in 1977, when their existence became anything but dull. After a yo-yo start, they had battled their way to the First Division two years previously. Their style, cultivated by former player Dave Bassett and maintained by Bobby Gould, was direct, flirted with illegality and won them few admirers. Their attitude was borrowed from fellow South London hard-nuts Millwall. No one liked them, and they didn't care.

1987–1988

Luton's solace after their semi-final defeat was the fact that they had already booked a place at Wembley in the League Cup Final against Arsenal. Luton came from behind to win the trophy with a late winner from Brian Stein. Goalkeeper Andy Dibble was the other hero with a penalty save to keep Luton in the game at 2-1 down.

None of the above applied to their opponents. A record seventeenth league title had recently been added, and the last fifteen years had issued a constant stream of glory, with European Cups and Championships a-plenty. The charm of the FA Cup is that, unlike the League, it has never become the exclusive preserve of one team. Liverpool had won the trophy in 1974 and 1986, but this hardly matched their return from other competitions. No team cared less for reputation than Wimbledon.

The Dons lack of respect was obvious even before kick-off. The baiting, out-psyching and downright abuse, led by Vinnie Jones, began in the tunnel. Liverpool were taken aback, and remained so for much of the next ninety minutes.

The game started scrappily and continued in similar vein until the thirty-seventh minute, when Wimbledon won a free-kick near the left edge of Liverpool's penalty area. Wise's free kick curled towards the front of the six-yard box, where it glanced off the head of the onrushing Sanchez past a flat-footed Grobbelaar and into the far corner of the goal.

The roars that greeted Wimbledon's winner seemed strangely muted. The Dons' average home attendance was barely a third of their opponents. Most of the ground was a sea of red.

All was hardly lost at that moment. More than an hour of the match remained and Liverpool, though shaken, stirred. On the hour they looked to be back in it, and in fortunate circumstances. The extended fingertips of Beasant looked to have diverted the ball from Aldridge's foot but the Liverpool striker tumbled in the challenge. Referee Hill pointed to the spot, then spent some minutes dampening predictable Wimbledon fury.

It may have been the delay that unsettled Aldridge, as he dusted himself down and waited to take the penalty. Whatever the reason, his spot-kick, although well to Beasant's left, was at such a height that the 6ft 4in keeper could dive and turn the ball round the post in one movement. Wise's baiting of Aldridge, as the horror-struck striker stared forlornly at the turf, left a typically sour taste.

Despite most descriptions to the contrary, this doesn't qualify as a major upset alongside the final victories of Sunderland in 1973 or Southampton in 1976. Wimbledon were a good side who had finished seventh in the First Division. The surprise element was provided by the downfall of the mighty Liverpool.

What could not be denied was that Wimbledon had earned their victory. Not one of the team had any comparable experience to draw on and this was a perfect retort to traditionalists who had sniffed at their suitability to sit at the top table.

THE DARKEST HOUR

EVERTON:
Southall, McDonald, Van Den Hauwe, Ratcliffe ©, Watson, Bracewell **(McCall 58 (2))**, Nevin, Steven, Cottee, Sharp, Sheedy *(Wilson 77)*

LIVERPOOL:
Grobbelaar, Ablett, Staunton *(Venison 91)*, Nicol, Whelan ©, Hansen, Beardsley, **Aldridge (1)**, **(Rush 72 (2))**, Houghton, Barnes, McMahon

The football significance of 15 April 1989 is nil. The game lasted less than ten minutes before being abandoned. As Liverpool boss Kenny Dalglish was to remark later: 'Football is irrelevant now.'

Liverpool had been drawn to play Nottingham Forest in the FA Cup semi-final and Hillsborough was designated as a venue. Nothing unusual here, as the Sheffield ground had staged thirty similar ties in its long history and the South Yorkshire police should have taken all arrangements in their stride.

Liverpool, despite a larger home support, were allocated the smaller Leppings Lane terrace, while Forest's fans had the run of the larger Spion Kop. The absurd excuse given by South Yorkshire police was that Leppings Lane faced west and would therefore be nearer to the majority of fans travelling from Merseyside. Why they thought an extra 100 yards would make any difference in a journey of over 50 miles is anyone's guess.

Twenty minutes before the game, the late arrival of many Liverpool fans at the Leppings Lane turnstiles caused lengthy queues. In an effort to speed the human flow, the police herded all latecomers into the central pen of open terracing, whilst surrounding areas remained relatively empty. The effect was disastrous.

Hemmed in by fences on three sides, and with a relentless surge of people pushing from behind, the resulting crush turned from dangerous to critical, then to fatal. As the game kicked off, ninety-five people were losing their lives.

After six minutes, and with a few lucky escapees having clambered over the fence, the referee led the players back to the dressing rooms. At first, the knee-jerk explanation was that hooliganism was suspected. It was only when advertising hoardings were converted into makeshift stretchers and the dead and injured started to be laid out on the pitch that the awful realisation dawned.

The next few weeks passed in a haze of recriminations and grief. Anfield was transformed from a football ground to a shrine of remembrance, with the Kop an emotional sea of scarves, flowers and heart-rending tributes. Liverpool played no football for weeks. It was the last thing on anyone's mind.

The Sun peddled a tale that some Liverpool fans had stolen from the bereaved, playing on the stereotype of the 'thieving Scouser.' It was a nasty and inappropriate slur. Copies of the paper were ritually burned on Merseyside, but the paper, owned by Rupert Murdoch's News International, took years to publish an apology.

Many of the police officers on duty that day received large amounts of compensation for stress incurred at work. Pitifully small sums were paid to bereaved families for the loss of their loved ones. The Hillsborough Justice Campaign still fights to obtain justice for victims' families. That such a campaign is necessary remains a disgrace.

The secondary tragedy of Hillsborough, apart from the loss of life and the devastation it brought to the bereaved, was that it could so easily have been prevented. This was not the first major disaster at a British ground. The lessons of Burnden Park in 1946 and Ibrox in 1971 had been ignored. The latter had resulted in the Safety of Sports Grounds Act, but this was legislation for its own sake, without any attempt at enforcement. Bradford and Heysel four years earlier had resulted in blame and buck-passing from all sides, but no concerted action.

The legacy of the disaster was a public enquiry, the usual whitewash that slapped a few wrists but brought no one to account. The real progress was the Taylor report, so named after the Lord Chief Justice brought in to provide a dispassionate analysis. In a thorough and excellent report, Taylor, after bemoaning the fact that his was the ninth such report, identified the principal reasons for Hillsborough. Its result was the conversion of First and Second Division grounds to all-seater stadia, the end to perimeter fencing and a realisation that, contrary to tabloid opinion, not all fans were Stanley knife-wielding thugs. Taylor also rubbished the identity-card scheme championed by Margaret Thatcher and a succession of ill-informed puppets masquerading as Ministers for Sport.

No one remembers the 1989 FA Cup for the football. It was dwarfed by the tragedy of Hillsborough and the subsequent emotion surrounding the second, thrilling, all-Merseyside final. The rest of the competition has dwindled into history as a footnote. In other years, that wouldn't have been the case. This year served as many shocks and stories as any other.

For Durham's Brandon United, this was their year in the sun. The club formed in 1958 as the works team from the town's waste paper company reached the first round for only the second time. A tie against Doncaster Rovers was virtually a trip down Wembley Way. They even survived to make the second round draw before Rovers beat them 2-1 in the replay.

Altrincham, Bognor Town, Runcorn and Enfield humbled league opposition in the first round. Kettering were the stars of the second round, knocking out Bristol Rovers 2-1. The Northamptonshire team followed up with victory over Halifax in the third round, before taking a bow at Charlton.

The big one came at Gander Green Lane, never the venue of legends. Suburban Surrey has never laid claim as a soccer hotbed. Only the FA Cup could

1988-1989

Sutton were already a team with previous Cup history. In 1970 they had reached the fourth round before losing 6-0 at home to Don Revie's Leeds. In 1988 they had seen off league opposition in Aldershot and Peterborough before going out gamely in extra time to First Division Middlesbrough.

transform a notch on the commuter belt into the focus of football attention. Coventry couldn't even use the excuse of needing to concentrate on the League. Most of their twenty-odd years in the top flight had been spent in saving their skins from the clutches of relegation. This year was different; they delighted in mid-table obscurity and finished in the dizzy heights of seventh place. This was just one of those days.

Just to rub it in for the Sky Blues, Match of the Day turned up. Just as Newcastle had felt the glare of the cameras at Hereford on the very occasion they would have ticked the box marked no publicity, so Coventry's humiliation was beamed into the living rooms of grinning neutrals throughout the land.

Coventry started as the form side, having thrashed Sheffield Wednesday five days earlier. They trooped off at half-time a goal in arrears, left-back Tony Rains having headed Sutton into a shock lead. The pitch may have been a gluepot, but that hardly excused their performance. Doubtless a tongue-lashing from John Sillett would straighten them out for the second half. And so it proved. Coventry re-emerged with socks pulled up and within minutes were level through David Phillips. Sutton's moment in the sun had passed, it seemed. The home enthusiasm in the 8,000 crowd abated as they braced themselves for inevitable defeat.

On the hour, a moment of respite for Sutton saw them mount a rare attack. The ball was flung into the box, where the baby-faced Matthew Hanlan slid in to steer the ball past Steve Ogrizovic. Pandemonium ensued. Coventry protested with some justification that Ogrizovic had been impeded, but the referee had turned a blind eye.

Sutton were then forced to endure the longest half-hour of their lives as Coventry abandoned all caution in pursuit of an equaliser. It was a tribute to the Conference side that, on such an energy-sapping surface, they matched Coventry for fitness and created the better chances in that final quarter. After thirty minutes the final whistle brought a surge of ecstasy and relief that could

The match programme contained a sombre introduction from FA chairman Bert Millichip, who explained the decision to continue with the final. He dedicated the match as a memorial to those who had died at Hillsborough.

1988-1989

have powered the whole of Surrey for weeks. The only lights that were going out were on Coventry.

While their team may not have covered themselves in glory, the 2,000 or so travelling Coventry fans deserved a pat on the back. To a man they stayed in the tiny ground and gave their opponents a rousing standing ovation.

Things went less swimmingly for Sutton in their next match, at Norwich. In fact they drowned, Malcolm Allen scoring four times and Robert Fleck adding a hat-trick in an 8-0 spanking.

A few other leading lights blew a fuse in round three too. Spurs, in the throes of rebuilding, lost to a Bradford City side drifting in division two. Middlesbrough, later to be relegated from the top flight, put the cherry on a miserable campaign by falling 2-1 at home to Fourth division Grimsby. Two goals from substitute Marc North completed a great comeback.

The fourth round saw the top brass reassert themselves, so the headlines were provided by Manchester City. Faced with a filthy day, a cloying pitch and the tight stadium at Griffin Park, they threw in the towel. Brentford beat them 3-1, with two from Gary Blissett, who repeated the dose at Blackburn to send the Bees through to their first quarter-final since 1949. Their reward was handsome – a trip to Anfield. A win was never a serious possibility, and Liverpool won 4-0. Their fans were magnanimous at the final whistle and Brentford departed the scene with a bag of cash and applause ringing in their ears.

At the same stage, Everton knocked out holders Wimbledon at Goodison Park, a Stuart McCall goal dividing the teams. For once the two Merseyside teams avoided each other in the last four. Liverpool drew Nottingham Forest for the second successive semi-final. Everton were paired with Norwich. Under normal circumstances, the Canaries would have started as under-dogs, but these were heady times at Carrow Road. City finished the league season in fourth place, their highest position ever. In a scrappy game Everton, drawing on all their years of Cup tradition, prevailed through a single goal from Pat Nevin. Norwich, as in

After seventeen seasons of Cup humiliation as the non-leaguers' bunny, Crewe scaled the heights of the third round once more. Their reward was a home tie against Aston Villa and a chance to welcome back David Platt, who had left Gresty Road the season before. Crewe fought manfully but lost 3-2.

1988-1989

their last semi-final appearance thirty years previously, had been edged out within sight of Wembley.

Forest made their date with Liverpool by beating three good Second Division sides and Manchester United without conceding a goal. Gary Parker's winner at Old Trafford meant another trophy-free season for the Old Trafford faithful and put manager Alex Ferguson under some pressure.

Forest did concede in the re-arranged semi-final. This time John Aldridge scored the spot-kick and added another for good measure to see Liverpool through.

In the days following Liverpool's semi-final victory, there remained considerable doubt as to whether this final would take place at all. The shadow cast by events at Hillsborough had been long enough to render thoughts of postponing the game until the start of the following season. After consultations between the FA and Liverpool, the match went ahead. Everton provided the most fitting of opponents and the city united in heart-warming fashion as Everton fans put aside a hundred years of rivalry to show due respect for the dead and bereaved.

Everton must have taken heart from the Liverpool team sheet. The surprising relegation of Ian Rush to the bench removed their scourge of the decade and nemesis of the final three years earlier – or so they thought. They reckoned without the determination of John Aldridge. Rush's replacement had a score to settle from twelve months earlier, when his penalty miss had ultimately handed Wimbledon the trophy. It took him only four minutes of this year's final to make amends.

Eighty-five scoreless minutes followed when the game looked destined to be filed in that overflowing drawer of routine one-nils, when it suddenly warmed up. Dave Watson, marauding up front in a desperate Everton gamble, fired a shot that Grobbelaar could only parry. Substitute Stuart McCall, who had replaced Paul Bracewell on the hour, lunged ahead of Steve Nicol to prod the ball home.

Having forced extra time, the momentum looked to be with Everton, but one vital factor needed to be accounted for. Ian Rush was on the field, having replaced Aldridge after seventy-two minutes. Twenty-two minutes into extra time, he controlled Nicol's cross on his chest, then pivoted past Kevin Ratcliffe as the ball dropped to smash the ball past Neville Southall.

Lesser sides would have crumpled, but Everton redoubled their efforts and were rewarded eight minutes later. Ratcliffe's free-kick was cleared by Alan Hansen's head but the ball dropped to McCall. The Scot's instant chest-and-volley looped into the corner of the net.

1988-1989

Six days later Kenny Dalglish failed narrowly to become the first manager to lead a Double-winning side twice. In the league season's final match Liverpool merely had to avoid a two-goal defeat to nearest challengers Arsenal at Anfield. Michael Thomas, later a Liverpool player, scored an injury-time clincher for the Gunners in the most exciting finish to a league season anyone could remember.

1988-1989

Coventry remain the most recent top-division side to have been knocked out by a non-League club. Manchester United have come the closest in the years since in their tie with Exeter in 2005.

McCall had become the first substitute to score twice in an FA Cup final, but his was an exclusive club for just two minutes. John Barnes broke down the left and delivered a wicked cross. The ball met with a glancing header that flashed past Southall for Liverpool's winner. The scorer was a man whose goal celebrations had become only too familiar for Evertonians – Ian Rush.

EAGLES SHOW THE RIGHT STUFF

FINAL, 12 MAY 1990, WEMBLEY

Crystal Palace **3** Manchester United **3**

PALACE:
Martyn, Pemberton, Shaw, Gray *(Madden 117)*, **O'Reilly (1)**, Thorn, Barber *(**Wright 69 (2)**)*, Thomas ©, Bright, Salako, Pardew

MAN UTD:
Leighton, Ince, Martin *(Blackmore 88)*, Bruce, Phelan, Pallister *(Robins 93)*, **Robson © (1)**, Webb, McClair, **Hughes (2)**, Danny Wallace

FINAL REPLAY, 17 MAY 1990, WEMBLEY

Crystal Palace **0** Manchester United **1**

PALACE:
Martyn, Pemberton, Shaw, Gray, O'Reilly, Thorn, Barber (Wright 64), Thomas ©, Bright, Salako *(Madden 79)*, Pardew

MAN UTD:
Sealey, Ince, **Martin (1)**, Bruce, Phelan, Pallister, Robson ©, Webb, McClair, Hughes, Danny Wallace *subs: Robins, Blackmore*

M any FA Cup tournaments follow a familiar pattern. A few early upsets add the spice, a couple of titanic clashes maintain the interest as the fifth and sixth rounds unfold, but the semi-finals and final are fuelled more by occasion than quality and excitement. This year, the Cup turned upside down.

The season belonged to two teams, and neither of them won the trophy. Oldham and Palace might have both fallen to Manchester United, but their colossal performances in the latter stages gave the season's competition its heart. For United the win has historic significance. If Alex Ferguson hadn't delivered a trophy that year, his tenure at Old Trafford may well have been over. Then, who knows? It could have been United and not their rivals across the City who spent their way to penury and lower league football.

Searching for early shocks was like panning for gold. Aylesbury beat Southend and Welling embarrassed Gillingham; that was the sum total of the first round's excitement. Whitley Bay stepped in to add much-needed romance in round two by turning over Preston but the plug was pulled on their party when the third round draw sent them to Spotland, where Rochdale won 1-0.

Coventry, after their horror show at Sutton twelve months previously, were again the third round fall guys. Third Division Northampton stole a 1-0 win, leaving the Sky Blues to their familiar relegation battle.

By the fifth round, a few unfashionable sides were starting to dream the impossible. Fourth Division Cambridge United, after two draws with Bristol City, cruised to their first quarter-final 5-1, Dion Dublin scoring twice. Oldham brought the national press to a forgotten corner of the north-west with three tenacious battles against Everton. The Second Division side, thanks to Roger Palmer and an Ian Marshall penalty, reached their first quarter-final since 1915.

Also in the sixth round were Crystal Palace, reviving memories of their charge to the semis in 1976. Back then the Eagles were headline grabbers: Big Mal strutted his stuff, while Leeds and Chelsea provided high-profile scalps. This year's run was decidedly low-key. Three home ties against Portsmouth, Huddersfield and Rochdale had provided a fortunate, if unglamorous passage. Their luck held in the sixth round, as they were sent to Cambridge, the lower orders' sole representative. Geoff Thomas earned them a narrow win and they had stolen into the last four.

Joining them there were Oldham. The Latics, unlike

Palace, were hogging the limelight. Their reward for beating Everton was the visit of Villa to Boundary Park. The visitors were flying high in the league, but had their wings clipped by a vastly more committed home side. In the end, Oldham cantered to victory, goals from Rick Holden, a talented but inconsistent winger, and Neil Redfearn, as well as an own goal.

The semi-final draw kept Oldham and Palace apart, but no one seriously expected either to line up at Wembley. The purists purred at the prospect of Manchester United and Liverpool providing a repeat of their final thirteen years earlier.

The Liverpool juggernaut was about to start grinding to a halt, but they were still the side to beat. They progressed by drawing away and relying on their formidable form at Anfield to see them through. Witness the third round tie against Swansea; a feeble goalless draw at Vetch Field followed by an 8-0 thrashing with the inevitable Ian Rush hat-trick.

Manchester United had won through in some style, winning every tie at the first time of asking, all of them away from home. Mark Robins scored the only goals in a fine third round win at Forest, Brian McClair chipped in with the winner in a 3-2 battle at Newcastle in the fifth and the only goal at Bramall Lane in the last eight.

At the Maine Road semi Oldham gave it everything. Earl Barrett, Ian Marshall and Roger Palmer put them within touching distance of Wembley. United were rescued by Danny Wallace, so three days later they returned to lock horns again. Andy Ritchie, rejected by United, proved a point by scoring against them, but Brian McClair and an

extra-time strike by Mark Robins finally broke Oldham hearts. Under normal circumstances, this 3-3 thriller in the first match would have made all the headlines. That it was forced on to the undercard was a tribute to the fare served up at Villa Park.

When Liverpool and Palace met at Anfield earlier in the season, Palace had been put to the sword 9-0, which remains their record league defeat. Added to which, Palace were still missing their best player Ian Wright, who was out with a broken leg. It's a wonder the bookies were taking bets. At half time, the form book remained unblemished. The teams were separated by Ian Rush's fourteenth-minute goal, although Palace derived some comfort from the sight of him limping off after half-an-hour.

The fun and games started in the second half. Mark Bright shot Palace level, and suddenly Liverpool looked rattled. When Gary O'Reilly took advantage of defensive hesitancy to force home from close range, the Reds' setback had become a crisis. Like all great sides, Liverpool failed to panic, and just moved into an extra gear. As Palace retreated, they passed, moved and waited. On eighty-one minutes, Steve McMahon brought Liverpool level, and two minutes later Palace's efforts looked in vain as Steve Staunton tumbled in the box and the referee pointed to the spot. John Barnes's conversion had surely sealed Palace's fate.

The script at this point should read that Liverpool kept possession, played out time and booked their Wembley clash with United, leaving Palace gallant and rueful losers. The twist was provided by Andy Gray, whose header brought the scores level three minutes from time. After ninety minutes of breathless fare, a lull in extra time allowed everyone to get their breath back. The first period passed largely without incident, as if both teams had slugged themselves to a standstill. With the second period four minutes old, Palace won a corner at the Holte End.

The near-post flick-on has been a set-piece tactic for decades. Its effectiveness has never been reduced because it is so hard to defend. Andy Gray's kick swung in from the left, Andy Thorn applied the touch and Alan Pardew, arriving unchallenged at the far post, headed home. After eleven agonising minutes, the ecstatic rejoicing that greeted Palace's victory contained more than a hint of disbelief. As their theme song, 'Glad All Over', thundered round Villa Park, a banner unfurled by delirious fans captured the euphoric mood. It read 'Thank you God, I can now die in peace.' For Palace fans, this was a victory that meant everything. They had never reached an FA Cup final before, and they had never played at Wembley.

Palace arrived at Wembley brimming with self-belief; United came determined to keep their boss in a job. Palace's confidence looked fully justified inside twenty minutes, as Gary O' Reilly rose to steer Phil Barber's free-kick past Jim Leighton via Pallister's head. United levelled after thirty-five minutes when Brian McClair broke wide and his centre was headed goalwards by Bryan Robson. Again a defender intervened; John Pemberton's touch took the ball past Nigel Martyn.

Just after the hour United were rewarded by the persistence of Neil Webb. Throwing himself at Andy Thorn's clearance, the midfielder earned a slice of

History has recorded this final as another David v Goliath contest. It was nothing of the sort. United's league season was a poor one. They stuttered to thirteenth place, level on points with Palace, who finished the season well after gaining promotion the previous year. Their third place finish the season after was comfortably their highest ever.

luck as he inadvertently ricocheted the ball into the path of Mark Hughes. Within a split-second, the ball was rocketing past Martyn into the net.

Palace were behind for the first time, but Steve Coppell, playing his last card, threw on a barely-fit Ian Wright to bolster their attack. His telepathy with fellow-striker Mark Bright was to pay dividends almost immediately. From Bright's pass, Wright burst between the statuesque Mike Phelan and Gary Pallister to smash home the equaliser.

In extra-time Palace seized the initiative from the off. John Salako's cross left Leighton clutching at straws and thin air, as he so often did when the ball was in the air. The talismanic Wright volleyed his second and the Eagles' third. Wright's match, like his career, had started late, but he had made up for lost time in both senses. This game would change his career.

Palace hung on until seven minutes from time, but their chance of victory in their first final was denied them by Mark Hughes. Racing on to Danny Wallace's through-ball, he slipped the ball past Martyn into the far corner.

The first match had been breathless stuff played at breakneck speed. The replay was an anti-climax and deserves only the briefest of footnotes. Ferguson made a tough decision and left out Jim Leighton, replacing him with on-loan Les Sealey. The decision was a good one; Leighton had been a weak link in the first game. Sealey rewarded Fergie with a solid game but Leighton never forgave his manager and moved on. Full-back Lee Martin became the answer to an oft-repeated quiz question, as this unlikeliest of scorers stole into an unguarded corner of the box to shoot the only goal. The Eagles' wings had been finally clipped.

GAZZA

NOTTM FOR:
Crossley, Charles, **Pearce** © **(1)**, Walker, Chettle, Keane, Crosby, Parker, Clough, Glover *(Laws 108)*, Woan *(Hodge 62)*

SPURS:
Thorstvedt, Edinburgh, Van Den Hauwe, Sedgley, Howells, Mabbutt ©, **Stewart (1)**, Gascoigne *(Nayim 18)*, Samways *(Walsh 82)*, Lineker, Paul Allen **OG Walker**

im Buzaglo, anyone? His name probably inspires a few stirrings of grey matter in your keener-than-average fan. For supporters of West Bromwich Albion, however, he is Darth Vader and Dirty Den rolled into one.

This Albion side were in the doldrums. Kicking around the lower reaches of Division Two, a Cup run would have provided much-needed relief and boosted ever-dwindling attendances. A draw at home to Isthmian League Woking looked to have provided the lowest of hurdles. Colin West gave the Baggies a half-time lead, and Albion passed the hour mark without alarm. Suddenly, though, the wheels fell off. Tim Buzaglo, a man whose principal sporting achievement had been to play cricket for Gibraltar, scored a hat-trick inside eleven minutes for the visitors. Substitute Worsfold strolled on to the field and picked his spot immediately to add Woking's fourth. Darren Bradley's last-minute consolation was greeted with a mixture of abuse and derision by the home supporters. The Albion fans greeted the end of the game with a huge ovation for Woking before hoisting Buzaglo aloft and carrying him around the ground for a lap of honour. Their calls for the resignation of the manager and the board were partially successful – unsurprisingly the board decided that manager Brian Talbot was the culprit, not themselves.

Woking were one of only two non-league teams in the second round. The other was Barrow, there by dint of a spot of Geordie-bashing, having seen off Bishop Auckland and Whitley Bay in the first two rounds. Bolton spoilt their fun. The only other non-league team to cause a stir were Bolton's neighbours Chorley, who added the scalp of Bury to that of Wolves five years earlier.

Woking's exploits reaped a handsome dividend as they were drawn at home to Everton in the third round. They switched the tie to Goodison and were rewarded by a 34,000 attendance. After a narrow 1-0 defeat, the home fans applauded them from the field. It was a bad season for Watford. Elton sold up, and they were hammered 4-1 in the third round by Third Division Shrewsbury. Shrewsbury then beat Middlesbrough for good measure before going out with a fight at home to Arsenal. Not literally, although the Gunners were docked points for brawling with Manchester United that season. They love each other, really.

Cambridge once again carried the poor relations' baton into the later rounds, reaching the last eight for the second successive season. The latest disciples of the long-ball game, manager John Beck had turned them into a real handful. Three Second Division sides were pummelled into submission with increasing ease; Sheffield Wednesday, who were promoted that season under Ron Atkinson, were blown away at the Abbey Stadium, Dion Dublin scoring twice in a 4-0 win. It took all Arsenal's resilience to see off Cambridge; Dublin scored again, but a goal from Kevin Campbell was followed by a winner from captain Tony Adams.

This set the Gunners up for a North London semi-final against Tottenham. Spurs' campaign had been about one man. Any assessment of Paul Gascoigne's career is usually accompanied by the phrase 'Jekyll and Hyde', an epithet that was never more deserved than in this season's competition. This was the year after Italia 90, the stage where Gascoigne had been propelled from the supporting cast to leading man. He revelled in the early rounds, scoring twice against Oxford in the fourth and Portsmouth in the fifth. When Spurs made hard work of their quarter-final against Notts County, it was Gazza who bailed them out with the winner. This sent them to Wembley, chosen as a semi-final venue for the first time. The reason was Tottenham's draw against Arsenal, a game that the whole of North London was desperate to watch. The bigger the stage, the more Gascoigne enjoyed himself. With the game only a few minutes old, Spurs were awarded a free-kick thirty-five yards out. It looked beyond Gascoigne's range, but his blistering drive arrowed over the wall and appeared to gather more pace as it bent into the top corner past England keeper David Seaman. It was a goal worthy of winning the final itself, and is rightly viewed as one of Wembley's finest ever. With Gary Lineker on target twice, Spurs ran out comfortable 3-1 winners.

They lined up at Wembley against Nottingham Forest, who in their third semi-final in four years, had finally won through against West Ham. The Irons had scored lots of goals in their run to the final and seen off Luton and Everton, two ordinary First Division sides. Nottingham Forest weren't world beaters, but they were desperate to win the FA Cup; it remained the only major trophy to have eluded Brian Clough and the great man was nearing retirement. In the end it was a cakewalk; West Ham's talented strikers never got a look in; full-backs Stuart Pearce and Gary Charles even found time to saunter forward and score two of Forest's four goals.

The final looked an intriguing contest, and Brian

Clough would have to draw on all his nous to work out a game plan to contain Gascoigne. In the event, Gazza did it all for him. Gascoigne started the game like a hyper-active two-year-old in the throes of a sugar rush. Within two minutes he could and should have been sent off after a chest-high, two-footed challenge. A few minutes later he lost control of the ball on the edge of the Forest penalty area. As Gary Charles shaped to challenge, he launched himself at the full-back. It was a horrible tackle, the sort that could have ended Charles's career. It nearly finished Gascoigne's. He got up to take his place in the wall but then collapsed and was carried distraught from the field, the cruciate ligaments in his right knee a ruptured mess. That he wasn't shown a red card was an act of mercy or forgetfulness on referee Milford's part.

When Pearce blasted home the resultant free-kick, Tottenham's afternoon was rapidly turning sour. Things looked up when Mark Crossley brought down Gary Lineker, but the England centre forward missed the penalty. Crossley was the game's second player lucky not to get a red card – maybe Mr Milford remembered that he hadn't punished Gazza and compensated by reprieving Crossley.

Tottenham were rescued eight minutes into the second half when Paul Stewart applied a slick finish to a good move. Clough, oddly, declined to gee up his players after ninety minutes, simply chatting to a policeman instead. His sang-froid appeared misplaced as Tottenham started to look the stronger side. Their winner came from the unlikeliest source. Des Walker, a rock in central defence for both Forest and England, looked to be dealing with a far-post corner but suffered a fatal moment of indecision. Unsure whether to head clear or cushion the ball to Crossley, he ended up doing neither and put it into the top corner of the goal. Tottenham had lost their previous final to Gary Mabbutt's own goal. Now, courtesy of Walker's, Mabbutt lifted the trophy as captain.

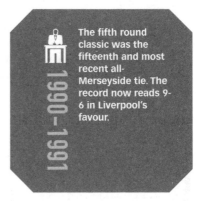

The finest tie of that season's competition had little bearing on the destiny of the Cup, but huge impact on who was top dog on Merseyside. They didn't know it then, but the Merseyside giants, who had won eight out of ten league titles in the last decade, were to fall upon leaner times in the nineties. When the draw threw them together for the fifteenth time in the FA Cup, the familiar scent of battle was in the nostrils.

The final had already been destined to be Gascoigne's last for Spurs. The club were steeped in debt, after disastrous attempts at diversifying their business. After Italia 90, Gascoigne was their only rising stock. Lazio's £7.5m offer proved irresistible, although Gazza's injury nearly scuppered the deal. Italy was about to discover the joys of raspberry-blowing and comedy breasts.

1990-1991

But although the heat was turned up, the contest failed to ignite. A tense, tight affair produced few moments of quality and even less by way of goalscoring chances. It finished scoreless, so three days later the teams crossed Stanley Park to try again. By half-time, the tie had a goal at last, Peter Beardsley's opportunism having put Liverpool in front. Still the game lacked a cutting edge and there was little to suggest the drama that was to unfold in the second half.

It started with Graeme Sharp's equaliser, which put a rocket under both teams. Goodison came alive; the pace quickened, tackles flew in with greater urgency and the volume control was turned up to eleven. With nineteen minutes left, a marvellous twisting run and finish from Beardsley looked to have won it for Liverpool, but Sharp replied almost immediately with his and Everton's second. When Ian Rush scored the game's third goal in six minutes, the home fans must have viewed his celebrations with a sense of deja-vu. It was as if the Finals of '86 and '89 had returned to haunt them. But one major difference for the Everton of 1991 was the arrival of Tony Cottee. The former West Ham striker had been on the fringes of the England squad in the late eighties and was still a player near his peak. With the clock showing ninety minutes, he seized the Toffees' last chance to send the match into extra-time.

Liverpool must have felt like they had won it again when John Barnes scored a memorable fourth. With the game in its 103rd minute there seemed little danger when the winger took up possession near the touchline. He turned and shot in the same movement, the ball curling as if magnetised beyond Neville Southall's outstretched fingers into the far corner of the net. Surely the game was up for Everton. After falling behind four times, they could only be running on empty. With the match deep into extra-time, it was Cottee again who provided its eighth goal. The sense of joy, relief and disbelief from the Gwladys Street End was unconfined.

As if the game had failed to produce enough drama, its aftermath produced the biggest story of the season. Within forty-eight hours of the final whistle, Kenny Dalglish had resigned as manager, citing pressures of work. Later the same year he returned to the game at Blackburn, a decision that left a taint on an otherwise glorious chapter at Anfield.

A week later, Goodison Park staged the second replay, won by Everton with a single goal from Dave Watson. It all came to naught for Everton in the quarter-finals. They lost 2-1 to Second Division West Ham, an unhappy return for Tony Cottee.

1991

POMPEY'S PAIN

1992

LIVERPOOL:
Grobbelaar, Jones, Burrows, Nicol, Molby, Wright ©, Saunders, Houghton, **Rush (1)**, McManaman, **Thomas (1)** subs: *Marsh, Walters*

SUNDERLAND:
Norman, Owers, Ball, Bennett, Rogan, Rush (*Hardyman 69*), Bracewell ©, Davenport, Armstrong (*Hawke 77*), Byrne, Atkinson

The early rounds threw up some intriguing if unlikely derbies. The first round saw Fulham entertain Hayes, who stunned their hosts with a 2-0 victory. Al-Fayed and Keegan were still some years away. In round two, Barnet thumped Enfield 4-1 in the other North London derby. This after Enfield won away at Aldershot; the Shots would resign from the league later that season after going bust. Another rare derby saw Reading and Slough play twice before the Third Division side pulled through.

One of the bitterest of rivalries was played out in South Wales, where Swansea and Cardiff, neither exactly in clover in the early 90s, played at Vetch Field; the Swans prevailed 2-1 in the first FA Cup meeting between the two since 1914.

Southern League Crawley made the third round for the first time, their run including a 4-2 win against Northampton. Two goals from Whittington had surprised the Cobblers, but instead of turning to London, the Sussex side made the short hop south to Brighton. The fairy tale ended with a 5-0 defeat.

The other non-league heroes were Farnborough Town. By defeating Torquay in a second round replay, they earned a money-spinning tie with West Ham. Ceding home advantage looked to be no handicap, as they forced a 1-1 draw. The Hammers squeaked home with the only goal in the replay, Tony Morley sparing them the lottery of penalties.

The penalty shoot-out had been introduced as a way of settling ties if teams were still level after extra time in the first replay. Traditionalists bleated, but two clubs slugging it out for three games or more rarely produced a classic, and was often tedious in the extreme. Newcastle would have settled for a third game against Third Division Bournemouth. The Magpies lost their third round replay 4-2 on penalties at St. James' Park. The tie had actually kicked off three times but the second attempt was abandoned as the ground became enveloped in fog. This defeat was a precursor to another new chapter in the Newcastle soap opera. Ossie Ardiles, such an intelligent footballer, was proving a hopeless case as a manager. The Newcastle board pledged to stand by their man, then, true to form, replaced him three days later with Kevin Keegan.

Three other top flight clubs fell to supposedly inferior opposition at the first hurdle. Wimbledon, more used to upsetting the apple-cart themselves, were turned over at Plough Lane by Bristol City, while Oldham, another of the upstarts of the eighties, lost a humdinger of a replay at Leyton Orient 4-3 in extra time.

Oh, and Arsenal lost. Who can forget the small matter of a 2-1 defeat at Fourth Division Wrexham for the reigning champions? Arsenal don't have a history of getting toppled by the little guys, so when they do it sticks in the memory. There were no excuses; unlike the current fashion, the champions weren't fielding a team of juniors. Their European Cup hopes had already been dashed by Benfica (the Champions League was still a twinkle in a Uefa accountant's eye), Coventry had dumped them out of the League Cup and a barren league spell had yielded one point from nine over Christmas. In short, the Gunners' season had turned pear-shaped. The Cup represented their last hope of salvation.

Wrexham welcomed the draw as a much-needed source of income since a mid-table spot in Division Four was not exactly attracting hordes to the Racecourse Ground. For much of the game, cash looked their only consolation. Arsenal controlled the first half and took the lead just before the break after Merson's wriggling run and pull-back had presented Alan Smith with a tap-in. The second half fast petered out. Arsenal, boasting the country's meanest back four, kept the ball, kept it tight and regarded Wrexham's honest endeavour with only the mildest flickers of irritation. They reckoned without a couple of wily veterans.

With only eight minutes remaining, Gordon Davies drew O'Leary into a foul on the right edge of the penalty

area. Mickey Thomas, with thirty-seven years and twelve clubs on the clock, unleashed a drive that rocketed past the wall and an astonished Seaman into the far top corner. His team-mates swore that the old scallywag had tried the same thing time after time in training and hadn't yet hit the target!

Two minutes later Wrexham's joy turned to unadulterated delirium. Davies broke down the right and his cross was hooked past a statuesque Arsenal defence by Steve Watkin. Wrexham basked in their most memorable moment of Cup glory. For George Graham, defeat was 'the lowest point of my career.'

The last sixteen saw the Second Division well represented. Only Bolton from beneath it were still in the frame, and they went out in a 3-2 extra-time thriller at the Dell after an equally rousing 2-2 home draw. Saints had beaten Manchester United on penalties in the previous round; United became the first top division club to lose in that manner. Of the Division Two sides, Portsmouth soldiered on with a good 4-2 replay win over Middlesbrough; a promising young winger called Darren Anderton added two goals to the two he scored in round four against Orient.

Sunderland made a better fist of flying the north east flag than Newcastle. Centre-forward John Byrne had found the Cup to his liking and goals against Port Vale, Oxford and West Ham sent the Black Cats to their first quarter-final in sixteen years. Opponents Chelsea had gone ten years without consecutive FA Cup wins, but had become the capital's last representatives for the first time since 1970. Clive Allen put the Blues in front, only for Byrne to sneak an equaliser with ten minutes remaining. Peter Davenport and Gordon Armstrong finished the job for Sunderland in the replay.

With Portsmouth winning through against a declining Nottingham Forest, and relegation-threatened Norwich beating Southampton, the semi-final line-up had Liverpool as the shortest-price favourites in years.

At Highbury Anderton attracted the attention of a wider audience. Portsmouth had drawn the short straw of Liverpool, and no-one gave them an earthly chance. That the teams were still locked together after 120 minutes was due to a fine display and goal from the youngster. At Villa Park another two hours failed to produce a result, or even a goal; as in the first match, Pompey were the better side. Portsmouth, if they could beat their nerves, were a few penalty kicks from their first post-war final. But the nerves won, 3-1.

Sunderland revived memories of their 1973 heroics by winning first time against Norwich. With Byrne on target again, he relished the prospect of becoming the first player since Peter Osgood in 1970 to score in every round.

It was never a serious hope. Sunderland, despite being bombarded with replays of Ian Porterfield's goal against Leeds, never looked like finding the net in the final. After a tame first half, Michael Thomas and Ian Rush scored, and Liverpool squeezed the life out of the game to collect their fifth trophy.

1992

CUPS RUNNETH OVER FOR ARSENAL

1991

1993

ARSENAL:
Seaman, Dixon, Winterburn, Linighan, Adams
©, Jensen, Davis, Parlour *(Smith 66)*, Merson,
Campbell, **Wright (1)** *(O'Leary 90)*

SHEFF WED:
Woods, Nilsson, Worthington, Palmer, **Hirst (1)**,
Anderson © *(Hyde 85)*, Waddle *(Bart-Williams*
112), Warhurst, Bright, Sheridan, Harkes

ARSENAL:
Seaman, Dixon, Winterburn, **Linighan (1)**,
Adams ©, Jensen, Davis, Smith, Merson,
Campbell, **Wright (1)** *(O'Leary 81) sub: Selley*

SHEFF WED:
Woods, Nilsson *(Bart-Williams 118)*,
Worthington, Palmer, Hirst, Wilson *(Hyde 62)*,
Waddle (1), Warhurst, Bright, Sheridan, Harkes

ere's where sorting the Davids from the Goliaths gets a bit tricky. With the advent of the FA Premier League for the 1992–1993 season, the Football League decided to re-name their own competition. They did so again in 2004, for no obvious reason. Here's how Sir Humphrey Appleby might explain it to that old simpleton, Prime Minister Jim Hacker: 'It's really quite straightforward Prime Minister. In 1992, with the formation of the Premier League, the football league was left without a First Division. So, unwilling to be party to a headless competition, the Football League decided to call the Second Division the First Division instead. Logically, therefore, the Third Division became the Second Division, and the Fourth Division became the Third Division. In 2004, the Football League decided that the First Division didn't sound important enough, especially when there was a possibility that some big, important teams might be playing in that division. So the First Division, formerly the Second Division, became the Championship. The Second Division, formerly the Third Division, became the First Division; and the Third Division, formerly the Fourth Division, became the Second Division. So, for example, when Luton won the First Division in 2005, they were promoted to what used to be the First Division, giving them an opportunity to be promoted to what also used to be called the First Division. You see, Prime Minister?'

'I see, yes, Humphrey. Thank you. One question. Why?'

'Revenue streams, Prime Minister, it's all about revenue streams.'

'Money, Humphrey? You're saying the modern version of our national game is all about money?'

'Yes, Prime Minister.'

For Cardiff, meanwhile, the memory of their 1927 victory was never more distant. Bath City turned up at Ninian Park and drowned the Bluebirds 3-2 in the first round. Two other league sides were embarrassed in round one by opposition even closer to home. Altrincham won an up-market derby against Chester, but the greater humiliation was reserved for Torquay. The Gulls were stuffed 5-2 at home to Yeovil, who recorded a record fourteenth victory by a non-league side over league opposition. They extended it in the Second Round by winning at Hereford.

Of the three non-leaguers who reached the third round, two were handsomely rewarded. Marlow travelled to Tottenham, where a 5-1 defeat was incidental to the

Buckinghamshire side's first appearance in round three for 106 years. North London's other aristocrats travelled to Yeovil in a repeat of their 1971 tie; a hat-trick from Ian Wright eased Arsenal through 3-1. Pity Marine, though. The Northern Premier League side could only curse their luck in being sent to Crewe, where they lost 3-1.

Holders Liverpool didn't make it past the third round. Signs of increasing fragility at Anfield were confirmed by the result of their tie with third tier Bolton. Wanderers, making strides under Bruce Rioch, took a 2-0 lead at Burnden Park, only to be pegged back by an own goal and an equaliser from Ian Rush. If Liverpool thought Bolton had shot their bolt they were jolted back to reality by John McGinlay's header after three minutes at Anfield. Andy Walker wrapped the tie up towards the end. Bolton went out at Derby after another good win at Wolves. They would be back for more the following year.

The fourth round draw threw up a clash of the titans. Leeds, who had taken advantage of Man United's late collapse to win the 1992 title, travelled to Highbury and purred into a 2-0 lead through Gary Speed and Lee Chapman. Arsenal fought back through Ray Parlour, then drew level in emphatic style thanks to Paul Merson's twenty-five-yard special. At Elland Road, it all looked in vain when Leeds led with eight minutes left. Alan Smith chose a timely moment to end a three-month drought before Ian Wright grabbed the winner in extra time.

After such escapology, Arsenal were tagged as the team with their 'name on the Cup', a notion that grew ever more plausible with victories over Premier League Forest and Ipswich. This left them with the little matter of a semi-final at Wembley against Tottenham. Unlike 1991, there was neither

Gascoigne nor Lineker to rattle their cage. The match was a shadow of the game two years earlier, settled by Tony Adams' header with fifteen minutes left.

The first semi, also at Wembley, had settled another local difficulty. United and Wednesday met in the Cup's first Sheffield derby for thirty-three years. Wednesday had a comfortable route to the final; United had to settle a couple of tough ties to earn their place. Glyn Hodges winner saw Manchester United off at Bramall Lane, and money-bags Blackburn were beaten on penalties after two goals from Mitch Ward saw the teams level after extra time.

The game was predictably tetchy, and thin on quality; goals from Chris

1992-1993

The final marked the end of David O'Leary's Arsenal career. The Irish centre-half capped twenty years at Highbury, including a club-record 558 league appearances, with a winner's medal at Wembley. He was romantically but justifiably brought on as a substitute.

Waddle and the veteran Alan Cork cancelled each other out in normal time, before Mark Bright sent the Owls to their first final since 1966.

The two Finals were dull affairs. Ian Wright deserves a commendation for playing and scoring in both games despite a broken toe. Both efforts were equalised, and Wednesday might have won either game, only to rue their missed chances. As the unedifying spectacle loomed of an FA Cup final settled by penalties, Arsenal won a corner in the last minute of extra-time. Merson picked out Andy Linighan's head, the centre-half's header finding the net via the despairing gloves of Chris Woods. For Wednesday, who had also lost the League Cup Final to the same opponents earlier in the season, it was a cruel finale. Linighan's 120th-minute winner is the latest in Cup final history. For Arsenal, it was a unique double – no other side had won both domestic cups in the same season.

ERIC LE ROI

CHELSEA:
Kharine, Clarke, Sinclair, Kjeldberg, Johnsen, Burley (*Hoddle 65*), Spencer, Newton, Stein (*Cascarino 78*), Peacock, Wise © *sub: Hitchcock (g)*

MAN UTD:
Schmeichel, Parker, Bruce ©, Pallister, Irwin (*Sharpe 84*), Kanchelskis **(McClair 84 (1))**, Keane, Ince, Giggs, Cantona **(2pp)**, **Hughes (1)** *sub: Walsh (g)*

1993-1994 saw the reign of King Eric at its height. Cantona, with trademark upturned collar, knocked in twenty-five goals with the air of a lord deigning to dine with the peasants. His two penalties at Wembley, tucked away with the minimum of ceremony, brought the curtain down on a momentous season for him and his club.

Bringing the curtain down is an appropriate term, because United provided plenty of amateur dramatics along the way. A collapse in form and discipline had seen a handsome Christmas lead in the league whittled away. A seventeen-month unbeaten home run was broken by Chelsea in March. Cantona was sent off in successive matches and Andrei Kanchelskis was dismissed in the League Cup Final defeat to Aston Villa. In the Cup semi-final at Wembley, unfashionable Oldham were a few minutes away form reaching the final after a messy game, but a moment of brilliance from Mark Hughes rescued United, and they eased through the replay at Maine Road, a far better venue than Wembley for a semi-final between two Greater Manchester teams. The league form steadied after that, and Ferguson's men finished as comfortable champions.

The team standing between United and the double were Chelsea, the only side to beat them twice in the league. Manager Glenn Hoddle had obviously done his homework. Chelsea were the better team in the first half and might have gone in at half time a goal to the good, had Gavin Peacock's dipping twenty-yarder not cannoned off the bar.

As the second half began, the Blues' failure to capitalise on their good approach play cost them. They held on until the hour mark, then as Dennis Irwin surged into the box, he was upended by Eddie Newton with a challenge so agricultural he may as well have been driving a tractor.

A goal behind, Chelsea immediately abandoned their plan of containment. It played into United's hands, who had the firepower in Giggs and Kanchelskis to rip apart opponents by breaking at pace. So it proved, and nine minutes later Chelsea were three down. David Elleray's award of a second penalty from forty yards away as Kanchelskis was brought down three yards outside the area, was rough justice. Hughes and McClair completed the victory. A harsh scoreline, but United had taught Chelsea a lesson and were hardly in a mood to be charitable. Their eighth Cup completed their first Double.

Six months earlier, back in Colchester, Sutton were

recreating a glory of their own. The Isthmian Leaguers from Surrey revived memories of 1989, Coventry and all that, by winning at Colchester and Torquay to reach the third round. They fought hard at Meadow Lane before going down 3-2 to Notts County.

Joining Sutton in the third round were Bromsgrove who, despite a goal from Crisp, had their chips against Barnsley, and Bath City who gained an honourable draw at the Victoria Ground before losing 4-1 to Stoke in the replay.

The non-leaguers with staying power were Kidderminster. They had reached the third round without meeting a league side, so a derby match with illustrious neighbours, Birmingham, was a draw made in heaven. It was a celestial performance to match; Neil Cartwright and Jon Purdie earned the Harriers a momentous win, leaving Birmingham with the eight-year-old ghosts of Altrincham rattling around St. Andrews. The fourth round presented Kidderminster with a disappointing draw but a real opportunity: Preston at home. The former 'Invincibles' were bottom tier no-hopers these days, and played their role as supporting cast to perfection. Delwyn Humphries carved his niche in Kidderminster history with the only goal, elevating the Harriers to a clique of five non-league clubs who have reached the fifth round. West Ham were just the sort of side to come a cropper against 'humble' opponents, but a disciplined performance and a Lee Chapman goal ended Kidderminster's dream.

The fifth round saw the end of Cardiff's challenge too. An ordinary third tier team, they had followed up a great away win over Middlesbrough with an even better victory over Premier League Manchester City. Their young striker, Nathan Blake, made the headlines with a fantastic solo goal.

Another whose stumble nearly rivalled Birmingham's was Chelsea. Barnet, having surrendered home advantage, forced a 0-0 draw and came close to winning the tie in the dying seconds. Booed off by their supporters, Chelsea made a proper job of the replay, winning 4-0. As is often the case, an early scare fuelled the impetus for a run. Gavin Peacock carried the baton, scoring in both fourth round games against Sheffield Wednesday.

Chelsea were one of only seven top flight clubs in the last sixteen. Wimbledon fell to Manchester United and a poor Ipswich team lost in a replay to Wolves. Aston Villa faced Bolton with some trepidation; Wanderers had already put out two Premiership, sides, and Villa were coming off the back of a defeat by Tranmere in the first leg of their League Cup semi-final.

Bolton's fun started in the very first round, when only two goals in the last ten minutes from Owen Coyle prevented an untimely exit at the hands of Gretna Green. A better performance was needed against Everton in round three. A 1-1 draw shouldn't have been good enough, but Everton, despite going 2-0 up, were pipped in extra time, and Coyle again got the winner. Arsenal, of all teams, didn't learn. Two-one up with fifteen minutes to go at Burnden Park, they too conceded a late goal, this time to Andy Walker, returning from nearly a year out with injury. Wanderers were outstanding in the replay, goals from John

McGinlay, Jason McAteer and Walker put paid to Arsenal's chances, and left egg on the face of former manager Bruce Rioch, now at Highbury. Villa were right to be nervous; they were beaten by a thumping free-kick from centre half Alan Stubbs.

None of the second tier clubs drew each other in the last eight: Manchester United beat Charlton; Bolton's season ended in anti-climax when they lost at home to Oldham; Peacock was on target again as Chelsea put out Wolves with the only goal; and only Luton carried the fight forward for the underdogs by beating West Ham in a replay. All three goals were scored by winger Scott Oakes, ably assisted by former Chelsea favourite, Kerry Dixon.

An emotional welcome for Dixon from the Chelsea faithful was the highlight of the semi-final for Luton; Peacock did the damage again, scoring both goals in a 2-0 win. Chelsea's long winter looked to be over. After twenty-four years and more than their fair share of humiliation, at least the had made the final again.

TOTTENHAM HOTSPUR OR BYE

EVERTON:
Southall, Jackson, Hinchcliffe, Ablett, Watson © , Parkinson, Unsworth, Horne, Stuart, **Rideout (1)** (*Ferguson 51*), Limpar (*Amokachi 69*) *sub: Kearton (g)*

MAN UTD:
Schmeichel, Gary Neville, Irwin, Bruce © (*Giggs 46*), Pallister, Sharpe (*Scholes 72*), Keane, Ince, McClair, Hughes, Butt *sub: Walsh (g)*

I t seems hard on Everton to relegate their hard-won fifth Cup to the status of prologue. They beat hot favourites and holders Manchester United, and thwarted them in their pursuit of consecutive Doubles. Three-times beaten finalists since 1989, they deserved to see blue rather than red ribbons adorn the old trophy. Truth is, though, the real story of this season's Cup was to be found off the pitch.

Tottenham were not a team on whom financial fortune had smiled of late. Their diversification a decade earlier into areas of business unrelated to football seemed a futuristic model at the time but on reflection looked the epitome of eighties greed. It had ushered in the harsh financial era of Alan Sugar as chairman. For a while, the ship seemed to steady, but in 1994 a fresh storm broke.

The FA had unearthed 'financial irregularities' in Spurs accounting, which took the form of illegal loans to players. Under pressure to throw the book, they dealt Spurs a £600,000 fine, docked them twelve league points before the start of the season, and expelled them from the FA Cup for one year. On appeal, the points deduction was reduced to six, the fine increased to £1.5 million, but the Cup ban remained.

Alan Sugar dug in his heels. So did the FA. The case went to independent arbitration and dragged on for months, so much so that it remained unresolved when the third round draw took place six months later. This led to the preposterous announcement by FA Secretary Graham Kelly, as Spurs' ball was drawn from the bag: 'Bye or Tottenham Hotspur'.

The farce was lent extra piquancy by Spurs' potential opponents. Altrincham from the Conference had put out Wigan to earn the right to rub shoulders with the big boys; only this big boy appeared to be grounded. In the end, as usual, the FA ended up with egg on its face and Tottenham were reinstated. After such beginnings, their date with destiny at Wembley looked virtually preordained. Altrincham and Sunderland were despatched, but Southampton looked to have halted the procession in the fifth round. After forcing a 1-1 draw at White Hart Lane, they led 2-0 at half-time in the replay. Tottenham's response was to bring on Ronnie Rosenthal, whose reputation had been built on dangerous appearances coming off the bench at Liverpool. What followed was one of the more extraordinary turnarounds in Cup history. Two rockets from Ronnie brought Spurs level and he completed his hat-trick in extra-time. In the second period, goals from Sheringham, Barmby and Anderton lent an air of unreality to the score-line that even Tottenham diehards found hard to grasp.

After such heroics, who would bet against Tottenham now? A trip to Anfield in the sixth round proved no problem – it was no longer the intimidating venue of old. The inspirational German striker Jürgen Klinsmann and Teddy Sheringham saw them to a 2-1 win.

Everton, forced to scrap in the bottom half of the table, started the semi-final as firm underdogs. Daniel Amokachi, who had entered the fray only as a seventieth-minute substitute, sank Spurs with two goals as Everton ran out 4-1 winners.

The earlier rounds had been a bit of a breeze for United, even without Cantona, but their passage to the final was hardly free from controversy. Their semi-final had been marred by the pre-match death of Crystal Palace fan Paul Nixon, who was killed after fighting between fans in a pub car park in Walsall. Bad blood had simmered since the infamous League game at Selhurst Park in January, which had seen Eric Cantona banned for nine months following his attack on a spectator. The game ended in a draw and Palace fans boycotted the replay at Villa Park. The 17,987 attendance was the lowest for a post-war semi-final. Before the game, appeals for calm had been widely issued. The word is not in Roy Keane's lexicon. He was sent off for stamping on Gareth Southgate, and Palace's Darren Patterson followed him down the tunnel after retaliating. It was just the incident that such an emotional occasion did not need. Both players were charged with bringing the game into disrepute. The small crowd went home happy as United won 2-0 with goals from their redoubtable centre-half pairing of Steve Bruce and Gary Pallister.

At Wembley Everton again took second billing, but won the game on the half-hour. Matt Jackson broke down the right, and his cross landed on a plate for Graham Stuart. He hit the bar from a few yards out, an inexplicable miss, but the incoming Paul Rideout headed the rebound past Peter Schmeichel. With the title slipping away to Blackburn, United's second double was kept on ice.

NORMAL SERVICE RESUMED

LIVERPOOL:
James, McAteer, Scales, Wright, Babb, Jones
(*Thomas 85*), McManaman, Barnes, Redknapp,
Collymore (*Rush 74*), Fowler *sub: Warner (g)*

MAN UTD:
Schmeichel, Irwin, Phil Neville, May, Keane,
Pallister, **Cantona** © **(1)**, Beckham (*Gary
Neville 85*), Cole (*Scholes 65*), Butt, Giggs *sub:
Sharpe*

T he missing link was back. Much had been made of
Cantona's absence the previous year, as United
failed to break down a workmanlike Everton. This
season he was back and mercifully let his football
do the talking.

Back in November, the competition had no need of
King Eric to create incident and headlines. Oxford United
spanked Dorchester Town 9-1, while Shrewsbury's players queued up to score against Marine. Seven were on
target in an 11-2 pasting, so Marine's offer of help with
an own goal was hardly necessary.

Walsall and Torquay served up a second helping of
defensive chaos in round two. With their replay locked at
4-4 after normal time, Walsall upped the ante with four
more. One can only wonder if Torquay misread the rules
of the competition and trooped off after ninety minutes
for a second replay.

Sheffield United, from the second tier, sprang a surprise by putting out Arsenal. Carl Veart's goal settled the
tie in a replay. Port Vale had a chance to emulate them
when they drew Everton in the fourth round; they had
won a terrific replay with Crystal Palace 4-3 in the third.
In Ian Bogie they had a player whose name was tailor-
made for a headline. Bogie picked his spot to earn a 2-2
draw at Goodison Park, then he opened the scoring in
the replay. Although Graham Stuart equalised, Everton's
bogey man was Northern Ireland winger Jon McCarthy,
who smashed a winner in off a post to revive memories
of Vale's win over Spurs eight years earlier. Round five
looked an impossible mission for the men from Burslem,
but dogged defending at Elland Road gained them a
lucrative replay. At Vale Park the task of taking the game to
Leeds was beyond them. Gary McAllister's double eased
Leeds into the quarter finals.

It was a last eight devoid of romance and even the
four all-Premiership ties went the way of the side with
better league form. At Elland Road, Leeds hosted a
Liverpool team for whom Stan Collymore and Robbie
Fowler were proving Anfield's best little-and-large
double act since Keegan and Toshack. Between them
they contributed eleven to the Reds' FA Cup goal tally.
Rochdale and Shrewsbury were hit for seven and four
respectively and even the step up in quality provided by
Leeds proved no obstacle. They played it canny in the
first game, then cantered to a 3-0 victory in the replay
with two from Steve McManaman and one from
Fowler. Villa, in their first semi-final for 26 years, were
on the end of a beating by the same scoreline at Old

1995-1996

Cinderford Town stepped up for their fifteen minutes of fame by reaching the first round proper for the only time in the club's seventy-four-year history. The Southern League side pulled off a surprise by putting out Bromsgrove Rovers from the Conference. Gravesend and Northfleet stole their thunder in the Second Round.

Trafford. Fowler scored twice this time, Jason McAteer adding a third.

On Villa's turf, Chelsea and Manchester United served up a better contest. The Blues led at half-time through Ruud Gullit's header but Andy Cole equalised early in the second half. The game turned on a lapse from Chelsea's midfielder Craig Burley, who attempted a bizarre back pass from near the half-way line. It bounced woefully short of keeper Dmitri Kharine and David Beckham applied the pinpoint finish.

Liverpool and Manchester United had forged an enmity in the eighties worthy of the Old Firm. Rather than inspire the final, it stifled it. The most entertaining part of the day was the mirth engendered by the cream suits the Liverpool players were sporting before the game. Their tailor, in attempting to create a late spring, lounge-lizard look, succeeded only in turning them into well-dressed programme sellers.

A disappointing encounter looked destined to drift scorelessly into extra time, when United won a corner with five minutes left. Beckham's cross was punched out by James and would have counted as a clearance had it fallen to any other player than Cantona. Lurking on the edge of the box, he adjusted his body shape to perfection, thus ensuring that his volley lost none of its power but maintained a low trajectory. It flew past James for the winner. With a customary sense of timing, Eric had grabbed the glory.

1995-1996

Gravesend and Northfleet evoked memories among older fans by reaching the third round for the first time since 1963. Excitement mounted as they drew Villa at home. They took the cash rather than glory, switching the tie to Villa Park and losing 3-0.

CUP GOES CONTINENTAL

CHELSEA:
Grodas, Petrescu, Minto, Sinclair, Lebouef, Clarke, Zola (*Vialli 89*), **Di Matteo (1)**, **Newton (1)**, Hughes, Wise © *subs: Hitchcock (g), Myers*

MIDDLESBROUGH:
Roberts, Blackmore, Fleming, Stamp, Pearson ©, Festa, Emerson, Mustoe (*Vickers 29*), Ravanelli (*Beck 24*), Juninho, Hignett (*Kinder 74*)

A s the English game moved towards the end of the century it was becoming increasingly dominated by overseas players. Eric Cantona was the catalyst; his influence on Manchester United was so huge that other teams searched abroad for similar talismanic figures. Tottenham found one briefly in Jürgen Klinsmann and David Ginola was about to charm the Toon army. Patrick Vieira and Dennis Bergkamp would soon arrive at Arsenal to provide them with the steel and subtlety to complement the goalscoring of the young French stars, Nicolas Anelka and Thierry Henry.

Chelsea, as befitted a side from the cosmopolitan Kings' Road, were at the forefront of this new import business. Not just players; they had an overseas coach, Ruud Gullit having stepped up to player-manager after the departure of Glenn Hoddle for the England job. Gullit had persuaded some of his friends from Serie A to join the revolution; Gianluca Vialli, Roberto di Matteo, and, crucially, Gianfranco Zola, were all strutting their stuff at Stamford Bridge. There was a risky side to this policy, and Chelsea's Cup final opponents were a stark illustration.

There was a right and a wrong type of player to buy. While Juninho, all twinkling toes and heart and vigour, was lighting up Teesside and leading Middlesbrough's Cup run, their other imports were thumbing their noses at an inexperienced manager and letting the club, for all its millions, slide into the second tier. Ravanelli scored goals, but not enough to compensate for the negative effect of his constant carping and conceited demands. When relegation beckoned, the White Feather waved a white flag. Mikael Beck and Gianluca Festa simply weren't good enough, and Emerson was a downright disgrace. Buy right, buy success – ask Chelsea now. Buy wrong, come back down to earth with a bang.

The Cup didn't exactly start with a bang. First round day came and went without the tweaking of a single league nose. Sudbury Town and Woking revived interest in their respective replays. Sudbury held Brighton for 120 minutes, and then sent them out 4-3 on penalties. Woking had drawn 2-2 with Millwall, but a trip to the New Den looked a tall order for the Conference side.

The Cup has a habit of allowing faded stars a last hurrah, and Woking boasted a popular ex-pro in their ranks. Nineteen years earlier, a long-haired winger

There were a few other high-scoring performances in the season; Carlisle put six past Shepshed; Bristol City beat St Albans 9-2 (four for Agostino); Middlesbrough won 6-0 at home to Chester; Sheffield Wednesday thrashed Grimsby 7-1; and Bolton won 6-2 in a replay against Luton.

1996-1997

named Clive Walker had ripped Liverpool apart as Chelsea had upset the form book. The golden locks had long since disappeared, but the ageing Walker showed Millwall a clean pair of heels with his second goal of the tie. Off went Woking to the Abbey Stadium, where Walker again opened the scoring against Cambridge. His team ran out 2-0 winners and reached the third round for the second successive season.

Unlike last year, Woking had the excitement of visiting a Premier League ground. They took several thousand to Highfield Road, but Eoin Jess looked to have done just enough for Coventry as the game entered its last minute. Up popped Steve Thompson with the equaliser to send Woking into the dreamland of the fourth round draw. Their prospective trip to Blackburn was cruelly taken away, when an own goal handed Coventry a 2-1 win.

Even after Woking's defeat, the Conference was represented in the fourth round. Hednesford Town flew the flag after seeing off Southport, Blackpool and York; Joe O'Connor was the hero for the Pitmen with the winner in the first two ties. Hednesford shocked Premier League Middlesbrough when O'Connor scored again to give them the lead at the Riverside. Surrendering home advantage looked to be no problem, until they too were undone by an own goal. Middlesbrough eventually squeaked home with the help of yet another own goal, but not before O'Connor scored yet another to confirm his cult status in the Staffordshire town.

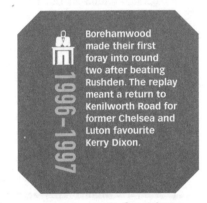

Borehamwood made their first foray into round two after beating Rushden. The replay meant a return to Kenilworth Road for former Chelsea and Luton favourite Kerry Dixon.

1996-1997

Wrexham were thumbing their noses at their betters again; a draw at home to West Ham should have been the end of their Cup, but the Hammers are always prone to a flaky day, and Wrexham scored the only goal to march on.

Away wins at Peterborough and Birmingham sent the North Wales standard-bearers into the fifth round.

The draw threw them up against Chesterfield, another team from the third tier, and guaranteed the winner the riches of a semi-final spot. Chesterfield had beaten a poor Nottingham Forest team in the fourth round. Even more impressively, they had beaten Bolton at Burnden Park, with an outstanding individual hat-trick from their powerful young forward, Kevin Davies. The Spireites came through the battle of the underdogs and set up a semi-final with Middlesbrough.

Middlesbrough were struggling in the Premiership; manager, Bryan Robson, had spent millions, but most of it went on imports with egos that outstripped their

Di Matteo's strike, timed at forty-three seconds, was the quickest-ever in a Wembley Cup final.

1996-1997

commitment. Only Juninho showed any pride that season, and the little maestro scored crucial goals in the ties against Man City and Derby.

This season's comeback kings were Chelsea. In their fourth round tie against Liverpool, another smash and grab from Fowler and Collymore left them with a 2-0 deficit at Stamford Bridge. Mark Hughes, so often a thorn in Liverpool's side, led the great escape. Gianfranco Zola and a rare double from Gianluca Vialli sent the Reds reeling. It gave Chelsea a momentum that no team could stop.

The Blues had luck on their side too. At Filbert Street it was Chelsea's turn to squander a two goal lead. But with a replay at Stamford Bridge, hopes remained high. Leicester, showing all of manager Martin O'Neill's fighting spirit, had other ideas. They dug in until Erland Johnsen burst into their area with three minutes remaining. The centre-half looked to be going nowhere, until his heel was clipped by the most innocuous of touches. With O'Neill dancing an apoplectic jig on the touchline, Frank Lebouef stroked home the penalty.

At a foggy Fratton Park, two goals from Dennis Wise saw Chelsea steer a safe passage to Highbury, where notorious party-poopers Wimbledon lay in wait. The Dons were still a good side, but no longer had the physical armoury to intimidate the Kings Road fancy-boys. Chelsea had stumbled at the same hurdle last year, but this time they had Gianfranco Zola. In his first English season he was in the form that was to earn him the Football Writers' Player of the Year award. With Chelsea already two up, he took possession twenty-five yards out with his back to goal. In an instant, he executed a Cruyff-like turn and curled the ball into the corner of the net. The Blues were back at Wembley for the second time in four seasons.

At Old Trafford, things hadn't gone according to script. This was a glorious semi-final, fulfilling all the great Cup traditions. The underdogs matched the big shots, fortunes swung back and forth and there were goals a-plenty. But what a pity that David Elleray had to intervene. Middlesbrough, for all their top-division millions and swanky new stadium, were hardly doughty Cup fighters. Their 121 years had produced not a single major final. This looked to be their big chance to deliver.

If Middlesbrough had a game plan, it soon lay in tatters. Chesterfield hassled and harried, reducing Emerson and even Juninho to bewildered passengers.

Brazilian it wasn't, but it was effective. The Spireites roared into a two-goal lead; Andy Morris followed up after Ben Roberts saved an effort from Kevin Davies, and their inspirational captain Sean Dyche converted a penalty. The tide looked unassailable, but Fabrizio Ravanelli suddenly turned it for Middlesbrough. His goal at last gave his team impetus, and it was Chesterfield's turn to hang on.

As the second half ticked on, the Spireites knew that if they could catch Middlesbrough on the break, the game would effectively be over. Their hopes were raised further by the dismissal of Vladimir Kinder, and Chesterfield took advantage of the extra man. When Jon Howard's shot crashed off the crossbar and landed two feet over the goal-line, they looked to have clinched it. Whether referee Elleray misinterpreted the linesman's signal for a goal remains a talking-point in North Derbyshire. The Harrow schoolmaster awarded Middlesbrough a free kick, although the source of the infringement baffled everyone. Elleray's post-match comments only deepened the mystery of Chesterfield's disallowed goal. 'I wasn't sure whether the linesman was indicating the ball had crossed the goal-line or whether he had spotted the same offence as me . . . although I can't remember what it was. In fact, there were eight or nine infringements I could have blown for before the player shot.' Television replays failed to reveal a single offence.

It was the twist of fate that Boro needed. Elleray was soon in action again, awarding the Premier League side a penalty that Craig Hignett converted. It was a borderline decision; the offence was clear but it was right on the edge of the box. When Gianluca Festa put them ahead it appeared that Middlesbrough could finally breathe easily. Just when it looked like Boro's Wembley date had been confirmed, Jamie Hewitt's diving header pinched Chesterfield a richly deserved equaliser with only seconds remaining.

The Spireites emotions at the end of extra-time were mixed. They had done themselves and the lower divisions proud, holding a Premier League side packed with Brazilian and Italian internationals and yet . . . Without Elleray's mistake, they might have become the first side from outside the top two divisions to reach an FA Cup final. Elleray had what he craved every time he took control of a game — attention.

The replay at Hillsborough could only be a let-down. Boro won a deserved but hollow victory 3-0. Beck, Ravanelli and Emerson were an unholy trinity of scorers; never before can three such unpopular players have taken their team to a Cup final.

Come the final, Middlesbrough ought to have been a broken side, having been relegated six days earlier. They had accumulated two points more than they required for safety but a three-point deduction for failing to fulfil a fixture at Blackburn returned to haunt them. On that occasion they had cited illness as the reason for not turning up. Within a minute of kick-off, the queasy feeling had returned.

After Boro's first venture forward, Roberto di Matteo picked up the ball inside his own half. Emerson should have intercepted him, but with the unconcerned Brazilian trotting alongside, Di Matteo continued his run deep into the opposition half and let fly from twenty-five yards. Roberts was stranded on his six-yard line as the ball dipped over him into the net.

Middlesbrough spent the next eighty-one minutes chasing the game, but without putting the brittle pairing of Frank Lebouef and Frank Sinclair under any serious pressure. With seven minutes left Eddie Newton found Dan Petrescu whose cross was met with an impeccable back-flick from Zola. Waiting to pick his spot and complete the move he had started was Eddie Newton. For the Chelsea midfielder, this was his moment of redemption. He had been the villain of the piece three years earlier, when his reckless challenge had gifted Manchester United a penalty and started his team's slide to defeat. This time he was part of a triumphant lap of honour, as the Blues paraded their first major trophy in twenty-six years.

ARE YOU WATCHING, MANCHESTER?

ARSENAL:
Seaman, Dixon, Winterburn, Vieira, Keown,
Adams ©, Parlour, **Anelka (1)**, Petit, Wreh (*Platt
63*), **Overmars (1)** *subs: Manninger (g), Bould,
Wright, Grimaldi*

NEWCASTLE:
Given, Pistone, Pearce (*Andersson 72*), Batty,
Dabizas, Howey, Lee, Barton (*Watson 77*),
Shearer, Ketsbaia (*Barnes 85*), Speed *subs:
Hislop (g), Albert*

Without uppity non-leaguers, where would the Cup be? Emley, despite being formed in 1903, had waited eighty-nine seasons to enter the first round proper. In 1991, their first round tie against Bolton had produced a swift exit. Six years later, they had obviously learned from the experience.

The Northern Premier League side punched above their weight immediately, although they needed penalties to see off Morecambe from the Conference. In the second round Emley were sent to Sincil Bank for a tie against Third Division Lincoln. They came away with a 2-2 draw, then shredded their fans' nerves for a second time. As against Morecambe, the replay finished 3-3 after extra time; again it was Emley who triumphed, winning the shoot-out 4-3.

They deserved the luck of the draw, and got it with a visit to Upton Park, where Premier League West Ham awaited. With five minutes played Emley looked sunk. Frank Lampard had shot the Hammers in front and centre-half Neil Lacey had been forced off with injury. Gradually, though, the non-leaguers found their feet. West Ham, notoriously susceptible to lesser opposition, found themselves under pressure not only from Emley but from their increasingly frustrated supporters. On fifty-six minutes, chemical worker Paul David headed in Iain Banks' corner, and dissent became open revolt. It took a John Hartson header nine minutes from time to rescue the Hammers, but it was Emley who left the field to a deserved ovation.

At the other end of the food chain, the tie of the third round pitched holders Chelsea against reigning champions Manchester United. On paper it looked a tight contest. In reality, the Blues were torn apart by one of United's finest-ever performances. David Beckham rifled two, Andy Cole and Teddy Sheringham got on the scoresheet, and when Cole got his second and United's fifth with fifteen minutes remaining, some of the home fans had seen enough. They missed a spirited ending by their team, although Chelsea's resurgence was largely due to United taking their foot off the gas. The Blues were flattered by 5-3.

Arsenal nearly joined Chelsea on the third round scrap-heap. Port Vale had frustrated them at Highbury, and then held them 1-1 at Vale Park. Only the penalty shoot-out weakened their resolve. Arsenal breathed deeply, and took it 4-3.

Stevenage Borough were the last non-league side left standing. Victories against Cambridge and Swindon

For the next seven seasons, only once would Chelsea avoid either Man United or Arsenal in the Cup. That was in 2000 and they won it.

1997–1998

earned them the right to host Newcastle in the fourth round. The Magpies attitude was sniffy. They complained to the FA that, even with temporary seating, a capacity of 8,000 at the Broadhall stadium was insufficient to meet their fans' ticket demands. The affair descended into a war of words between the respective chairmen, so much so that the football arrived not a moment too soon. Grazioli earned Stevenage a creditable draw, before they lost gallantly 2-1 at St James's Park.

Arsenal were still making life difficult for themselves. It took another replay to see off Crystal Palace and they faced the lottery of another shoot-out against West Ham in the sixth. Again their nerve held. By comparison, the semi-final against Wolves brought light relief. Liberian striker Christopher Wreh, a stand-in for Dennis Bergkamp, opened the scoring early on. After that Arsenal locked the game up and threw away the key.

Wolves were again left cursing the semi-finals. Since their last final appearance in 1960, this was their fourth defeat out of four. This season's defeat to Arsenal was their second at Villa Park, having lost to the Gunners in 1979. Wolves still couldn't battle their way back into the top flight, but they had proved their mettle that season by beating two Premier League sides. Wimbledon were edged out in a replay at Molineux, and Don Goodman's winner had pulled off a great sixth round win at Elland Road.

Turn and turn about. After hauling back Newcastle in 1997, it was Manchester United's turn to sacrifice a healthy lead in the Premier League. Their record of two Doubles was now shared by their hated rivals Arsenal. Shooting for three trophies at the turn of the year, United ended up with nothing.

1997–1998

Another second tier team made it to the semi-finals when Sheffield United crept through after a penalty shoot-out against Coventry. Coventry's penalty-taking was risible; one scored in four attempts. Newcastle, after the shenanigans with Stevenage, had progressed unfussily through the competition. They beat Tranmere and Barnsley, conquerors of Manchester United, and an Alan Shearer strike gave them another low-key victory over the Blades. The Geordies earned their first final appearance since 1974 mainly through Shearer's goals.

The turning point in the final came just after the hour. Arsenal were a goal to the good, Marc Overmars having nutmegged Shay Given midway through the first half. Suddenly, Martin Keown's slip allowed Shearer a clear run on goal. His shot beat Seaman, but hit the post and rebounded to safety. Five minutes later, Nicolas Anelka found himself in a similar position at the other end. He made no mistake, the game was over, and the Double belonged to Arsenal.

TREBLE CHANCE

THE LAST 16

Arsenal **2** Sheffield Utd **1**

Huddersfield (2) **1** Derby (2) **3**

Manchester Utd **1** Fulham **0**

Sheffield Wed **0** Chelsea **1**

Newcastle (0) **1** Blackburn (0) **0**

Everton **2** Coventry **1**

Barnsley **4** Bristol R **1**

Leeds (1) **0** Tottenham (1) **2**

QUARTER FINALS

Arsenal 1 Derby 0

Manchester Utd (0) 2 Chelsea (0) 0

Newcastle 4 Everton 1

Barnsley 0 Tottenham 1

SEMI FINALS

Arsenal **1** Manchester United **2**
at Villa Park

Newcastle **2** Tottenham **0**
at Old Trafford

FINAL, 22 MAY 1999, WEMBLEY

Manchester United **2**
Newcastle United **0**

MAN UTD:
Schmeichel, Gary Neville, Phil Neville, Johnsen, May, Beckham, **Scholes (1)** (*Stam 77*), Keane © **(Sheringham 9 (1))**, Giggs, Cole (*Yorke 61*), Solskjaer *subs: van der Gouw (g), Blomqvist*

NEWCASTLE:
Harper, Griffin, Charvet,Dabizas, Domi, Lee, Hamann (*Ferguson 46*), Shearer, Ketsbaia (*Glass 79*), Speed, Solano (*Maric 68*) *subs: Given (g), Barton*

aken at statistical face value, this appeared to be a pretty ordinary year. A semi-final line-up of Manchester United, Arsenal, Tottenham and Newcastle was a victory for the Cup's old guard. Of the two non-league teams that made it to the third round, Yeovil's presence was virtually taken as read, and Southport's defeat to Leyton Orient failed to hold many back pages. This being the FA Cup, drama was never far below the surface, and the top teams hogged almost all of it for themselves.

It was an uncharacteristically quiet Third Round, with Coventry providing the fireworks by scoring seven against Macclesfield. New kid on the block, Darren Huckerby, was too quick, and scored a hat-trick. The first hint of what was to come arrived with the fourth round draw. Manchester United v Liverpool dwarfed the other fifteen ties. With just a minute to go, United trailed to a goal from Michael Owen, but a late, late show from Dwight Yorke and Ole Gunnar Solskjaer sent Old Trafford into a frenzy. It would be a fourth consecutive trophy-free year for the Merseysiders.

The other big boys made steady progress. Tottenham put Wimbledon away in a replay – for the Dons life amongst the elite was coming to an end; the third tier and Milton Keynes awaited them. Spurs drew a tough one at Leeds in the fifth round. Tim Sherwood's goal forced a replay and Darren Anderton, in a rare spell away from the treatment room, and David Ginola ended the Yorkshire club's interest. Newcastle had been drawn at home in every round – although they only beat Blackburn in a replay at Ewood Park. They were particularly impressive in a 4-1 home win against Everton in the quarter-final; two goals from the excitable Georgian international Temuri Ketsbaia set them on their way.

Arsenal, after victories at Preston and Wolves, faced what looked a straightforward task against Sheffield United at Highbury. With quarter of an hour remaining, the Blades were standing toe to toe with the champions at 1-1. When Lee Morris fell injured, United keeper Alan Kelly kicked the ball into touch for him to receive treatment. Ray Parlour attempted to restart the game in the now customary manner by throwing the ball back to his opponents. Most players had moved towards the Arsenal half, but not Marc Overmars. The Gunners' winger stole the ball, dashed down the wing and squared for the now incoming Kanu to slot home.

The match took minutes to restart, while the understandable storm of protest was brought under control. The referee was powerless to disallow the goal, as Arsenal had broken an unwritten code rather than an official rule. Overmars excused himself by claiming not to have known Kelly's kick into touch was deliberate. Curiously, he was in a minority of one.

Arsene Wenger's offer to replay the game was sporting, fair and accepted. The sight of Overmars, never likely to be a candidate for Players' Player of the Year at any club, opening the scoring stuck in everyone's throat, but Arsenal repeated their 2-1 victory and the episode finished with almost everyone's honour intact. Kanu managed a less controversial effort in the next round, which was enough to see off Derby and take Arsenal into the last four.

Manchester United's quarter-final was a less straightforward affair. They hosted Chelsea who, despite playing a man short for fifty minutes after Di Matteo was sent off, held out for a goalless draw. Scholes evened up the numbers late on with a red card, but the game was niggly rather than full-blooded. Having made life difficult for themselves, United's assured, professional display at Stamford Bridge saw them run out 2-0 winners with both goals coming from Dwight Yorke.

The semi-final draw matched Arsenal and Man United, so Newcastle faced Spurs at Old Trafford with both sensing an opportunity. The tie pitted the

wits of Tottenham's David Ginola against his former club, and much was expected of the Frenchman after goals in each of the three previous rounds. At Old Trafford Alan Shearer proved that flair is no substitute for reliability, striking twice in extra time to send Newcastle into their thirteenth final.

The first match between the top two finished scoreless, but was no tepid affair. The Gunners' Nelson Vivas had been sent off after elbowing Nicky Butt. Roy Keane was left cursing his luck after a marginal offside decision had denied him a winner. His misfortune was football's gain as it ensured a scintillating replay.

The teams returned to Villa Park only three days later, as United had an appointment in Europe the week after. After a high-octane start, a trademark David Beckham swirler from twenty yards gave Seaman no chance. The goal seemed to redouble both team's efforts, and the game flowed from end to end but without a clear chance worthy of the name.

The replay result was a repeat of the teams' only previous semi-final meeting. In 1983, also at Villa Park, Bryan Robson and Norman Whiteside had seen United to victory.

1998-1999

With just over twenty minutes remaining, Arsenal drew level in fortunate circumstances. Dennis Bergkamp's effort was taken away from Peter Schmeichel by a deflection off Dutch international team-mate Jaap Stam. The game had turned in an instant and for the rest of normal time the momentum was with the Gunners.

Nicolas Anelka appeared to have put Arsenal in front but his strike was chalked off. On seventy-four minutes Roy Keane was dismissed for a second bookable offence, and the heart looked to have been ripped out of United. In injury time, Ray Parlour's surge into the box was checked by Phil Neville's lunge, and Arsenal had won a penalty.

In retrospect, to choose a Dutchman for such an important spot-kick may have been Arsenal's undoing. Holland's international record in shoot-outs is as woeful as England's. Bergkamp's penalty was by no means appalling, but it lacked pace, height and direction! Schmeichel guessed right and his massive frame easily diverted the ball round his left-hand post.

A game that looked to have been moving inexorably into Arsenal's grasp suddenly lurched back towards United. With the game on a knife edge, it looked increasingly likely to be settled either by a mistake or a moment of individual brilliance. On 109 minutes, the moment duly arrived. Vieira's tired pass was horribly misplaced and rolled into the path of Ryan Giggs. Although just in his own half, Giggs' momentum carried him thirty yards before any Arsenal player could react.

Ask any Premiership defender in the last dozen years what confrontation he feared more than any other, and most would instantly recall the sight of Ryan Giggs bearing down on them at full tilt. Even so, the Welsh winger on this occasion was faced with one of the most settled and parsimonious defences in

Rushden & Diamonds from the Conference continued a remarkable rise by hosting Leeds United in a third round tie at Nene Park. The club, a merger between two local sides, had only been formed in 1992. Manager Brian Talbot, twice a Cup winner, led his Diamonds to a replay before Leeds overcame them 3-1 at Elland Road.

the country. He weaved through them as if they were a pub team, leaving Tony Adams a prostrate spectator as he fired past Seaman into the roof of the net. If one moment defined the FA Cup in the nineties, this was it. It won United the tie and powered them to a record fifteenth final.

Unfortunately for Alan Shearer, United carried on where Arsenal had left off the previous year. Not even the loss of Roy Keane through injury inside ten minutes could turn the match Newcastle's way. Within two minutes of the Irishman's departure, his replacement, Teddy Sheringham put United one-up, and they sealed a comfortable victory eight minutes into the second half. Nikos Dabizas fluffed a clearance and Sheringham's pass set up Paul Scholes to fire past Steve Harper. United's tenth Cup had been won at a canter.

1999

FAREWELL TO WEMBLEY

2000

VILLA:
James, Delaney, Ehiogu, Southgate ©, Barry, Merson, Taylor (*Stone 79*), Boateng, Wright (*Hendrie 88*), Dublin, Carbone (*Joachim 79*) *subs: Enckelman (g), Samuel*

CHELSEA:
De Goey, Melchiot, Desailly, Lebouef, Babayaro, Di Matteo (1), Wise ©, Deschamps, Poyet, Weah (*Flo 87*), Zola (*Morris 90*) *subs: Cuducini (g), Terry, Harley*

Since 1923 Wembley had been the cathedral of the FA Cup. So many phrases in football's lexicon had derived from the old stadium: The twin towers, the road to Wembley, the hallowed turf, Wembley Way, even a best-forgotten jingle from Chas 'n' Dave. From next year, it all had to change. In this most nostalgic of seasons, Wembley's most frequent visitors turned their back on tradition.

Manchester United had been invited to compete in the inaugural Fifa Club World Championships in Brazil. The snag was the start date – January 2000. Rumours abounded that the government were leaning on United to accept, as they feared a rejection would be frowned on by the governing body and jeopardise England's bid to host the 2006 World Cup finals. Whatever their reasons, United chose Brazil and faced a barrage of criticism, much of it from their own supporters and former players.

Manchester United's loss was Darlington's gain. With the draw imbalanced by United's withdrawal, one second round loser had to be reinstated to ensure a full third round quota of sixty-four. Their place in future pub quizzes was assured. Darlington became the first team to lose in successive rounds of the competition. Having gone down 3-1 at Gillingham, they went out 2-1 at Aston Villa.

After such upheaval, traditionalists were reassured by the sight of West Ham exiting to lowlier opponents. Tranmere administered this season's bout of toe-curling, with Manchester City cast-off Nick Henry scoring the only goal.

Henry's former employers fared little better than West Ham. After cruising past Chester, City were thumped 5-2 at Maine Road by Leeds. Shaun Goater had fired them in front after only two minutes and City led 2-1 before Alan Smith, Harry Kewell, twice, and Bowyer crushed feeble home defending.

Arsenal blew their chance to capitalise on United's absence. After Leicester had held them to scoreless draws in the fourth round, the Gunners were spiked 6-5 on penalties. Liverpool, too, threw away a golden opportunity when they went down to a Nathan Blake goal at home to Blackburn.

In the goal-scoring stakes, Leeds were trumped by Newcastle. The back-to-back beaten finalists seemed determined to finish the job properly this year, thumping Tottenham 6-1 in a third round replay and then put four past Sheffield United. A trip to Blackburn saw Alan

Shearer return to the club where he had won his only winner's medal, the Premiership title in 1995. He duly reminded Blackburn of what they had been missing, scoring both goals in a 2-1 win. A 3-2 win at Tranmere took Newcastle's Cup tally to sixteen in five games, and sent them to Wembley for the third year in succession, this time for a semi-final. Tranmere were there a week later, but narrowly lost the League Cup Final to Leicester. It was a momentous season for John Aldridge's Rovers, but it ended blank.

Chelsea, waiting for the Magpies' in the semi, had also racked up an impressive goal tally, with Hull and Gillingham being hit for six and five respectively. Gus Poyet led the way with a hat-trick against Forest in the third round. The Uruguayan's forays from midfield proved the undoing of Newcastle, heading the winner after seventy-two minutes, six minutes after his opening strike had been cancelled out by Robert Lee.

The other semi-final revived the fortunes of two teams whose Cup glories could best be savoured through the Pathe newsreel. Aston Villa, though seven times winners, had only tasted glory once since 1920, and their last success had been against the Busby Babes in 1957. Villa didn't have it easy on the way through, meeting three Premiership sides. Southampton at home, Leeds 3-2 in a humdinger, and Everton 2-1 showed their pedigree; the highlight was a terrific hat-trick from the maddeningly inconsistent on-loan striker Benito Carbone to put out a strong Leeds team. He scored the winner in the next round as well,

By withdrawing from the Cup, Manchester United ignored the option to field a junior side in the early stages. Their first-team could have returned by the Fifth Round, and even a third-choice United might have coped with most teams.

1999-2000

The FA also trampled on tradition by moving the third round from its customary slot in early January to two weeks before Christmas. A ridiculous experiment was quickly abandoned and normal service was resumed the following year.

1999-2000

Newcastle's semi-final defeat was their fifth in succession at Wembley. Since triumphing three times in the fifties, they had lost three FA Cup finals and a League Cup Final to Wolves in 1976.

1999-2000

Bolton had last lifted the trophy a year after Villa, and it would have been fitting if, holding the record as Wembley's first winners in 1923, they could return for the stadium's last final. Eidur Gudjohnsen scored in every round as Bolton picked their way thorugh a comfortable draw. But there was to be no fairy tale. A sterile, nervy encounter juddered to a halt after 120 scoreless minutes. Dean Holdsworth had scooped over an open goal late in the game after Gudjohnsen had waltzed through Villa's defence to put him in. Carbone, after his heroics en route, put in a derisory performance and was substituted to catcalls from the stands. The penalty shoot-out was embarrassing for Bolton; their penalties blazed high, wide and not very handsome, handing Villa their tenth final appearance.

As a finale, Chelsea and Villa served up a hugely underwhelming spectacle, albeit not untypical of most of Wembley's previous encounters. A repeat of its popular 1-0 score-line was the order of the day after David James's attempt to punch Zola's free kick cannoned off Southgate into the path of Roberto Di Matteo. Chelsea's hero of 1997 stabbed home from a few yards out and Wembley's last final before the wrecking-ball had been won.

2000

DROUGHT ENDED

2001

THE LAST 16

Sunderland **0** West Ham **1**

Tottenham **4** Stockport Co **0**

Arsenal **3** Chelsea **1**

Bolton (1) **0** Blackburn (1) **3**

Southampton (0) **3**
Tranmere Rovers (0) **4**

Liverpool **4** Manchester C **2**

Leicester **3** Bristol C **0**

Wycombe W (8-7 pens) (2) **2**
Wimbledon (2) **2**

QUARTER FINALS

West Ham **2** Tottenham **3**

Arsenal **2** Blackburn **0**

Tranmere Rovers **2** Liverpool **4**

Leicester **1** Wycombe W **2**

SEMI FINALS

Tottenham **1** Arsenal **2**
at Old Trafford

Liverpool **2** Wycombe W **1**
at Villa Park

FINAL, 12 MAY 2001, WEMBLEY

Arsenal **1** Liverpool **2**

ARSENAL:
Seaman, Dixon (*Bergkamp 90*), Keown, Adams ©, Cole, **Ljungberg (1)** (*Kanu 85*), Grimandi, Vieira, Pires, Henry, Wiltord (*Parlour 76*) subs: *Manninger (g), Lauren*

LIVERPOOL:
Westerveld, Babbel, Henchoz, Hyppia ©, Carragher, Murphy (*Berger 77*), Hamann (*McAllister 60*), Gerrard, Smicer (*Fowler 77*), Heskey, **Owen (2)** subs: *Arphexad (g), Vignal*

A tournament that ended up catching Arsenal by surprise started gathering its League victims early. Six were picked off in the first round, including a couple of spectacular falls from grace in the Potteries. Stoke drew at home to Nuneaton Borough and failed to learn the lesson, losing 1-0 in the replay. Their only solace came from the fortunes of their rivals Port Vale. After a 4-4 draw at Canvey Island, Vale too failed to heed the warning and came a cropper in the replay 2-1. Canvey Island lost in a rarely-played local derby with Southend in round two. Brentford were humbled at home by Kingstonian, who added Southend in the third round to their scalping belt with a goal from Eddie Akuamoah. A tie against third tier Bristol City looked winnable until Tony Thorpe's equaliser deep into injury time. Another late goal in the replay put an end to Kingstonian's best Cup run. There were plenty of less seismic upsets too: Bury lost at Northwich and Yeovil added their ritual League scalp, hammering Colchester 5-1. They followed up with a 1-0 win at Blackpool in the next round, before going out to Bolton. Blackpool were the Somerset team's twentieth and last league victims before they finally achieved league status after romping away with the Conference in 2003. A big, big hand, please, for the top dogs of giant-killing.

The rout continued in a minor key in the second round. In addition to Yeovil, Dagenham and Redbridge won at Lincoln, while Morecambe overcame Cambridge. The Daggers came mighty close to joining Kingstonian in the fourth round. A plum tie at near-neighbours Charlton looked like the stuff of dreams when, with a minute remaining, they led through McDougald's goal. John Salako threw the Addicks a lifeline but they still faced an uphill battle in the replay. After ninety scrappy and fruitless minutes, it took Shaun Newton's goal in extra time for Charlton to breathe easily.

Another tighter-than-expected London derby was at Brisbane Road. Leyton Orient held Spurs for eighty-nine minutes before Gary Doherty converted a set piece to send Tottenham into round four and deny the O's a lucrative replay.

With all the money sloshing around at the top end of the football pyramid, the bookies only gave a handful of teams a chance of winning the trophy. By the fifth round, half of them were out. Newcastle fell at the first hurdle against Aston Villa, who were beaten by Leicester

2000-2001

Tranmere's Paul Rideout had already carved his niche in FA Cup history. He had scored the winner for Everton in the 1995 final against Manchester United.

in the next. Leeds and Liverpool met in the fourth round, Liverpool winning with surprising ease through Nicky Barmby and Emile Heskey. The much-maligned Heskey was enjoying the competition; he had scored twice against Rotherham in the round before and was one of four Liverpool scorers in the easy win over Man City in round five. Manchester United were undone by Paolo Canio in the fourth round; his perfectly-timed run and finish at Old Trafford was enough to seal a famous victory for West Ham. The sight of Fabien Barthez, rooted to the spot with arm raised vainly for offside as Di Canio outfoxed him, summed up a witless afternoon for the champions.

The Hammers' 'reward' in the fifth round was an even longer away trip and a 4am start for their fans. Their tie at Sunderland was selected by TV for a lunchtime kick-off but it was the home side that were still asleep when, with quarter of an hour remaining, Freddie Kanoute put West Ham into the last eight.

Another creditable away performance saw Tranmere hold Southampton to a goalless draw. The replay at Prenton Park produced one of the competition's most extraordinary matches. The game kicked off with local hopes high. Tranmere were a good Cup team, and had proved doughty fighters at Southampton. Given similar discipline and a fair wind they had more than a chance. By half-time, such optimism seemed hollow.

2000-2001

Wycombe's manager Lawrie Sanchez was able to draw on considerable personal experience. His winner for Wimbledon in the 1988 final against Liverpool had pulled off a major surprise.

For forty-five minutes, Southampton opened up Rovers at will. Hassan Kachloul started the rot, gathering a Chris Marsden pass and advancing unchallenged to smash home a cracker from twenty-five yards. Kachloul turned provider for Saints' second fifteen minutes later, crossing to the far post where the waiting Jo Tessem could hardly miss. Neither marker nor challenge was within a country mile. A goal arrived on the stroke of half-time. For Tranmere, it could have been a life-saver, and enabled them to regroup at the interval with their opponents within touching distance. In the event, Southampton scored it, Dean Richards forcing home after Tessem's header had evaded a clutch of defenders. 3-0 – game, set and match.

2000-2001

Arsenal and Liverpool had also met in the finals of 1950 and 1971. For Liverpool this was revenge at last after two previous defeats.

But John Aldridge vented his spleen at half-time and the improvement in his team was marked. For all Tranmere's endeavour, almost a quarter of an hour passed with no dent in the deficit. When Paul Rideout's outstretched boot diverted an Andy Parkinson drive past Paul Jones, it seemed mere consolation. Eleven minutes later the veteran Rideout rose to head home a corner from Jason Koumas and things started to look interesting. Still, Southampton's Premiership squad boasted enough class and experience to weather this little storm. Apparently not.

With ten minutes left, the 13,000 crowd was in uproar, as Rideout completed his hat-trick by turning home another cross from Parkinson. The unthinkable became fact three minutes later when another former Everton man, Stuart Barlow, scrambled home to send the majority of Prenton Park into a frenzy. It was untidy but it completed a great night for the Wirral club. Forever in the shadow of Everton and Liverpool, this was a night when the spotlight shone brightly on the third team in Merseyside.

A sixth round tie with Liverpool was a fitting reward, but not even the ex-Everton contingent could raise themselves enough to clinch this one. In a 4-2 win, Liverpool had four different scorers again – and none of them had scored in the 4-2 win in the previous round!

The sixth round did spring a surprise, but not on the Wirral. Wycombe Wanderers had earned their first quarter-final by holding their nerve against Premiership Wimbledon. Wycombe had come from 2-0 down to draw the first tie, and Paul McCarthy had equalised in stoppage time in the replay. Their brinksmanship continued when a momentous penalty shoot-out ended 8-7 in their favour. As another big day at Leicester approached, Wycombe had an injury crisis on their hands. In desperation, manager Lawrie Sanchez posted an appeal for a striker on the club's website, a curio that was picked up by a BBC journalist and broadcast on Ceefax.

Sanchez' plea was answered by the agent of one Roy Essandoh. This hardly looked like the arrival of a messiah. The Belfast-born striker's previous experience of British football had been at East Fife and Motherwell, and he had plied his trade most recently for the less than mighty VPS Vassa in Finland. On the basis that beggars couldn't be choosers, Sanchez offered him a fortnight's contract.

On the day, Wycombe fought gamely. Although Muzzy Izzet equalised Paul McCarthy's goal, Wanderers were hanging on as the game reached injury time. From a free-kick wide on the left, Essandoh stole in to head Wycombe's winner. So frenetic were the celebrations that midfielder Steve Brown collected his second yellow card for removing his shirt. He joined his manager in the tunnel where an over-excited Sanchez had already been banished from the dugout by referee Steve Bennett.

The semi-finals had a curious look about them. Arsenal and Tottenham received a last-four pairing for the third time in eleven seasons; Spurs were there courtesy of two goals from forgotten man Sergei Rebrov in a 3-2 win at West Ham. Liverpool counted their blessings after being left with Wycombe.

But Liverpool found Wycombe a tough nut to crack, taking seventy-eight minutes to break down stubborn resistance. Once Emile Heskey breached the dam, Robbie Fowler added a second within minutes. Keith Ryan managed a deserved consolation in the dying moments, but Wycombe's adventure was over. At Old Trafford Gary Doherty drew first blood for Tottenham, but goals from Patrick Vieira and Robert Pires saw Arsenal home.

The final was the first held at Cardiff's Millennium stadium. After seventy-two minutes the tradition of Wembley was maintained as the game failed to match its billing. When Freddie Ljungberg put the Gunners in front, it looked unlikely that a hitherto blunt Liverpool could raise their game sufficiently. With seven minutes remaining, the normally reliable Gunners' defence made a hash of clearing a free-kick from Gary McAllister. The ball broke to Michael Owen, who smashed home. Six minutes later, a rejuvenated Owen chased Patrik Berger's pass, outpaced Lee Dixon and from the left edge of the box, spotted enough daylight between David Seaman and the far post to thread the ball precisely between them. Arsenal had been undone by two great finishes from a top class player. They would have been disappointed to lose to such a humdrum Liverpool side.

A DULL YEAR

THE LAST 16

Middlesbrough **1**	Blackburn **0**	
Everton (0) **2**	Crewe Alex (0) **1**	
Newcastle **1**	Manchester C **0**	
Arsenal **5**	Gillingham **2**	
Tottenham **4**	Tranmere Rovers **0**	
Preston **1**	Chelsea **3**	
West Brom **1**	Cheltenham **0**	
Walsall **1**	Fulham **2**	

QUARTER FINALS

Middlesbrough **3**	Everton **0**
Newcastle (1) **0**	Arsenal (1) **3**
Tottenham **0**	Chelsea **4**
West Brom **0**	Fulham **1**

SEMI FINALS

Middlesbrough **0**	Arsenal **1**

at Old Trafford

Chelsea **1**	Fulham **0**

at Villa Park

FINAL, 4 MAY 2001, CARDIFF

Arsenal **2**	Chelsea **0**

ARSENAL:
Seaman, Lauren, Campbell, Adams ©, Cole, **Parlour (1)**, Vieira, **Ljungberg (1)**, Wiltord (*Keown 90*), Bergkamp (*Edu 72*), Henry (*Kanu 81*) *subs: Wright (g), Dixon*

CHELSEA:
Cuducini, Melchiot (*Zenden 77*), Desailly ©, Gallas, Babayaro (*Terry 46*), Gronkjaer, Lampard, Petit, Le Saux, Hasselbaink (*Zola 68*), Gudjohnsen *subs: De Goey (g), Jokanovic*

anvey Island isn't a name that automatically springs to mind when thoughts turn to Cup exploits. The Isthmian League side had made their first polite entrance in 1996, when they reached the first round. Last season had seen them create a ripple with the defeat of Port Vale. This season, they made a bigger splash. Neil Gregory was their hero, scoring the only goal on both occasions as they knocked out Wigan and Northampton, both from the third tier. Stepping up another league proved a bridge too far, and they went out 4-1 at Burnley.

Joining them in the third round were Dagenham and Redbridge who had thrashed a woeful Exeter 3-0. They faced Premiership opposition for the second successive season but failed to frighten Ipswich as they had Charlton, going down 4-1.

The drama of the early rounds lay in penalties rather than shocks. Forest Green and bottom division Macclesfield couldn't be separated after their first round replay, so the contest went on with penalties, and on . . . and on. All twenty-two players had a turn, and still the scores remained level. At 10-10 Kevin Langan, having already scored once, missed. The veteran Lee Glover netted for Macclesfield and they squeaked through. What remained of the crowd just about made it home for early morning tea and cornflakes. Macclesfield's manager Dave Moss revealed after the game that he had made his players practise spot-kicks at some length. This included a march from the centre circle for each penalty taker, with team-mates baying abuse for that authentic, big-match atmosphere.

The tie of the third round was Manchester United's visit to Aston Villa, lent extra piquancy by the return of the Villa goalkeeper, Peter Schmeichel, to Old Trafford. Schmeichel had been synonymous with United's dominance in the previous decade but was now playing out the dregs of his career at Villa Park. After a scoreless first half, his team took a firm grip in proceedings within ten minutes – Ian Taylor and a Phil Neville own goal putting Villa two up. United had one vital ace up their sleeve, and Ferguson played it. Ruud van Nistelrooy came off the bench and the game was transformed. Regular super-sub Ole-Gunnar Solskjaer fired home with thirteen minutes left, then two stunning efforts from the Dutchman destroyed Villa.

As United recovered, Leeds faltered. They had earned their visit to Cardiff the easy way but lined up at Ninian Park rather than the Millenium Stadium. They left in disgrace. After Mark Viduka had given them a twelfth-minute lead, they folded to goals from Graham Kavanagh and Scott Young, the second with only three minutes remaining. Alan Smith collected a red card and Leeds misery was complete when their supporters reacted to defeat less than magnanimously. Their positioning in the ground was nonsensical, right next to a notoriously combustible section of the home support. Chairman Sam Hamman, a man more interested in posturing than common sense, insisted on his customary but unwisely inflammatory stroll behind the opposition goal, but there remains no excuse for the louts. This sort of incident was meant to be a thing of the past.

Leeds's embarrassment masked Portsmouth's. A season away from romping away with the Division One title, Pompey saw a one-goal half-time lead against bottom tier Orient turned into a 4-1 thrashing at Fratton Park.

In the fourth round, Manchester United were handed another tough draw away to Middlesbrough. All their good work at Villa Park came to naught, as goals in the last five minutes from Whelan and Campbell saw the home side run out winners. One talking point was the attendance, a mere 17,624. This would have been unthinkable even a few years previously for such an attractive tie, and discussion abounded that the Cup was being sidelined by the saturation of Premiership and Champions League coverage. Another particular factor was the Boro fans displeasure that their season tickets no longer included Cup ties as part of the package. Having forked out once, many fans felt cheated at having to do so again; the pattern repeated itself at many other grounds.

Chelsea, having relied on Carlo Cudicini to keep them in the third round against a boisterous Norwich, hit their stride in the replay. Their 4-0 win was crowned by one of the Cup's great goals from the magical Gianfranco Zola; a mid-air scissors kick worthy of the lead dancer at Ballet Rambert. Even the disappointed visiting fans applauded a breathtaking moment from a player who illuminated the English game. West Ham ran the Blues close in round four but John Terry's goal at Upton Park won a replay in which the Blues had twice come from behind. After an early scare, Preston were dismissed at Stamford Bridge, which sent the Blues for a quarter-final at Tottenham. A few weeks earlier, Chelsea had been hammered 5-1 at White Hart Lane in the League Cup. Spurs had scored four in each of the last two rounds and must have fancied their chances but Chelsea ran out 4-0 winners. Chants of 'Normal service is resumed,' echoed from the away end.

At Villa Park, the Blues faced neighbours Fulham. The Cottagers had crept through the draw, defeating last year's heroes, Wycombe, and the last of this season's real underdogs, Cheltenham. Again, Chelsea relied on John Terry. The centre half's goal three minutes before half-time was good enough to earn Chelsea their second final in three years. They faced their third London derby in four ties but the opposition were a class apart.

Arsenal had already run away with the league title. Their progress to Cardiff had been largely serene. Newcastle took them to a replay, and Middlesbrough had lost only through Gianluca Festa's own goal in the semis, but Arsenal suffered no undue alarms in either game.

At Cardiff, Chelsea handicapped themselves by starting with the clearly unfit Hasselbaink. After sixty-eight minutes the Dutchman belatedly made way for Zola. Two minutes later Ray Parlour advanced from central midfield to curl a fine twenty-yarder beyond Carlo Cudicini's reach and Arsenal never looked back. Ten minutes on Freddie Ljungberg repeated the dose, thus becoming the first player since Spurs' Bobby Smith to score in successive finals.

A boring and routine final ended a boring and routine competition. Arsenal's third Double had been completed without much of a flourish.

The big clubs were starting to rotate their squads in the FA cup, as well as the League Cup, which was now seen as a reserves tournament by the Champions League contenders around the turn of the century. It wasn't just the top four, either. Clubs with smaller squads embroiled in relegation battles were starting to play makeweight teams in the Cup competitions. In 2001-2002, Bolton met Spurs in both Cup competitions, losing 6-0 in the League Cup and 4-0 in the FA Cup. Wanderers' reserves may have been good enough for Stockport, but they were cannon-fodder for a mid-table Premier League side with serious thoughts of Cup silverware.

The argument is a tricky one; money talks in modern football, and survival in the Premiership with the TV money and place money is the easiest way to balance the books. Moreover the big clubs, especially those in Europe, play too many games and the domestic Cup competitions offer a chance to rest key players. Unless, of course, your squad contains the Bionic Man or Frank Lampard. This is about money, too, as Uefa look to expand their competition to rake in ever more cash.

Against that any sport which becomes purely about money is destined to destroy itself. The life-blood of the game is its fans, both the live and armchair variety, and if the game devalues itself and becomes a less attractive spectacle those fans will desert.

The big clubs, it is true, provide great drama and great football – the Premiership is a fantastic product, whatever carping journalists may write. Those same big clubs need to respect the endeavours of those less fortunate than themselves. When a lower division or non-league club draw a big side, their players and fans deserve to play against and watch some of that big team's star players. Thierry Henry has scored only three goals in the FA Cup because he has hardly ever played in it. Like many other overseas stars, he probably regards the Cup weekends as a well-earned rest. This is not a slur on Henry, who is a consummate professional and a decent man. Players arriving from Europe have been raised in a tradition where the domestic cup is a second-rate B-feature not a star turn in its own right.

There isn't an obvious antidote. Maybe a rule could be made stating that if a player doesn't play at least a full half in round three or four, but plays in other competitions during that time, he is ineligible for the Cup for that season. The big clubs would then have to pick some of their stars earlier in the competition, rather than just in the semis and final when they realise it's all that remains of their season.

2002

ARSENAL DO IT THE HARD WAY (EXCEPT FOR THE FINAL)

2003

ARSENAL:
Seaman, Lauren, Luzhny, Keown, Cole, Parlour, Silva, Ljungberg, **Pires (1)**, Bergkamp (*Wiltord 77*), Henry *subs: Taylor (g), Toure, Van Bronckhorst, Kanu*

SOUTHAMPTON:
Niemi (*Jones 66*), Baird (*Fernandes 87*), Michael Svensson, Lundekvam, Bridge, Telfer, Anders Svensson (*Tessem 75*), Oakley, Marsden, Beattie, Ormerod *subs: Williams, Higginbotham*

The FA Cup final used to be one of only two live games broadcast in a season (England v Scotland being the other, another discarded tradition). Now the former blue riband match arrives at the fag end of nine months' continuous transmission. Mind you, if Arsenal v Southampton had been one of the two games shown on TV in a season, the viewing public would have been severely short-changed. (Especially if the other was England against the current Scotland team with Sven using seventy-two substitutes.)

In the midst of all this modern upheaval, a throwback to the past arrived. This went beyond the black-and-white Matthews-and-Lofthouse era. Team Bath, the side representing the city's university, reckoned they had a tidy side so evoked the spirit of the Victorians by becoming the first club from the academic world for 122 years to play in the FA Cup. Not since Oxford University lost to Clapham Rovers in the 1880 final had a college side made an appearance.

Not only did they enter but five games later Team Bath were in the first round. Their home tie with Mansfield was screened live on Sky and 5,500 people filled the campus ground at Claverton Down. The Stags threatened to overwhelm the students after roaring into a 4-0 lead but respectability was restored with two late goals from the students. One of them, a twenty-five-yard howitzer from midfielder Carl Heiniger, attracted a professional contract from German club KSV Hessen Kassel. He became the first of several Team Bath players to sign professional forms. The season would end in triumph as Team Bath finished league champions of the Screwfix Direct Western League Premier Division. And we haven't made that up.

The theme was continued in the Yorkshire spa town of Harrogate. The town had never before been represented in the first round proper and now here they were with two qualifiers. Harrogate Town fell to a heavy defeat at Farnborough but the splendidly named former works team, Harrogate Railway Athletic, beat Slough Town before falling with honour intact at home to Bristol City. City had already put out the equally Corinthian-sounding Heybridge Swifts 7-0. Jason Roberts, Scott Murray and Leroy Lita was a forward line to worry good league sides so neither the Swifts nor Athletic were disgraced.

Another 'works team', Ellesmere Port's Vauxhall Motors, held QPR to a goalless draw at Chester's Deva Stadium and took their bow in the replay at Loftus Road, where they sensationally knocked out Rangers 4-3 on penalties after a 1-1 draw. 'That's probably the worst day I've had at the office,' lamented Rangers boss Ian Holloway, a man not known for his phlegmatic approach. A defeat at Macclesfield was a tame end for the Merseysiders.

While the lesser non-league lights fell, Dagenham & Redbridge marched on. The Conference side reached round three for the third successive season. This time they went one better, drawing 2-2 at Second Division Plymouth before finishing them off 2-0 in the replay. Junior McDougald terrorised the Argyle defence, scoring in both matches; the other goal in the away match was scored by Paul Terry, brother of Chelsea's John. A narrow defeat at Norwich in round four ended Dagenham's interest. They were joined in the fourth round by Farnborough Town, who had knocked out Darlington. Their 3-2 win in a good old-fashioned cup tie came courtesy of two from Danny Carroll and one from Rocky Baptiste. Their reward was immense, a home draw with Arsenal. The tie was switched from Hampshire to Highbury; cue accusations of cynicism aimed at a club with a regular home attendance of 600! Farnborough were rewarded with a 35,000 crowd.

The sight of Arsenal running out at Highbury in a blue strip was a strange one. The Gunners were technically the away team and therefore had to wear their change kit. That was the last extraordinary occurrence as Campbell and Jeffers put Arsenal two-up at half-time. By then Farnborough were reduced to ten men after Christian Lee had found Francis Jeffers too hot to handle and hauled back the Arsenal striker as he bore down on goal. On seventy-one minutes, with the Gunners three up, Rocky Baptiste earned himself a niche in Cup history by scoring for the Conference side, a goal greeted with loud cheers from all sides of the ground. The ease with which he turned Pascal Cygan was a warning Arsene Wenger still hasn't heeded. Bergkamp and Lauren found the net before the end but the finest day in Farnborough's history had been no disgrace.

With the non-leaguers going out, the underdog's baton was handed to Rochdale; wins over second tier Preston and Coventry won them a fifth round appearance for only the second time. The journey ended with a 3-1 defeat at Wolves.

The tie of the fifth round wasn't difficult to spot. Manchester United v Arsenal needed no hype but the event proved no contest. Arsenal controlled the game and goals from Edu and Wiltord without reply were an accurate reflection of their superiority. United's day was summed up by a moment from Ryan Giggs. When confronted eighteen yards out with an open goal having rounded the keeper, he skied his shot into the Stretford End for the miss of the season. It was an odd performance; United had been dismissive of earlier opposition, winning 4-1 against Portsmouth and 6-0 against West Ham.

After seeing off United Arsenal hosted Chelsea in the sixth round. They recovered from John Terry's third-minute goal to lead at half-time, only to be pegged back by a scrambled Frank Lampard effort six minutes from time. At

Stamford Bridge Terry found the net again, this time at both ends. Goals from Wiltord and Lauren saw Arsenal run out comfortable winners. They had beaten the last remaining opponents of real significance. Newcastle had fallen to a George Ndah winner at Wolves in the third round. Liverpool, enduring another trophy-free season under the increasingly confused stewardship of Gerard Houllier, had given a hapless display in a replay at Anfield against Crystal Palace. A comical Stephane Henchoz own goal summed up their mood.

The semi-finals kept the two remaining Premiership sides apart. Sheffield United had reached the last four in both domestic Cups and faced the daunting prospect of Arsenal at Old Trafford. They were defeated far less easily than United and Chelsea, and may have forced a replay had David Seaman not produced the save of his career to scoop out Canadian international Paul Peschisolido's header. At the finish Freddie Ljungberg's first-half goal proved just enough.

In the other semi-final at Villa Park, Watford faced their third Premiership side in Southampton. The Hornets had already put paid to top division stragglers West Bromwich Albion and Sunderland, but were undone by Brett Ormerod and an own goal. Marcus Gayle's strike two minutes from time was only a consolation.

Arsenal lined up at Cardiff for their sixteenth final against a Southampton side hoping to repeat their last appearance in 1976, when Bobby Stokes's goal had upset the form book against Manchester United. They won that game because they believed they could. This time they turned up devoid of belief and failed to put their lively manager's game-plan into effect. Gordon Strachan's body language on the touchline was the most watchable feature of the afternoon as Robert Pires's thirty-eighth minute goal won it for a subdued Arsenal.

LIONS TAMED

THE LAST 16

Liverpool (1) **0** Portsmouth (1) **1**

Arsenal **2** Chelsea **1**

Manchester Utd **4** Manchester C **2**

Fulham (0) **3** West Ham (0) **0**

Sunderland (1) **2** Birmingham (1) **0**

Sheffield Utd **1** Colchester **0**

Millwall **1** Burnley **0**

Tranmere Rovers **2** Swansea **1**

QUARTER FINALS

Portsmouth **1** Arsenal **5**

Manchester Utd **2** Fulham **1**

Sunderland **1** Sheffield Utd **0**

Millwall (0) **2** Tranmere Rovers (0) **1**

SEMI FINALS

Arsenal **0** Manchester Utd **1**

at Villa Park

Sunderland **0** Millwall **1**

at Old Trafford

FINAL, 1 MAY 2004, WEMBLEY

Manchester United **3** Millwall **0**

MAN UTD:
Howard (*Carroll 84*), G.Neville, Brown, Silvestre, O'Shea, **Ronaldo (1)** (*Solskjaer 84*), Fletcher (*Butt 84*), Keane, Giggs, Scholes, **Van Nistelrooy (2)**

MILLWALL:
Marshall, Ryan (*Cogan 74*), Ward, Lawrence, Elliott, Sweeney, Livermore, Wise (*Weston 89*), Ifill, Cahill, Harris (*McCammon 75*)

'Accrington Stanley will play Huddersfield Town.' This was a tie that rolled back the years. The days of Accrington as a league club had ended with acrimonious bankruptcy in 1962, forcing their resignation from the Fourth Division, never to return. It took thirty-one years for the Lancashire side to reach the third round again, but a 6-1 defeat to Crewe in the second round in 1993 hardly covered them in glory. A year later they were back in the first round but lost at home to Scunthorpe.

This time the years really were rolled back. An injury-time winner did for Huddersfield, then Bournemouth were eliminated in another cliff-hanger at the Crown Ground. Accrington scraped home 5-3 on penalties, and were back in the third round for the first time since 1961. To be drawn with Colchester was a huge disappointment, and their 1-0 defeat in a replay left the Conference side dreaming of what might have been.

A roll-call of those who fought honourably for the tradition of giant-killing included Hornchurch, Ford United, Burton Albion, Stevenage, Telford and Scarborough. Stevenage's win over ailing Stockport was no massive shock, and Port Vale just salvaged their pride when they won their replay 2-1 against lowly Ford United. They promptly lost it again by losing at home to Scarborough in the next round. Burton will have enjoyed their long trip back from Torquay after winning 2-1, and Hornchurch meant Darlington exited to non-league opposition for the second year running. Telford had made a habit of beating league teams but Brentford were a decent third tier side, and 3-0 was emphatic.

The third round draw was spiteful to all the non-league sides, but two turned misfortune to their advantage. Telford won 1-0 at Crewe with a goal from much-travelled striker Lee Mills. Scarborough endured and survived a trip to Southend, drawing 1-1 and knocking out the Shrimpers 1-0 in the replay through Mark Quayle's late goal. The spoils of victory were immense, as a home draw against Chelsea awaited the winners. The McCain Stadium was filled to bursting for this one with 5,379 inside and many thousands more watching on live TV. The predicted massacre looked on the cards when John Terry headed Chelsea into a tenth-minute lead, but by luck, pluck and sheer endeavour, Scarborough held on. They may have had a second-half penalty, but William Gallas's block was adjudged ball to hand.

The pot wasn't stirred too much in the third round; Gillingham beat Charlton and Tranmere won a replay at the Reebok Stadium after Sam Allardyce declined to put out a competitive team once he had reached the League Cup final.

Aston Villa and Manchester United were drawn at Villa Park for the second time in three years. It was a tale with a familiar ending. Although they took the lead through Gareth Barry, two second-half goals from Paul Scholes sent Villa spinning out early yet again.

The fourth round thinned out the Premier League's representation by pairing a few of them. Liverpool beat Newcastle in the clash of the nearly men; the unlikely hero was Bruno Cheyrou, derided by Liverpool fans as the worst of a number of suspect buys by Houllier, but temporarily forgiven. Fulham beat Everton in a replay and Arsenal thrashed Middlesbrough, the other League Cup finalists. The other all-premiership tie had Spurs face Manchester City for the second year running.

By half-time, this game was wrapped up, and an often critical home crowd basked in a rare bout of smugness. Tottenham were three-up and City had ended the half a man light, as Joey Barton's backchat had tried the patience of referee Rob Styles once too often. It had been all too easy. Spurs took only two minutes to open up City's defence, Ledley King turning to lash the ball past debutant keeper Arni Arason. When Robbie Keane fastened on to Stephen Carr's pass and swept the ball home, the game was not twenty minutes old. Christian Ziege curled in a free-kick two minutes before half-time and there looked no way back for City. Nicolas Anelka was so disinterested and inept that he had already made way for Jonathan Macken.

Spurs had already suffered at the hands of a Manchester comeback in recent years. Two seasons earlier United had overturned a three-goal deficit at half-time to overpower them 5-3 in as fine a second-half display as anyone could remember. But that was United, the team of Van Nistelrooy, Beckham and Scholes. A line-up containing Jihai, Dunne and Tarnat should not have been presented with a lifeline.

Tottenham's charity started two minutes after the break. Backing off Michael Tarnat, they allowed the midfielder to wait for Sylvain Distin ghosting in at the far post. Tarnat's clever chip found Distin's head, and he applied a neat finish. Spurs's assurance turned to hesitancy. City's midfield started to boss the game and just past the hour carved out a deserved slice of luck. Paul Bosvelt latched on to a weak King clearance but his goal-bound drive represented little threat until it cannoned off Antony Gardner's leg and sped past Kasey Keller.

Spurs were in full-on panic mode. With ten minutes left Robbie Fowler's canny pass sent Shaun Wright-Phillips clear, and City's brightest star outpaced Johnnie Jackson with ease before lifting the ball over Keller into the net.

At last Spurs were roused. It looked as though they might have stirred themselves sufficiently to conjure up a winner, but City had one last counter-attack up their sleeve. Deep into extra-time, Wright-Phillips dribbled the ball into the Spurs half before feeding Tarnat, who knocked a diagonal cross towards the far post. Substitute Jonathan Macken timed his run to perfection. What his header lacked in power it made up for in precision, looping across Keller before squeezing into the corner.

City's manager danced for joy on the touchline, and no-one begrudged Kevin Keegan his moment. He has always worn his heart on his sleeve, and this game summed up his managerial career; a mixture of brilliant, bravura attacking and bungling ineptitude. Bless him!

United's win at Villa took them to Northampton, another tie that recalled memories of times past. In 1970 George Best had helped himself to six goals in an 8-2 victory. This win was no less emphatic, if at 3-0 a little more prosaic. United's opponents in the fifth round raised the stakes and the temperature. Neighbours City visited Old Trafford and contributed to a full-blooded Cup tie in every sense. United's 4-2 victory was achieved despite playing more than 45 minutes with ten men. Gary Neville had seen red, and a red card, after Steve McManaman had choice words following the United full-back's theatrical tumble in the box. Rather than argue the finer points of the rule book, Neville butted him. After living up to his billing as a man who doesn't suffer Scousers, he departed to a misplaced but heartfelt ovation. Perhaps it would have been more appropriate had one of McManaman's team-mates supplied the aggro; since his move from Real Madrid, the contribution of this gifted but lightweight player to City's cause had been an insult to their fantastic supporters..

If Villa were fed up with United, Chelsea were positively sick of Arsenal. The Gunners put them out for the fourth successive season, and again after Chelsea had taken the lead at Highbury. This time it was Adrian Mutu, with his last-ever goal for the Blues, who gave them another false dawn. A familiar tale unfolded in the second half, as two excellent goals from Jose Antonio Reyes sent Arsenal into the quarter-finals. There they faced Portsmouth at Fratton Park, and tore them apart. So classy was their performance that when Thierry Henry was substituted in the second half, he departed to a standing ovation from home supporters not normally known for their magnanimity. Portsmouth manager Harry Redknapp could only shrug his shoulders and wish Arsenal all the best. Before the game they thought they had a chance; they were in decent form and effectively ended Liverpool's season in a replay in the previous round.

For the second successive season, the semi-final draw was made up of two teams from the Premiership and two from the First Division. Last year the two peer groups had been kept apart. This season Arsenal faced Manchester United at Villa Park. United were in the unusual situation of starting a match as underdogs. The Gunners had been in majestic form, approaching the end of their historic unbeaten league season; United simply had a point to prove. When Paul Scholes shot them ahead after thirty-two minutes, it was a lead they were determined to keep. For Arsenal, who had one eye on a Champions League clash with Chelsea, it was one game too many.

In the other semi-final, Sunderland and Millwall were both delighted to be playing each other. With United and Arsenal both guaranteed places in next season's Champions League, both teams were one victory away from a Uefa Cup place. The omens favoured Sunderland. The tie was a repeat of their semi-final in 1937, which Sunderland had won 2-1 before lifting their first FA Cup. This time the tables were turned. Australian international Tim Cahill, earning rave reviews in Millwall's midfield, scored the only goal on twenty-six minutes.

The final was the fifth for the Lions' player-manager Dennis Wise. His first was sixteen years previously in 1988 as part of Wimbledon's Crazy Gang. He had also lifted the Cup as captain of Chelsea in 1997 and 2000. He was upstaged by Roy Keane as United's captain was appearing in his sixth final, a post-war record. Only Arthur Kinnaird, with nine appearances for Wanderers and Old Etonians in the nineteenth century, has appeared in more.

It seemed unthinkable that Keane would not pick up his fourth winner's medal, such was the disparity in class between the teams. United lived up to their billing as 1/10 favourites by cantering to a 3-0 victory. Millwall, in their first final, held superior opponents until a minute before half-time. Once Cristiano Ronaldo had opened the scoring with a text-book header, the result was never in doubt. Ruud Van Nistelrooy converted a penalty just after the hour, then produced a final flourish with nine minutes left.

For all the disdain shown to the FA Cup by United and Arsenal in recent seasons, both were grateful and relieved for the finals of 2003 and 2004. Each had surrendered their Premiership title to the other, so victory at Cardiff represented their last chance for silverware. As United paraded their record eleventh trophy, it seemed as though the FA Cup was enjoying the last laugh.

2004 SHOOT-OUT 2005

MAN UTD:
Carroll; Silvestre, Ferdinand, Brown, O'Shea *(Fortune, 77)*; Scholes, Keane, Fletcher *(Giggs, 90)*, Ronaldo; Rooney, van Nistelrooy

ARSENAL:
Lehmann; Cole, Toure, Senderos, Lauren; Vieira, Fabregas *(van Persie, 86)*, Gilberto; Pires *(Edu, 105)*, Reyes; Bergkamp *(Ljungberg, 65)*

Penalty shoot-out:

MAN UNITED		ARSENAL	
Van Nistelrooy	Scored	Lauren	scored
Scholes	Saved	Ljungberg	scored
Ronaldo	Scored	Van Persie	scored
Rooney	Scored	Cole	scored
Keane	Scored	Vieira	scored

The third round produced one of the biggest shocks of recent years and it wasn't even due to a defeat for a big team. TV money has so polarized the top and bottom of individual leagues now that it is almost inconceivable that a non-league side could beat a top Premiership team, especially one of 2005's 'Big Three'. But it nearly happened.

Exeter City dropped out of the league at the end of the 2002-2003 season. They had kept a decent squad with a number of ex-league professionals to try and fight their way back from the Conference. The squad was good enough to see off Grimsby and Doncaster and cause delirium in Devon when the draw threw the Grecians up against Manchester United at Old Trafford.

The script was pretty predictable: a work-out out for United's reserve squad, win 2-0 and a nice pay-day for Exeter followed by gracious smiles from Sir Alex and on to more serious matters like the Champions League and stopping Chelsea from running away with the title. The script was thrown away and an abysmal display from the reserves was forthcoming, which even the introduction from the bench of Scholes, Smith and Ronaldo could not transform. Exeter's Andy Taylor, a former United youth team player, even came close to scoring twice, with a volley and a curled free-kick. A blasting from Sir Alex for his hapless team, and an enforced midweek trip to St James's Park for a replay. Cue the end of improvisation and back to the script: 2-0 workout etc, and a great and well-deserved write-up for Exeter, not to mention the clearance of their £750,000-plus debt.

Some of United's Premiership colleagues didn't get a second chance. Scott Vernon's fifteenth minute goal meant Oldham went on to represent Greater Manchester in the fourth round, not Kevin Keegan's Manchester City. Sheffield United, a redoubtable Cup side, beat Aston Villa 3-1 despite going a goal behind early in the second half; Andy Liddell was the two-goal hero. West Ham and Sunderland against Norwich and Crystal Palace were always going to be tight, and both went the way of the second tier side. Liverpool whinged about the late call-off of their game at Burnley, and then lost the replay after a laughable display capped by a comedy own-goal from Djimi Traore.

If this round prompted notions of a Cup filled with romance and glory for an unsung side, the fourth round quashed them abruptly. Not one team beat another from a higher division and there wasn't a single tie to quicken

The early rounds were almost devoid of shocks. Slough Town beat Paul Merson's Walsall, and then went out down the road at Yeading. Hinckley Borough beat Torquay United and Halifax beat Cambridge (no great surprise this, as Cambridge were about to slip out of the league).

2004-2005

the pulse. Even the Hampshire derby, settled 2-1 in Southampton's favour by Peter Crouch's injury-time penalty, was a poor spectacle made worse by the bile and enmity of the supporters. An always poisonous atmosphere was made worse by the fact that Harry Redknapp had swapped Pompey for Southampton during the season. Portsmouth had the last laugh when a 4-1 league win in April helped put the Saints down. The last sixteen contained only five non-Premiership clubs. Defeats for Sheffield Utd, Brentford, Burnley and Nottingham Forest in their replays left only one, Leicester, courtesy of Dion Dublin's last-minute winner at Charlton.

The Foxes went out in a dreadful match at Ewood Park, leaving Blackburn in the semi-finals for the first time since 1960. Their opponents would be Arsenal, 1-0 winners at Bolton. Wanderers had beaten Arsenal at the Reebok in the league and were in terrific form, but a second minute goal followed by a moment of madness from El-Hadji Diouf cost them dearly. The Senegal striker reacted to petty provocation from Jens Lehmann, swung an arm, and saw red.

The semi-final was one-sided. Amidst complaints about Blackburn's overly physical approach Robin van Persie produced an entertaining cameo, scoring with two exemplary finishes after coming on as a late substitute.

Newcastle ended all talk of four trophies for Chelsea in round five, holding on to a 1-0 win after an early goal from Patrick Kluivert. A repeat in the next round against Tottenham saw the Magpies through to a semi against Manchester United. These goals were Kluivert's only contribution to a dire season for New-

Six divisions separated Yeading and Newcastle United, but the non-leaguers held the Magpies for fifty-one minutes before going down 2-0 in their third-round tie. The match was switched to Loftus Road and shown live on the BBC, bringing a bounty of over £150,000 for the Ryman Premier League outfit.

2004-2005

castle. No wonder Alan Shearer opted for another year to try to go out on a better note.

Man United, after their tribulations with Exeter, had come through with ease against Premiership opposition in every subsequent round. Middlesbrough, Everton and Southampton were seen off with an aggregate score of 9-0 as United made light of the absence of Van Nistelrooy. The Dutchman struggled on his return, but looked more his old self whilst scoring twice in a 4-1 romp in another one-sided semi-final. Newcastle had gone out of Europe and the FA Cup within a week – their season was over.

The third round paired two managers who knew each other's game inside out. Glenn Hoddle had managed Dennis Wise at Chelsea and the boss kept the apprentice in check as Wolves beat Millwall 2-0.

2004-2005

So we were set for a clichéd 'Clash of the Titans' final. Would the old rivals revert to the petty squabbling of so many of their recent encounters, or would we see a festival of brilliant, attacking football, like their league game in February?

In the event, it was a damp squib, with the only drama served up by the artificial finale of the final's first-ever shoot-out. The tabloid build-up had been inflammatory and predictable, with language better suited to a Mike Tyson fight than a game of football.

Arsene Wenger took the sting out of the contest with his team selection and tactics. With his attack denuded by the absence of the injured Henry, the Arsenal manager's response was to pack the midfield and use Bergkamp as a lone striker. It proved a waste of the Dutchman's ability to scheme and his lack of pace meant Ferdinand and Silvestre coped without breaking sweat.

A pattern was quickly established; United attacked and Arsenal relied on the occasional break. Ronaldo and Rooney carried the main threat, the latter coming the closest as a low, snap effort from the right edge of the box looked to be sneaking inside Lehmann's front post. A reflex parry diverted the ball on to the woodwork, and the Gunners breathed again. This was one in a string of saves that marked the German keeper's renaissance. Criticised throughout the season as their weak link and dropped for part of it, he chose this match for his finest performance in an Arsenal shirt. Jim Montgomery he wasn't, but in a lack-lustre team display his competent handling and increasing confidence set him apart.

Minutes from the end, United may have realised that this was not their day. Van Nistelrooy, for whom the game was a series of might-have-beens, saw a point-blank header stopped on the line by the flailing head of substitute Ljungberg. The game juddered to a scoreless stalemate and the real action was about to unfold.

Nine out of ten spot-kicks could have formed a training video. The exception was United's second, as Paul Scholes' effort was struck with neither the power nor trajectory to outwit a keeper who had guessed correctly. Lehmann did just that, diving right to

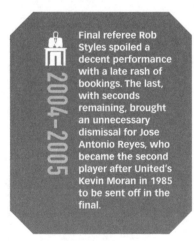

parry. Appropriately, the final penalties were taken by two old adversaries. Keane's nerveless conversion brought the scores level, only for Vieira's nonchalant finish to win Arsenal's tenth Cup.

Bibliography

The Complete Record of the FA Cup, Mike Collett, 2003
Rothmans Football Yearbook (now the Sky Sports Football Yearbook), various editions
The Sportman's World of Soccer, ed. Martin Tyler, 1975
Encyclopedia of British Football, Phil Soar and Martin Tyler, 1977
The Illustrated History of Manchester United, Tom Tyrrell and David Meek, 2001.
The Official History of West Ham United, Adam Ward, 2001.
The Official Illustrated History of Arsenal, Phil Soar and Martin Tyler, 2001.
Spurs, The Illustrated History, Bob Goodwin, 2003
Wembley: The FA Cup Finals, Glen Isherwood, 2003.
Football: The Golden Age, John Tennant, 2001.
Football Days, Peter Robinson, 2003.
Sunday Times Illustrated History of Football, 1998
The Observer on Soccer, Tony Pawson, 1989
F.A. Cup Giant Killers, Geoff Tibballs, 1994
Breedon Book of Football Records, compiled by Gordon Smailes, 2000
The Official Illustrated History of the F.A.Cup, Bryon Butler, 1996

DVDs

Numerous Cup final DVDs from the BBC and ITV Sport archives, distributed by ILC Sport Ltd.

Websites

A special acknowledgment is due to http://hometown.aol.co.uk and www.rsssf.com. The authors gratefully acknowledge the assistance of many official and unofficial websites from individual clubs, particularly for non Premiership and non-league teams.

Various newspaper articles were devoured and appreciated, both in hard copy and on-line.